"Paradise Lost: A Poem Written in Ten Books"

Essays on the 1667 First Edition

Medieval & Renaissance Literary Studies

"*Paradise Lost:*
A Poem Written in Ten Books"

Essays on the 1667 First Edition

_____

Edited by
Michael Lieb & John T. Shawcross

Duquesne University Press
Pittsburgh, Pennsylvania

Published in the United States of America by
DUQUESNE UNIVERSITY PRESS
600 Forbes Avenue
Pittsburgh, Pennsylvania 15282

Library of Congress Cataloging-in-Publication Data
Milton, John, 1608–1674.
    Paradise lost : a poem written in ten books.
      p. cm. — (Medieval & Renaissance literary studies)
    Summary: Vol. 1: "This authoritative text of the first edition of John Milton's Paradise
lost transcribes the original 10-book poem, records its textual problems and numerous differences from the second edition, and discusses in critical commentary the
importance of these issues"—Provided by publisher.
    Summary: Vol. 2: "Essays by ten Miltonists establish the significant differences in
text, context, and effect of the first edition of Paradise lost (1667) from the now standard second edition (1674), examining in particular the original text's relationship
to the literary and theological world it entered in 1667 and thus offering interesting
correctives to our understanding of Milton's thought"—Provided by publisher.
    Includes bibliographical references and indexes.
    ISBN-13: 978-0-8207-0404-3 (set : acid-free paper)
    ISBN-10: 0-8207-0404-0 (set : acid-free paper)
    ISBN-13: 978-0-8207-0392-3 (v. 1 : acid-free paper)
    ISBN-10: 0-8207-0392-3 (v. 1 : acid-free paper)
    [etc.]
    1. Bible. O.T. Genesis—History of Biblical events—Poetry. 2. Adam (Biblical
figure)—Poetry. 3. Eve (Biblical figure)—Poetry. 4. Fall of man—Poetry. 5. Milton,
John, 1608–1674. Paradise lost. 6. Milton, John, 1608–1674—First editions. I.
Shawcross, John T. II. Lieb, Michael, 1940– III. Title.
    PR3560.A2S53 2007
    821'.4—dc22

                                                              2007025652

∞ Printed on acid-free paper.

CONTENTS

PREFACE

This volume grew out of a lively and engaging session titled "The Discovery of a New Milton Epic: *Paradise Lost* 1667," organized on the occasion of the International Milton Congress, hosted by Duquesne University, March 11–13, 2004. The purpose of the session was to stress the importance of a long-overlooked document in Milton studies, that is, the first edition of *Paradise Lost*. Obviously, the title of the session was ironic. After all, how is it possible to speak of the discovery of a new Milton epic if the edition in question has been known all along? The answer is that an awareness of the *existence* of a work is not sufficient to qualify as evidence that it is really *known*. In this case, the lack of attention has been so much in evidence that the term "discovery" (rather than, say, "rediscovery") appeared to be entirely appropriate. Despite all the critical and scholarly effort bestowed upon the second edition of Milton's "diffuse epic," little effort has been exerted in bringing the first edition to the fore. The present collection is offered, in part, in an attempt to rectify this *lacuna*. ooh One might suggest that the purpose of this collection is archeological: it seeks to unearth what has long been buried. In keeping with this enterprise, the editors of this collection have also produced an edition of *Paradise Lost* 1667, one that can be used with confidence as the basis of future scholarly endeavors. Both undertakings—the collection and the edition—represent a "first" for Milton studies.

The purpose of these projects is not to "supplant" the second edition of *Paradise Lost* 1674 and its heirs. Quite the contrary is true. The collection and the edition are offered as a means of reasserting not only the significance of the 1667 edition as a poem with its own identity and value but also the way in which that edition provides fundamental insight into the nature of the later edition, how it is to be conceived and how it works. By focusing on the 1667 edition, one is likewise invited to come to terms with the contemporary political, social, religious, biographical, and literary contexts out of which *Paradise Lost* first emerged. Although one need hardly assert the importance of distinguishing the earlier contexts (those of 1667) from the later ones (those of 1674 and beyond), those distinctions are worth remembering.

Accordingly, the present volume makes a point of engaging the first edition of Milton's epic both as a "thing-in-itself" and as the product of the milieu to which it responds. With these goals in mind, the volume brings together ten previously unpublished essays that elucidate major aspects of the first edition of *Paradise Lost*. Of immediate interest is the text of *Paradise Lost*, that is, the poem as a "book." The first three essays here are concerned with the "material culture" that shaped the conception of the epic as it originally appeared in 1667, as well as the changes this edition underwent both in its subsequent issues (1668 and 1669) and in its publication as the second edition in 1674. Complementing these chapters, in turn, are the next four essays, all of which develop historical, literary, social, and political contexts against which the first edition of *Paradise Lost* may be placed. The concluding three essays round out the volume through detailed thematic and textual analyses that address the philosophical, theological, and structural implications of the epic in its original format.

The structure and logic of the volume are made evident by the issues that the individual essays address. Initiating the discussion of the first edition of *Paradise Lost*, Michael Lieb's essay functions both as an introduction to the volume as a whole and as an analysis of the changes incorporated in the poem from its first appearance to its later incarnations. As such, Lieb's essay lays the groundwork for the essays that follow. In his finely nuanced study, Joseph Wittreich focuses on the way in which the alterations that emerged between the 1667 text and those that appeared in 1668 and 1669 provide evidence that Milton's epic is "an oracle of its own history," an idea that Wittreich develops in his detailed account of the first edition and its subsequent issues. Rounding out this triad of approaches to the text of the poem in its original incarnation, Stephen B. Dobranski explores the relationship between Milton and his publisher, Samuel Simmons, which is evident in the changing faces of the title pages that preface the first edition of *Paradise Lost*. The underlying premise of each of these essays is that "meaning" resides as much in the poem as physical object as it does in the poetry itself. In order to come to terms with the later editions of Milton's epic, one must attend to the various aspects that constitute the changes the epic underwent in its initial appearances.

Elaborating upon such concerns, the second section of the volume engages the all-important question of milieu. The underlying assumption here is that a truly enlightened understanding of the first edition must take into account the historical milieu out of which the poem emerged. Achsah Guibbory's essay discloses how the 1667 edition of Milton's epic participated in the "cultural conversation" that distinguished the decade following the Restoration. In response to that task, Guibbory delineates the historical and literary setting against which one might most profitably place the first edition of *Paradise Lost*. Doing so, she demonstrates the extent to which Milton's epic is a work that must be read in the context of both the literature and the events of the time. Drawing upon the political life of the Restoration, Richard DuRocher, in turn, addresses the issue of regal attire both in the 1660s and in *Paradise Lost*. Specifically, DuRocher offers what he terms "contextual evidence" that associates Charles II with Milton's Satan, both of whom, it appears, adorn themselves with a "shared mode of dress and imperial styles." What results is a reading of the first edition as sensitive to the topical dimensions as to the larger thematic concerns of the epic. Essays by Laura Lunger Knoppers and Bryan Adams Hampton bring this issue of milieu to a close. Focusing on the social implications of the gardens and royal parks that flourished during the Restoration, Knoppers views Milton's depiction of his own "pleasure garden" or garden of Eden (from *"gan 'eden"* or *"garden of pleasure"* in Hebrew) in the context of the detailed descriptions of the pleasure gardens by Samuel Pepys, among others. Knoppers's essay thereby provides a renewed sense of how the Miltonic depiction of Eden implicitly comments upon "the commercialization of leisure" in the 1660s and beyond. Concluding the group of four essays that address the contemporary milieu, Hampton provides a way of locating the insurrection of the rebel angels in *Paradise Lost* within the "crackling atmosphere of persistent paranoia, political conspiracy, and importunate dissent" that followed hard upon the Restoration. In particular, Hampton contends that the politics of the Clarendon Code represents a contemporary context through which to approach Milton's portrayal of the dissenting angels in the first edition of *Paradise Lost*. All of the essays in this second group prove themselves germane to an understanding of the first edition of Milton's epic within its contemporary setting.

Rounding out the volume as a whole, the final three essays mount detailed thematic and textual arguments that engage the philosophical, theological, and structural implications of the epic as it originally appeared. Phillip J. Donnelly addresses essential questions about matters of structure and narrative treatment in the 1667 edition by highlighting Plato's *Republic*. Through an analysis of various aspects of this seminal work, Donnelly demonstrates the existence of a "sustained intertextual engagement" between the *Republic* and *Paradise Lost* 1667. At issue is what Donnelly calls the "architectonic symmetries" that bind the two works. So compelling is the architectonic relationship between them that Milton's epic does not simply reenact Platonic themes; rather, as a ten-book epic, it veritably subsumes the argument in Plato's great work. Moving from the philosophical dimensions of Donnelly's essay to the theological dimensions of Michael Bryson's essay, one is made aware yet once more of the primacy of Milton's epic in its first incarnation. Once again, the ten-book structure is at issue, but for Bryson the energies that shape the poem assume particular importance in the strain of negative or apophatic theology that underlies the depiction of God at various points in the narrative. Complementary accounts of the philosophical and theological implications of the ten-book epic, Donnelly's and Bryson's respective essays demonstrate the extent to which the first edition of *Paradise Lost* is its "own poem," one that demands to be read and understood on its own terms as well as in conjunction with the later editions of the poem. A coda to this third and final group of essays, John T. Shawcross's study comments implicitly upon the volume as a whole. Through an analysis of both structure and theme, Shawcross, like Donnelly and Bryson, reinforces the idea that Milton's epic in its first incarnation must be accorded the kind of careful attention that has been given its later incarnations over the centuries.

Paradise Lost 1667 can no longer be "silenced" as a poem that simply anticipates the "true" version that appeared some seven years later and that has subsequently been canonized as Milton's final statement. Drawing attention to the significance and complexities of the first edition, this volume seeks to justify the title of the session mounted on the occasion of the International Milton Congress: the essays gathered here amount in effect to "The Discovery of a New Milton Epic: *Paradise Lost* 1667." Having sought to accord that epic its due in the present collection, the editors hope to generate renewed interest in a work that later generations would not willingly let die.

Michael Lieb and John T. Shawcross
July 2007

Back to the Future
Paradise Lost 1667

Michael Lieb

I

When Milton declared in the 1667 edition of his ten-book epic *Paradise Lost* that his muse Urania would "fit audience find, though few" (7.31), little did he surmise how true that statement would prove to be for future generations of Miltonists who neither know nor care about the version in which Milton's "diffuse epic" first appeared.[1] Even those who do profess to care, however, are not necessarily the most knowledgeable in their treatment of first editions. Witness the legendary filmmaker Frank Capra, who considered himself a most savvy book collector. In his autobiography *The Name above the Title* (1971), Capra observes rather smugly that such collectors are a "tight-knit, snooty lot." They consider themselves superior to the simple book lover because they make a point of delving into the history of books. The best way to become "privy to the author himself," Capra maintains, "is to collect his first editions." Doing so, "one often opens the dossier on the writer: his botched beginnings, shattered hopes, dark dreams, frustrations, endurances; what drove him to write the book; what made the book a collector's item." To illustrate his point, Capra singles out the first edition of *Paradise Lost*:

> You probably have read Milton's *Paradise Lost*, and loved it. But wouldn't you love it more if you knew that the first edition of this

classic—with the title page reading *Paradise Lost* by JOHN MIL-
TON—was a complete failure? And that when the disgruntled publisher grudgingly printed a second edition, he lower-cased the author's
name to *John Milton?* And that when the second edition moved as slowly
as the first, the name on the third edition was further diminished to
J. Milton—and to just *J. M.* on the fourth edition? But then the book
began to sell. On the fifth edition the initials expanded back to *John
Milton,* and by the sixth printing the author's name was restored to
the upper-case glory of the first edition: JOHN MILTON. If you yawn,
and ask *why* that bit of trivia should make you love *Paradise Lost* more
than you do now—that's what makes us book collectors so snooty—
nobody understands us.[2]

Capra might be a great filmmaker, but one has doubts about his knowledge of the first edition of *Paradise Lost.* Yet one admires Capra
nonetheless for at least aspiring to come to terms with Milton's epic
in its original incarnation. However fit Milton's audience might
claim to be, those who have taken the trouble to read his diffuse epic
as it was first published are few indeed. Judging by the lack of attention bestowed upon the 1667 edition of *Paradise Lost* in the centuries
since its publication, one would hardly know that it had existed at
all, despite (or perhaps as the result of) the industry that has grown
up around the second edition of 1674.

To come upon *Paradise Lost* in its "original" form, then, is rather
like encountering a "new" epic, one we were aware existed all these
years but never thought necessary to read, let alone discuss. In the
traditions of canon formation so essential to the emergence of
Milton's reputation as a poet among poets, it is the later edition (along
with its heirs) that is commonly (and quite understandably) conceived
as the fulfillment of all his longstanding aspirations, as expressed in
The Reason of Church-Government, to "leave something so written to aftertimes, as they should not willingly let it die" (YP 1:810).
The result is that the epic of 1674 is canonized as the consummate
expression of Milton's poetic *oeuvre,* whereas the version published
some seven years earlier gets left out in the cold, if not entirely mar-
ginalized. One might almost be inclined to designate the epic of 1667
as nothing more than a "supplement" to the Miltonic canon or, better yet, an "apocryphon" in the sense not so much of that which is

deemed to be "spurious" as of that which is "secret" or "hidden away."
Name it what we will, this work haunts us by its presence, one that
calls out for renewed recognition and interpretation. In response to
that call, I propose not to dismiss the second edition outright, a
move that would rightly be considered foolhardy and self-defeating.
Rather, I offer a reading in which the first edition is viewed as a work
at once fully in command of its own destiny, distinguished by its own
shape, its own integrity, its own sense of beingness and, at the same
time, a work bound inextricably to that which is to come. In keeping with this approach, I contend that the later work cannot be fruit-
fully understood without a knowledge of its former self. Beneath the
skin of the later work (and helping to animate it) reside the spirit and
import of its progenitor. With such an approach in mind, I invite us
to travel "back to the future," there to discover an epic that is a vital
part of Milton's poetic canon.

   In order to realize the full significance of this journey, we must,
however, focus initially not only on the second edition but on the
editions that appeared later in the century. I adopt this approach to
establish a sense of the radical disjunction between the first edition
and its heirs. At issue is not only the transformation that the first
edition underwent in the subsequent editions but the extent to
which the whole revisionary process fostered a new culture of reception that has influenced studies of Milton and his *oeuvre* to this very
day. Only by approaching the issue in this manner shall we be able
to gain an understanding of what the first edition as a "cultural artifact" represents. I have in mind the physical object of the book, its
"attire," or how it represents itself in all its accoutrements. As we
proceed from the second edition to its later self-representations during the final decades of the seventeenth century, we shall behold a
"different" epic emerging, one that prompts us to view both the
poet and the poem from the perspective delineated not only in the
textual and structural changes that the epic was made to sustain but
in the apparatus through which it was offered for public consump-
tion. Because my primary focus is the first edition of *Paradise Lost*
in 1667, my discussion of the later editions will address itself only
to the most salient features, those that serve to point up the major
differences between the first edition of the epic and the editions that

it in turn engendered. I proceed in this manner to emphasize a crucial feature of the epic as it evolves from its *ur*-self to its later manifestations. That feature is one of change.

Even in a cursory account (as this will be) of the epic in its original form, change is the order of the day. This is already present in the way the first edition represents itself from one issue to the next.[3] As others have noted, between 1667 and 1669 there were no fewer than six issues of the first edition, accompanied by six different title pages.[4] On the title page of the first issue, for example, we find not the name of the printer Samuel Simmons but the names of three booksellers and their places of business: "*Peter Parker* under *Creed* Church neer *Aldgate,*" "*Robert Boulter* at the *Turks Head* in *Bishopsgate-street*"; and "*Matthias Walker,* under St. *Dunstons* Church in *Fleet-street.*" The name "*S. Simmons*" does not appear until the second issue of 1668, along with the names and the locations of the bookstalls of additional booksellers. What accounts for such variants as we move from one issue to the next is largely a matter of surmise, possibly having to do with Simmons's desire not to get caught in the act of publishing so controversial a figure as that divorcer and supporter of the regicides, John Milton.

Along with these variants, others are also of note. Whereas the title page of the first issue does not hesitate to identify the author in large bold type as "JOHN MILTON," a later title page sees fit to provide only the initials "J. M.," but Milton's name returns once again in succeeding title pages.[5] On the earlier title pages, the all-important claim to legitimacy ("Licensed and Entred according to Order") is prominently displayed; on the later title pages, no such claim is in evidence.[6] What does all this signify? One would be hard pressed to know. Even the title "*Paradise lost*" (thus printed)[7] is in some sense qualified by a descriptive statement in large bold type that changes between the time of the first issues in 1667 and the subsequent issues in 1668 and 1669. Whereas the earlier issues have "A POEM Written in TEN BOOKS," the later issues eliminate the word "Written" to state that this is "A POEM IN TEN BOOKS." Whatever the reasons for these unstable signifiers of provenance, legitimacy, and authorship, this is a work that represents itself in a manner that changes before our eyes.[8]

Underscoring this sense of flux is the "packaging" of the work, which is effectively reconfigured by the inclusion of new apparatus in the final issues of 1668 and 1669. This apparatus includes such material as a statement from the printer "*S. Simmons*" to the "*Courteous Reader,*" claiming that, although "There was no Argument at first intended to this Book," he has "procur'd it," for "the satisfaction of many that have desired it," as well as "a reason of that which stumbled many others, why the Poem Rimes not."[9] Confirming this statement are a series of prose summaries or "arguments" for each book, grouped together *ad seriatim* as part of the front matter, and, finally, both a defense of the verse employed in the epic and a list of "*ERRATA,*" all of which greets the reader even before he or she sets foot into the epic. These become "aids to reading" for a public not so much "surprised by sin" as inclined to "stumble" in the act of coming to terms with certain features of the epic as it originally appeared. Despite the sense of flux that arises from an examination of the issues, it would seem that the history of the publication of *Paradise Lost* between the time of the first edition and that of the second is one in which the work was nonetheless becoming more mindful of its charge and of the experience it sought to communicate. Involved in that process of "mindfulness" is the implicit collaboration between the poet and his printer to produce a work that would find a greater market.[10]

If the first edition begins to grow and change through the addition of certain accoutrements and paraphernalia, the second edition is one in which both the appearance and the text of the poem depart substantively from its progenitor. At first blush, the departures might not appear to be particularly significant; nonetheless, they are important enough to prompt the inclusion of a statement on the title page that this is a work that has been "Revised and Augmented by the Same Author." The phrase at once identifies the work as that which has appeared in an earlier form and at the same time declares its pedigree as that which is already known in one form but that now appears in another.[11] A brief glance at the alterations tells the tale. The title page now declares that this is "*Paradise Lost. A Poem in Twelve Books,*" that "The Author" is "*John Milton,*" that this is "The Second Edition," "Revised and Augmented by the Same Author," that the printer is quite clearly "*S. Simmons* next door to the *Golden Lion* in *Aldersgate-street*," and that the date of publication is 1674.

Beyond the title page, one frequently finds William Dolle's engraving of the poet based upon the portrait by William Faithorne; and, beyond that, two commendatory poems (one in Latin, by "S.B. M.D.," and one in English, by "A.M."). Whereas the first poem (putatively by Samuel Barrow, physician to General Monck's army in the 1650s) extols Milton's epic for encompassing the "story of all things" and emphasizes the war in heaven that culminates in the coming forth of God's "living chariot [*currus animes*]" with its wheels of "fierce lightnings" bursting from "those grim eyes," the second poem (by Andrew Marvell) explores the process by which the reader is made to come to terms with so daunting a venture as that undertaken by this "Poet, blind yet bold."[12] Following these items, the defense of the verse reappears to make its case yet once more. In keeping with the earlier edition, prose arguments for each book of the epic appear, but unlike the earlier edition, the arguments are no longer grouped at the beginning of the text. Rather, they are distributed *ad seriatim* before their respective books. One might suggest that this has the effect of creating a greater sense of balance, one in which exposition anticipates the particular narrative unit with which it is allied.[13] Most important, in the movement from the ten-book epic to the twelve-book epic, structural changes are implemented to reflect a new way of conceiving the action of the poem. The transformation is effected not through the addition of two wholly new books but by the division of existing books to reflect a new *Gestalt*, one in which books 7 and 10 of the ten-book epic are each divided into two: book 7 becomes books 7 and 8, whereas book 10 becomes books 11 and 12. (Although there has been much speculation about Milton's motives for undertaking these structural changes, no convincing argument has thus far come to light.)[14] These alterations, as we shall discuss, are supplemented by transitional passages and textual revisions amounting to some 15 lines.[15] If these changes do not appear to be so extensive as one might anticipate, that is because the epic as originally published is no longer the work that we know as *Paradise Lost*.[16]

The extent to which the earlier edition has been superseded by the later editions is discernible in those that appeared in the final decades of the seventeenth century. I refer to the monumental folio editions of 1688, 1691, and 1695.[17] Once again, I shall consider only the most salient of features of these editions. At issue is the way the later editions underscored the construction of Milton as a figure larger than life and his poem as a masterwork of major proportions. One feature of the editions in question is crucial: after the appearance of the third edition of 1678, the title pages of the final three editions (1688, 1691, and 1695) eliminate any reference to the 1667 edition. In short, that telling phrase "Revised and Augmented by the Same Author" is nowhere in evidence. It has been effectively erased from the table of memory that records the form in which both poet and poem were originally made known to the world. With that excision, that erasure, the *ur*-text is effectively silenced as well. A reader first coming upon the editions of 1688, 1691, and 1695 would hardly know that the ten-book epic of 1667 even existed. Rather, he would witness the poem in its new skin adorned by all the paraphernalia and accoutrements accorded only the most definitive of editions. The fourth, fifth, and sixth editions are remarkable in this regard. No longer are we presented with a text as quarto (the 1667 edition) or octavo (the 1674 and 1678 editions). In their place, we have before us sumptuous folios attired in all their finery, "so bedeckt, ornate, and gay" that one cannot but be in awe of such attention bestowed upon both poet and poem.

In keeping with the events of the time, the publication of the 1688 edition might be construed as something amounting to a "glorious revolution" all its own. A monument to the poetics of extravagance, this edition is obviously one upon which no expense has been spared. We need only glance at the final pages of the edition to confirm the manner in which Milton was appropriated by the moneyed class as the national poet in the making. Titled "The NAMES of the Nobility and Gentry That Encourag'd, by SUBSCRIPTION, the PRINTING [of] this Edition of Milton's *PARADISE LOST*," this section proceeds to list alphabetically (in double columns) over 500 subscribers, all of whom coupled their admiration with their pocketbooks. The list reads like a rollcall of who's who in the world of nobility and the arts. In his magisterial biography of Milton, David Masson cites from the list only the most notable of lords, earls, dukes, and ladies, not to mention poets, such as John Dryden, whose subscription helped to bring the edition to light. Because of the special efforts of the statesman and benefactor John, Lord Somers, this edition is sometimes called "the Somers edition."[18] Planned and executed by various individuals connected with Christ Church, Oxford, the volume is a testament to how Oxford, once the seat of royalist sentiment, supplanted Cambridge, once the seat of the radical poet.[19] The volume itself lives up to the highest expectations that extravagance can beget. "Adorn'd with Sculptures," it is graced by detailed illustrations that accompany each book. As the result of these illustrations (by John Baptist de Medina and others), Milton's epic enters the world of the visual arts as a signature and indeed a reading of the way key moments in the epic lend themselves to the artist's hand. In our encounter with Milton's epic, we now move first from the world of illustration to the discourse of prose argument before we enter the poem: once again, exposition (this time, visual and descriptive) anticipates performance. Ironically, the first illustration to greet us in that venture is none other than that of Satan himself in the posture of rousing his troops from the burning lake. The satanic school takes visual shape even before the narrator has had a chance to speak.

Reinforcing the visual dimension is the appearance of the frontispiece itself, handsomely rendered with an elaborately framed portrait of the poet (again, based on the work of William Faithorne), beneath which is placed Dryden's hyperbolic accolade:

> Three Poets, in three distant Ages born,
> Greece, Italy, and England did adorn.
> The First in loftiness of thought Surpass'd,
> The Next in Majesty: in both the Last.
> The force of Nature could no farther goe:
> To make a Third she joynd the former two.

Both visually and rhetorically, the poet of *Paradise Lost*, then, finds himself elevated to the pantheon of poets, where he assumes his rightful place above even Homer and Virgil. So exalted, he and his poem assume the kind of aura bestowed only upon the most imposing of luminaries. No call for an "S.B." or an "A.M." to offer interpretive tributes here. The paraphernalia that enshrines the poet in the 1688 edition precludes the need for such gestures. One can almost hear the volume challenging all oncomers: "Not to know mee argues your selves unknown." With this edition, finally, we are introduced to the entrepreneurial Jacob Tonson as co-publisher. Eventually securing full rights to Milton's poetry in 1691, as well as holding the rights to other important authors of the time, the talented Mr. Tonson made more money from *Paradise Lost* than any other work he published, and he succeeded in establishing what was to become a family dynasty of publishers throughout most of the eighteenth century. One might suggest that it was at least in part the result of Tonson's entrepreneurial efforts that Milton was marketed so successfully in the years to come.

The same sort of accoutrements that adorn the 1688 edition are largely replicated in the fifth and sixth editions of 1691 and 1695, respectively. But with the sixth edition, something even further happens to reinforce the sense of grandeur bestowed upon the poet and his poem: the aura of the visual ("Adorn'd with Sculptures") is reinforced by that of the exegetical. For here we find "Explanatory NOTES upon each Book, and a TABLE to the POEM, never before Printed." Produced by one "P. H." (Patrick Hume), the annotations are both voluminous and learned. As such, *Paradise Lost* is canonized as a scholar's poem, one that sanctions what has since become an institutional activity, that of inviting later scholars to produce their own learned commentaries.[20] In his discussion of the various editions that emerged in the eighteenth century, Marcus Walsh observes quite cogently that the kind of exegesis that P. H. undertakes in his "Explanatory NOTES" is consistent with the detailed and erudite hermeneutics that accompanied editions of the Bible during the Reformation.[21] If such is the case, Milton's epic assumed both the role and the magnitude of a scriptural text, at least in some quarters, by the end of the century and beyond. This reading is consistent with John T. Shawcross's telling observation that "many people in England seem to have learned their Bible with *Paradise Lost* at hand."[22] Not only was the poet elevated to the godly pantheon, but his poem achieved the status of a "sacred" text, one that found its aptest counterpart in the Bible itself. How much more might any poet desire?

I can't take you seriously Such is the *Nachleben* of Milton's epic between the time of the first edition in 1667 and that of the sixth edition in 1695. During that period, *Paradise Lost* underwent a transformation not simply in the adjustments Milton made to the text both verbally and structurally but in the self-representation of the epic as a work that excelled the "classics" and assumed something of a biblical aura.[23] It is difficult to know how Milton would have greeted this transformation. As much as he would have welcomed the apotheosis implicit in Dryden's epigram, the iconoclast in him might have felt some degree of discomfort. For there is a sense in which he found himself "High on a Throne of Royal State, which far / Outshon the wealth of *Ormus* and of *Ind*," an elevation that would no doubt have given him sufficient pause to eschew the idea of being raised by merit to that "bad eminence."[24] I cast my argument in these terms not to suggest that there was anything necessarily bad about the "eminence" that accrued to Milton in the final decades of the seventeenth century. He certainly merited such an elevation. It is simply that the more inclined we are to view *Paradise Lost* through the "adornments" that accompanied the later editions, the further we get from the poem that Milton published in 1667, a poem initially acknowledged by the 1674 and 1678 editions ("Revised and Augmented by the Same Author") but ultimately disregarded as having any ties whatsoever to their ultimate progenitor. It is this ultimate progenitor that engages us here, as we deconstruct the text as we know it and gaze for the first time on both poet and poem as they first appeared. Under these circumstances, one might be inclined to declare with William Butler Yeats that there is "more enterprise" in "walking naked."[25] The experience of reading this naked poem is one that gives rise to its own pleasures, its own insights, and its own meanings. Some of these I shall attempt to elucidate here.

II

A return to the 1667 as a physical "object" might initially be in order as a way of a moving into matters of theme and structure. For example, the fact of the publication of the 1667 edition as a quarto represents its own quiet statement (or understatement) about how the poem itself is to be understood.[26] In its original form as a quarto, the edition is remarkably unassuming and unprepossessing. Stark and bare in appearance, it is entirely (indeed, "fiercely") unencumbered by the presence of editorial apparatus, including prefatory material, apologies, glosses, plates, or illustrations,—in fact, anything that would call attention to it as a work of the first moment. The appearance of the first edition, then, invites a sense of the epic itself that is a far cry from both the textual changes and the additions that followed in its wake. The edition of 1667 is a volume the very physical dimensions of which belie the magnitude of the poetic universe that resides within. There is, of course, nothing untoward in the publication of volumes of such modest dimensions in the early modern period. The Bible itself had been issued in quarto and octavo format. It is simply that, coupled with the starkness and bareness of its appearance, the dimensions of the physical object serve to reinforce our sense of *this* edition as one that refuses to call attention to itself with anything that resembles pomp or fanfare. In keeping with this lack of pretension, the title page of the first edition is especially important in that it represents the first issue's only front matter.[27] This means that nothing lies between the title page and the epic itself. Such a circumstance is worthy of deliberation.

In what might be construed as our first encounter with the poem, we are invited to enact the following little drama, inspired by Milton himself. Wandering about London in 1667, we come upon a poem called *"Paradise lost"* (*thus printed*) in one of the bookstalls mentioned on the title page.[28] As we take the volume in hand, we are made aware that this is a poem by that blind, scurrilous poet John Milton. Glancing at the title of the work, we cry out in the spirit of Milton's own self-reflexive sonnet on his prose tract *Tetrachordon*: "Bless us! what a word on / A title page is this!" (*Sonnet XII*, 1–6). Who is he to write about losing paradise, and what does that mean? No matter that the text appears to be "woven close both matter, form, and stile," we are immediately suspicious.[29] Although we know who authored the work, we nonetheless ask who is the individual ultimately responsible for printing such a book? It is, one assumes, not the proprietors of the bookstalls. As far as the title page is concerned, Samuel Simmons might as well be in hiding. Is he nowhere to be found? Yes, but only in the later issues. Likewise in hiding is the full significance of the phrase that qualifies the title. I refer once again to "A POEM Written in TEN BOOKS," a statement significant not so much for what it does say as for what it doesn't say. Thus, although we are informed that the text following immediately upon the title *Paradise Lost* is "A POEM," we initially have no idea what *kind* of poem it is.[30] Nowhere does Milton designate it an epic, a term that he had earlier used with approbation in his prose works.[31] This does not mean that *Paradise Lost* is not an epic.[32] It simply suggests that Milton elects not to designate it as such on his title page, or rather he elects to designate it with a signifier so generic that it occludes as much as it reveals. How, then, are we to understand the idea that *this* poem (as opposed to others of the same kind?) is specifically "Written in TEN BOOKS"? I maintain that this additional bit of information does more to reinforce the fact of concealment than to elucidate how either the mode of composition or the length of the poem is to be understood. To be sure, ten-book narratives of one sort or another are available to hand and have been cited as models, but that fact does little to provide insight into the nature of the work that our wandering reader at first encounters.[33] Not knowing the specific kind of work that one has before him will not be elucidated by the knowledge of its length.[34] And what of the fact that it is "Written"? Of course, we exclaim, it is written! That is how poems get made. Why belabor the obvious? The answer, of course, is that in the very process of belaboring the obvious, the fact of writing further renders problematic a phrase that does more to conceal than to illuminate.

If we give ourselves a bit of leeway, we might be inclined to allow the signifier "Written" a bit more play. We have heard of this scoundrel Milton, and we know that he is blind. Overcoming our impulse to proclaim "No blind guides!" we consider the deep irony of the fact that this is a poem of a blind man. So in what sense is it "Written"? The answer, of course, is that it is not. Rather, it is dictated to the poet's amanuensis, who then transcribes it. In this sense, it is very much an "oral" performance. As we read into the poem, we discover that this is a poet who takes "dictation"; that is, he is the receptacle of that "unpremeditated Verse," dictated to him nightly by the Muse as he sleeps (1667 edition, 8.22–24), after which he calls for his amanuensis and demands to be *"milkd."*[35] The act of writing thereby assumes a deeply ironic cast. In keeping with the thematic perspective that Milton's epic endorses, we might suggest that what results from this process of dictation is none other than the "written Records pure" of "all the sacred mysteries of Heav'n," mysteries that cannot be understood "but by the Spirit" (1667 edition, 10.1401–06). If this reading sounds suspiciously *post hoc*, it nonetheless rings true as a means of anchoring the kind of poem that Milton believed himself to have authored. As such, it is a work that emerges from a process of "aurality" and "orality" by an inspired poet through whom the written text encodes the sacred mysteries of God. Thus conceived, "Written" becomes a signifier of Milton's own belief that his work is the embodiment of that which is occluded to all but a "fit audience" initiated into the ways of deciphering the hieroglyphic dimensions of a strange and mysterious poem "Written," as the title page indicates, "in TEN BOOKS." Fiercely unassuming in its appearance, the title page that bears this inscription haunts us (to use Milton's phrase) with an "aspect" that is "silent yet speaks."

In the 1667 edition of *Paradise Lost,* this occlusive outlook strikes us immediately as we move from title page to text. In that transition, we find ourselves entirely alone with the text, challenged to master its discourse, to understand its meanings, and to be attentive to its intricacies. This is no small matter. Whereas both the subsequent issues and the later editions of the epic provide prose summaries and other paraphernalia, the very first issue, as discussed, offers only the poem itself. Confronting the text *qua* text without the aid of summaries and the like is a daunting experience. As a result of that initial encounter, the reader is challenged to decipher its meanings, to come to terms with its secrets. In short, the reader finds himself or herself at this moment in a position very much like that of Adam, who is permitted to witness for the first time "the secrets of another world, perhaps / Not lawful to reveal" (1667 edition, 5.569–70). If Adam is in a sense our first "reader" of such matters, those who moved from the title page of the first edition of *Paradise Lost* to the text of the poem itself assume the role of first readers as well, that is, readers of "first things." It is almost as if in keeping with this conception of first things that the first proem to the first book of the first issue of the first edition of *Paradise Lost* focuses upon first or primal things: "Mans *First* Disobedience"; "That Shepherd, who *first* taught the chosen Seed, / In the Beginning how the Heav'ns and

Earth / Rose out of *Chaos*"; first endeavors ("Things unattempted yet
in Prose or Rhime"), inspired by that Spirit of which the poet sings,
"Thou know'st; Thou from the *first* / Wast present."

> "Say *first*," [sings the poet]
> for Heav'n hides nothing from thy view
> Nor the deep Tract of Hell, say *first* what cause
> Mov'd our Grand Parents in that happy State,
> Favour'd of Heav'n so highly, to fall off
> From their Creator, and transgress his Will
> For one restraint, Lords of the World besides?
> Who *first* seduc'd them to that fowl revolt?
> Th' infernal Serpent; he it was.   (line 1–34; italics mine)

In a sense, this is Milton's "*bᵉreshit*," his "in the beginning of things,"
his "in the first place." If the movement from the title page of the
1667 edition to the proem and "epic question" of the first book
yields nothing else, it must yield that sense of firsts available most
dramatically only through the kind of confrontation and engagement that the first issue of the 1667 edition provides. Nothing to
impede us here, no editorial paraphernalia, no prose summaries, no
interventions of the printer to the reader, no illustrations (satanic
or otherwise): just the text that announces itself in "firsts" is what
the reader is made to encounter, sink or swim. Already in that
inscription of first things, the "written text" begins to unfold itself
as the means by which one is to decipher the sacred mysteries of the
other world.

It was to this sense of otherness that the earliest readers of the 1667
edition attest. A fine example is the Norfolk Presbyterian baronet
Sir John Hobart, a supporter of the commonwealth but also a supporter of the Restoration of Charles II. Our knowledge of his interest in the first edition of *Paradise Lost* derives from his correspondence
(1668). There, Hobart makes a point of sharing his impressions of
Milton's newly published epic by observing that, whereas Milton is
a "criminal" who suffers now from "obsolescence," his epic is
nonetheless sublime. Not only is the "Theme" of his epic "above
hyperboles, or tropes" but the "raptures" his poetry inspires are of
a kind with those of the most venerated poets such as Homer and
Virgil. "I have been strangely pleased," he allows, "in a deliberate

and repeated reading of him [Milton], & more the last time than the
first, my incompetency of making comparison . . . confines my censure only to my own delight, which has been so excessive, that I can
say truly I have never read any thing more August."[36] This account
of the sublimity of the epic is also an attestation to the sense of
"strangeness," if not "otherness," it provokes. It is here that "strangely
pleased" assumes the quality of that which responds with a certain
delight, combined with a sense of awe, to that which is beyond its
grasp. Whereas Hobart feels compelled to engage the poem repeatedly in an act of multiple encounters, he is still left with that strangeness, that otherness, that only a poem that encompasses worlds
beyond hyperbole and trope is able to elicit. It is for this reason that
Hobart invokes the term "August," which as *augustus* implies that
which is "venerable," if not "consecrated." Giving rise to "raptures," it is a work that is *sui generis.* That Hobart was capable of *gag me.*
responding to the first edition in this manner suggests the extent to
which the earliest readers of Milton's poem would have understood
completely the nature of this strange, yet wonderful, artifact known
as *Paradise Lost.*

III

   Those initiated into the "mysteries" the poem encodes will be led
to understand precisely why this ten-book epic invites analysis on
its own terms. It is here that the structure of the epic becomes especially meaningful, indeed, of fundamental importance to Milton's original conception of the "shape" his poem would assume. We are
made to acknowledge that shape as a crucial aspect of what Milton
himself calls the "great Idea," a locution adopted to describe the process
by which his deity goes about the act of cosmic creation (1667 edition, 7.557). In keeping with this great Idea, Louis Martz some time
ago pondered the rationale behind the ten-book structure. Although
he stopped short of voicing Barbara Lewalski's more recent conjecture that Milton might originally have planned a twelve-book epic,
Martz nonetheless does "wonder why Milton ever produced his
poem with ten books in the first place," since a twelve-book epic (signaled by the phrase "Half yet remains unsung" in the proem to book
7 [line 21]) is more nearly in keeping with what Martz deems the

"symmetry of dividing the poem into two halfs of six books each" after the Virgilian model. Despite the obvious symmetry that might be attained through adherence to such a model, Milton chose in the first edition "to present the second half in an asymmetrical division into four books." Considering all those years that Milton planned his epic, Martz speculates that the poet must no doubt "have had some compelling design in mind when he offered us this poem in ten books."[37] The "asymmetry" of which Martz speaks would have come as a surprise to all those who have documented the fearful symmetry of the first edition.

In his structural analysis of that edition, John T. Shawcross is germane to our discussion. Although it would be redundant, if not impossible, to summarize his complex argument here, suffice it to say that in the ten-book version he sees a "pyramidic construction" that brings into sharp focus the "rising and falling action of the entire poem and the climax at the center." As such, the shape of the ten-book poem may be viewed as "a hieroglyph of the mountain of God."[38] At the summit of that mountain, the Son is described as having "Ascended" (1667 edition, 6.762) the "Chariot of Paternal Deitie" in order to overcome the rebel angels in the war in heaven. It is no accident that the very numerical midpoint of the poem as a whole falls on the word "Ascended," which split the 1667 version in half.[39] This hieroglyphic positioning is bolstered by the numerological underpinnings of the poem in its ten-book format.[40] Here, one finds "geometries and arithmetic metaphors" that suggest "mystic emanations arising from its creator."[41] If this mode of discourse strikes us at first blush as somewhat questionable, we need to acquaint ourselves with a host of others who think along the same lines. I have in mind such scholars as Gunnar Qvarnström, Maren-Sofie Røstvig, Claes Schaar, and Alastair Fowler.[42] In fact, it is a line of thinking that I have followed elsewhere in some depth in my explorations of the occult traditions that underlie the Miltonic conception of the "Chariot."[43] There is no need to rehearse this material here. I simply note in passing that Milton did indeed have "some compelling design" in mind when he offered us his poem in ten books. It should come as no surprise that the blind poet counted line numbers both for the 1667 edition and for the edition of 1674.[44] In fact, William B.

Hunter conjectures that Milton attempted, albeit unsucessfully, to revise in such a way that the Chariot would once again be at the numerical center of the twelve-book epic.[45] That Milton was ultimately unsuccessful in this task merely reinforces the view that he was at pains to preserve the structural matrices of both editions. Each may be said to reflect its own sense of architectonics, and one would not be very far wrong in reading one edition in the context of the other.

Having glanced at the structural implications of the ten-book epic, we should be aware of corresponding aspects as well. We recall that books 7 and 10 of the original edition were each divided into two books for the second edition: book 7 became books 7 and 8, and book 10 became books 11 and 12. With those divisions in mind, we need to regain a sense of what it was like to read a ten-book, rather than a twelve-book, epic. Short of undertaking the task of rereading the epic in its original form, we might remind ourselves of the alterations made to the text. The 1674 edition adds a total of some fifteen lines, eight of which account for the transition from ten to twelve books and seven of which represent alterations of one sort or another. Before the transition from book 7 to books 7 and 8, the original text moved from the great angelic celebration that climaxed Raphael's account of the creation of the universe to the intimate dialogue between Adam and Raphael concerning the nature of celestial motions, followed by Adam's account of his own experience of being created and the dialogue that springs from it. In the 1674 edition, the transition from book 7 to 8 is effected through a brief prose argument, followed by the editorial reflections of the narrator, who sets the stage for the action of book 8 and comments on the disposition of both Raphael and Adam at this point in the dialogue: "The Angel ended, and in *Adams* Ear / So Charming left his voice, that he a while / Thought him still speaking, still stood fixt to hear; / Then as new wak'd, thus gratefully repli'd" (1674 edition, 8.1–4). In the 1667 edition, the only transition that appears at this juncture is the result of the movement from Raphael to Adam: "To whom thus *Adam* gratefully repli'd" (1667 edition, 7.641). There is no prose argument to mark the transition from one book to the next, no narrative editorializing, nothing to disrupt the flow of thought from character to character. The result is that Adam's response in the 1667 edition to Raphael's description of

the creation of the universe and the angelic celebration that concludes
the description is immediately, indeed, almost inevitably, met by
Adam's questions concerning the precise workings of the celestial
bodies (1667 edition, 7.641–75). It is the inevitability of Adam's questioning that renders the 1667 edition more nearly compelling in
some respects. Not only are there no prose arguments and narrative
transitions to interrupt the flow of the action, but the sense of balance that the book as a whole reflects serves to reinforce the seam-
less movement from cosmic to personal as first Raphael and next Adam
recount their own individual experiences.

If the first major transition is that reflected in the division of
book 7 into books 7 and 8, the second is that reflected in the division of book 10 to books 11 and 12. There is no doubt about the logic
and propriety of such a division. Whereas in the 1674 edition book
11 recounts the course of postlapsarian history from the time of the
Expulsion to the time of the Flood, book 12 recounts the course of
postlapsarian history from the time of the Flood to the time of Christ
and beyond. Whereas the antediluvian history of book 11 culminates
in the Noachic covenant and the promise of new life on earth, the
postdiluvian history of book 12 culminates in the Christocentric
covenant and the promise of new life in the world to come. The sense
of balance could not be more logical and finely nuanced. To underscore this sense of balance, Milton provides both a prose argument
and a transitional stanza:

> As one who on his journey bates at Noon,
> Though bent on speed, so heer th'Archangel paus'd
> Betwixt the world destroy'd and the world restor'd,
> If *Adam* aught perhaps might interpose;
> Then with transition sweet new Speech resumes. (1674 edition, 12.1–5)

To be sure, the transitional passage is rich in its implications. The
trope of "bating" or pausing at "Noon" at once recalls the time of
the temptation and the Fall and looks forward to the Christocentric
reshaping of the event at noon with the Crucifixion as a sacrificial
act that underscores the new covenant.[46]

All this is missing in the 1667 edition. What it loses in transitional
passages, however, it makes up for in the sense of immediacy and

spontaneity that arises from Adam's inquiry about the significance of the rainbow:

> But say, what mean those colourd streaks in Heavn,
> Distended as the Brow of God appeas'd
> Or serve they as a flowrie verge to bind
> The fluid skirts of that same watrie Cloud,
> Least it again dissolve and showr the Earth. (1667 edition, 10.879–83)

In response to this question, Michael "indoctrinates" Adam into what might be called "the hermeneutics of the rainbow." It is a hermeneutics that moves from the physical to the spiritual as it expounds upon the nature of the Noachic covenant, a covenant that prefigures that coming of the Messiah to redeem mankind. In the form of the rainbow, God promises "not to blot out mankind, / And makes a Covenant never to destroy / The Earth again by flood" (1667 edition, 10.887–89). With the onset of the rainbow, mankind will be able to "call to mind his [God's] Cov'nant" until "fire purge all things new / Both Heav'n and Earth, wherein the just shall dwell" (1667 edition, 10.894–97). Immediately following the discourse concerning the rainbow, Michael summarizes all that Adam has beheld: "Thus thou hast seen one World begin and end / And Man as from a second stock proceed" (1667 edition, 10.898–99). Because there is no break, no imposition of book division, once again, there is no sense of discontinuity. In fact, the idea of Adam's ability to behold the rainbow at this point brings home what amounts to his inability to move beyond the rainbow as a symbol of God's self-presencing. For Michael says, "Much thou hast yet to see, but I perceave / Thy mortal sight to faile; objects divine / Must needs impaire and wearie human sense" (1667 edition, 10.900–902), a sign both of the limits under which Adam labors in his postlapsarian condition and the occasion for his assimilation of Michael's teachings not through the eye but through the ear. As a result of this oral / aural mode of communication, Adam is indoctrinated into the significance of "salvation history" that comes through the Word.

To be sure, all this is present in the 1674 edition with its book divisions that constitute the twelve-book epic, but the sense of flow achieved in the ten-book version is more dramatic, more effectively felt on the pulses as a result of the emphasis that the vision of the rainbow receives and, along with it, Michael's commentary, which in turn immediately takes into account the failure of Adam's "mortal sight." There is no pausing here to see "If *Adam* aught perhaps might interpose." Adam is silent, and his silence assumes its own significance as a sign that he has achieved the limits of mortal sight and is able to proceed no further without the support of his angelic guide. My point is that the resonance achieved at this moment is all but lost in the book divisions that structure the 1674 edition, but that, in turn, is able to compensate for the loss by providing a rich transitional passage that highlights the movement "Betwixt the world destroy'd and the world restor'd" (1674 edition, 12.3).

Among the other changes that Milton imposed upon the text of the 1667 edition are verbal alterations of one sort or another. One or two examples should suffice to point up the differences. In book 5 of both the 1667 and the 1674 editions, Raphael relates to the unfallen couple how the angelic hosts received God's "begetting" of the Son. If that event appears to be welcomed with the festivity of "song and dance about the sacred Hill" (5.619), not all are so pleased, as we well know, and that displeasure ultimately results in Satan's rebellion. Be that as it may, the angels turn "from dance to sweet repast," and the tables upon which are "pil'd / With Angels Food" and "rubied Nectar" greet them with

> Fruit of delicious Vines, the growth of Heav'n.
> On flowrs repos'd, and with fresh flowrets crown'd,
> They eat, they drink, and in communion sweet
> Quaff immortalitie and joy, secure
> Of surfet where full measure onely bounds
> Excess, before th' all-bounteous King, who showrd
> With copious hand, rejoycing in thir joy.   (1674 edition, 5.632–41)

Now, in the 1667 edition, the tables are likewise "pil'd / With Angels Food" and "rubied Nectar" with "Fruit of delicious Vines, the growth of Heav'n." But there is no "reposing" on flowers of any sort, nor are the angelic hosts crowned with "fresh flowrets." Rather than eating and drinking "in communion sweet," as the 1674 edition describes them, the angelic hosts of the 1667 edition "eat, they drink, and with reflection sweet / Are fill'd, before th'all bounteous King," who, once again, "showrd / With copious hand, rejoycing in thir joy" (1667 edition, 5.632–38).

The alterations that Milton made in the transition from the 1667 edition to the 1674 edition are particularly meaningful, for they suggest that this is not simply a festivity or celebration of God but in its own way a movement toward the vision of the celestial world of *Paradise Lost* as essentially sacramental in outlook.[47] This aspect of Milton's epic is embodied in what is called "communion sweet," a phrase much more telling than the rather nondescript "reflection sweet" of the 1667 edition. In fact, it is difficult to say precisely what the phrase "reflection sweet" means. "Communion sweet" is an entirely different matter. Anticipated by what is in effect the communion table ("Rais'd of grassie terf" and "heap'd" with "various fruits") that the unfallen couple prepare for their angelic guest within the confines of the Edenic world (5.388–95), the communion tables of the angelic hosts in heaven draw upon such sacramental ideas as the festivities of Passover (compare Exod. 12), as they prefigure the celebration of the Eucharist. Although one must be careful not to push these correspondences too far, they are at least implicitly present in the revisions incorporated into the 1674 edition of Milton's epic.[48]

Having examined what might be termed the move toward sacramentalism in the 1674 edition, I shall conclude with two other revisions that possibly highlight changes in outlook or perspective that the poet himself was undergoing between the first and second editions of his great poem. Because these revisions are of a kind, I shall consider them together. Both occur in the context of Adam's first true encounter with the meaning of death in the postlapsarian world, an encounter recorded in the tenth book of the 1667 edition. The first revision concerns the "shapes" of Death as Adam comes to behold it on the "Hill of Speculation." There, he witnesses for the first time the murder of one brother by another, both the immediate offspring of the fallen couple. "Have I now seen Death? Is this the way / I must return to native dust?" Adam asks Michael, who responds that Death assumes "many shapes," including those brought on by "Fire, Flood, Famin," as well as by "Intemperance," all the result of "th'inabstinence of *Eve*." Here, Adam suddenly witnesses a place that is "sad, noysom, dark, / A Lazar-house," or leper house, "it seemd," in which are placed those wracked by disease, "all maladies / Of gastly Spasm" and other forms of torment, which Milton enumerates as follows: "Convulsions, Epilepsies, fierce Catarrhs, / Intestine Stone and Ulcer, Colic pangs, / Dropsies, and Asthma's, and Joint-racking Rheums" (1667 edition, 10.483–85). As if this litany of horrors were not sufficient, Milton enumerates still more in the 1674 edition. Thus, between "Intestine Stone and Ulcer, Colic pangs" and "Dropsies, and Asthma's, and Joint-racking Rheums," he inserts the following: "Daemoniac Phrenzie, moaping Melancholie / And Moon-struck madness, pining Atrophie, / Marasmus, and wide-wasting Pestilence" (1674 edition, 11.485–87). Precisely what accounts for this list of additional diseases is not clear. Perhaps the memory of the plague continued to linger and made him ever conscious of his own mortality, as well as an ongoing sense of his own ailments, including not just blindness but also gout from which it appears he suffered greatly and which might well have contributed to his death.[49] Thus, it may not be too much of a stretch to consider the possibility that the inclusion of these additional diseases is not an arbitrary act of fleshing out an already graphic list but instead may reflect Milton's own frame of mind in the years culminating in his death.

It is precisely the wisdom that comes of suffering that no doubt prompts the poet to place in the mouth of Adam the words that he utters as a result of having witnessed the horrors that beset the human race in the generations to come. The 1667 edition provides an initial account of what Adam has learned: "Henceforth," he says,

> I flie not Death, nor would prolong
> Life much, bent rather how I may be quit
> Fairest and easiest of this combrous charge,
> Which I must keep till my appointed day
> Of rendring up.   (1667 edition, 10.544–48)

There is a profound sense of resignation in these words by a man who has not yet had the opportunity to spend even a day in the fallen world below, and yet he proves himself a superb student of what that world offers and of what that world denies. This sense of wisdom is deepened even further in the slight but notable revision ventured in the 1674 edition, which appeared very shortly (some four months or so) before Milton's own death. Once again, Adam shares his most profound insight. The lines are so close to those in the 1667 edition that one might miss them were he not on alert for the revision. "Henceforth," Adam confirms,

> I flie not Death, nor would prolong
> Life much, bent rather how I may be quit
> Fairest and easiest of this combrous charge,
> Which I must keep till my appointed day
> Of rendring up, *and patiently attend*
> *My dissolution.*   (1674 edition, 11.547–52; italics mine)

There is something almost unbearably poignant about these lines, here reinforced even further by the idea of Adam's "attending" his "dissolution." One cannot but think of Milton himself at the end of his long career as a poet, polemicist, and thinker contemplating his own death, an event that he must have sensed would not be too far off his authoring of these lines, along with the added verses that bring Adam's thought to a resolute close.

In my consideration of the first edition of *Paradise Lost*, I have gone back to the future in order to rectify what I feel has been a lacuna in our understanding of Milton's epic. That lacuna is one in which the poem published in 1667 has been effectively erased from memory in our determination to look upon the second edition and its heirs as truly canonical. In my own teaching of the epic, I customarily do no more than gesture toward the first edition as *there* but nonetheless as hardly relevant to our understanding of what Milton is about. As I hope to have demonstrated here, the first edition is important not only on its own terms but as an essential part of our understanding of what transpired in the later editions. It is for this reason that we need a renewed interest in the poem that Milton thought he was leaving to an aftertimes sufficiently responsive to his developing sensibility that the ten-book version of *Paradise Lost* might attract the attention it deserves. I am in no way suggesting that the first edition be viewed as supplanting the second. We must respect Milton's decision to revise and publish a later version of his epic as presumably "authoritative." On the other hand, a true journey back to the future must take account of the wellspring from which its own sense of identity and existence emerges. Only in that way will the future be fully understood.

"More and More Perceiving"

Paraphernalia and Purpose in *Paradise Lost*, 1668, 1669

JOSEPH WITTREICH

[A] Reader of Milton must be Always upon Duty; he is Surrounded with Sense, it rises in every Line, every Word is to the Purpose; There are no Lazy Intervals, All has been Consider'd, and Demands, and Merits Observation. . . .

His Silence has the Same Effect, not only that he leaves Work for the Imagination when he has Entertain'd it . . . ; but he Expresses himself So Concisely, Employs Words So Sparingly, that whoever will Possess His Ideas must Dig for them, and Oftentimes pretty far below the Surface.
—Jonathan Richardson Sr.

The text of *Paradise Lost*, in the different issues of the first edition, is an oracle of its own history—a history of alterations and accretions: changing signatures, modified legends, variant title pages with different pointings and type facings; additions or supplements, including a list of errata, observations on the verse form, and arguments initially printed not as headpieces to individual books but as prefatory material to them all; two separate states of "The Printer to the Reader," one in four, the other in six lines. Much of this information, conveniently summarized by John T. Shawcross, was made available to earlier readers of *Paradise Lost* by Jonathan Richardson Sr.[1]

in his recollection that Milton seems to have been repeatedly, even obsessively, revising his poem during and after dictation of it; then in the course of recasting what was first a tragedy into an heroic poem; then again while converting a manuscript poem into a book, in its first edition existing in seven different issues (that is, seven title pages, thus "issues"); and finally when in the process of transforming, with modest redefinition, this first into a second edition of *Paradise Lost.*

In his observations, Richardson imagines a Milton who was regularly revising his poem, initially by truncation: "I have been . . . told he would Dictate many, perhaps 40 Lines as it were in a Breath, and then reduce them to half the Number." Richardson goes on to tabulate variations within the different issues of the first edition, always remembering among the "little Additions" that "an Errata is Added, with a little Discourse concerning the Kind of Verse." For Richardson, those "Additions" are a reminder (1) that "the First Title, That of [16]67 was immediately follow'd by the Poem, Naked of Advertisement, Errata, &c.,"[2] and (2) that *little additions* accumulate to become a distinguishing feature of later states of the first edition and the chief hallmark of the second edition, with its new title page announcing the conversion of a ten- into a twelve-book poem, hinting at a Virgilian model for it, and with its portals now filled not only with the author's portrait and an address to his readers but also with preliminary poems doing some of the author's own work of mediation. The identifying feature of the different texts of *Paradise Lost*—what Richardson calls "Additions Chiefly"[3]—is a persistent feature of editions after Milton's death as evidenced by John Dryden's rhymed version of Milton's poem, William Hog's translation, John Baptist de Medina's and others' illustrations, and Patrick Hume's commentary on and indices to the poem, all published before the end of Milton's own century. As a book, *Paradise Lost* seems to be forever undergoing enlargement. Some people apparently wished it longer—and fully ornamented with erudition.

What makes Richardson's words, cited in the epigraph to this essay, a logical starting point for consideration of the integrity of the first edition of *Paradise Lost* is the fact that, as duly noted by Samuel Taylor Coleridge,[4] those words are prompted by Richardson's reflections on the evolving text of Milton's poem, even as they embrace his understanding that silences and omissions in Milton's text are as telling as alterations of and additions to it. If *Paradise Lost* is a poem in which Milton speaks as author and interpreter and, in the course of revising his poem, acts as editor and again as commentator, it is also a poem that "it Self does *More than Whisper*" so that, in Richardson's words, "Nothing [is lost] by its Author's Blindness."[5] At least not nearly as much is lost as is sometimes supposed.

I

The multiple title pages to the first edition of *Paradise Lost* are a good place to start a discussion of what Jerome McGann calls "radial reading," or active reading, which involves deciphering bibliographical codes and which, as "a function of the historicity of texts," investigates their reception history.[6] That history, in turn, as it gathers into focus alternative readings of a text, may also reveal the text's conflicting commitments, multiple and sometimes competing contexts, surface as well as hidden content, silences, and invisible features. Not just the poem but what surrounds it gives access to its meanings: the ceremonies and protocols of title pages and preliminary material, the use of italic and capitalization, of different type fonts and sizes, of generic and stanzaic forms, of rhyme schemes or the lack thereof. Rhyme schemes sometimes function as generic signals, or markers; and rhyme, dogged by controversy in Milton's time, was irrevocably involved with politics of which the poet's note on the verse is striking evidence.

We need to read both before and after, as well as between, the lines of a poem while remembering that protocols of printing, beginning with the title page, can establish unexpected and sometimes peculiar inflections. For example, a period is added after "Books" in the last four issues of the first edition of *Paradise Lost* thus making A POEM IN TEN BOOKS. (with period added, and diminished caps) a separately marked unit that, by virtue of type size and boldfacing, in its prominence overrides the poem's title, "Paradise lost," and even its designated ten-book structure. In short, this poem's formulaic subtitle, "A Poem in . . . Books," gives to *Paradise Lost* the broadest possible literary categorization. It is *a poem*, period. But perhaps the most striking feature of all on the title page, once its various elements are put in perspective, is the emphasis accorded "Paradise" by virtue of its (and not "lost) being capitalized. Nor is "lost" capitalized in the running heads for each page of each book of *Paradise Lost*.[7] For a long time, a cliché of Romantic criticism had it that Milton emphasizes the loss of paradise, the Romantics its recovery—a cliché that is effectively challenged when the title pages to the first editions of *Paradise Lost* and *Paradise Regain'd* are set side by side: **Paradise lost** / ᴘᴀʀᴀᴅɪsᴇ **REGAIN'D**. While "lost" (without a cap) is diminished, "Regain'd" is enhanced in importance by virtue of its appearance in distinctly larger type than "Paradise."

Yet the subtitle also anticipates an important emphasis and focus. The word "Book" will appear on every page of this poetic text as a reminder of the book's materiality, of the poem fulfilling the poet's idea in *Areopagitica* of "a good Booke" as "the pretious life-blood of a master spirit" (YP 2:493). The marked endings of each book—"*The End of the First Book*,"[8] for example, as well as the emphatic conclusion of the poem, "THE END"—are clogs in the narrative, forced stops, which in conjunction impart to *Paradise Lost* a powerful sense of an ending and which, together with other still points in the poem, force readers into contemplation and reflection. In "The Verse," Milton may promise a poem in which "the sense [is] variously drawn out from one Verse into another" [a4], and then from book to book; but with ruptures within and between some books, Milton creates impediments to his announced design, with commentary interrupting the narrative and impeding its flow and with enforced closure at the end of most books imposing unexpected "stops." Readers are thus bridled before they can press forward, but are also stopped in their tracks by the obstructive bulk of the longest books in the poem: the 1,290 lines of book 7 and the 1,540 (actually 1,541) lines of book 10.[9] In this way, Milton follows, even out-does, Spenser in putting the brakes on the fast pace of epic narrative; yet, this practice of a forced stop, of emphatic closure, goes back to the 1645 publication of *Lycidas* and *A Mask*. Nowhere in Milton's poetry is an ending more boldly marked than after *Lycidas*, where there are two rows of 15 stamps with an "E" between them. *Lycidas* and

A Mask seem to rival each other, and then *A Mask* appears to be relegated to an appendix, subordinating it in importance to *Lycidas.* This point is subsequently reinforced in the table of contents to the 1673 *Poems,* both by type size and type facing: **LYCIDAS** versus *A Mask.*

Initially, we learn nothing at all about the generic identity of *Paradise Lost,* its aspirations or castings, only that it will participate in the relative obscurity of poetry, although in "The Verse" we are apprised of Milton's invention, "*English* Heroic Verse without Rime," of its precedents in both "some . . . *Italian* and *Spanish* Poets of prime note" and "our best *English* Tragedies," before we encounter an open declaration of *Paradise Lost* as a "Heroic Poem" [a3v–a4]. Yet we can also infer from the coupling of title and subtitle that we are about to encounter a religious poem, not a theological tract—a secular scripture, so to speak. From attention given to this poem's rhymelessness, we may suspect, too, that this heroic poem (in its studied disorder and rebellious gestures) will be cast as a prophecy. Indeed, in its very rhymelessness, *Paradise Lost* resists a chief signature of false prophecy: both the false prophet, that "vast rabble of rhyming, clinching, versifying Prophets"; and the badge of false prophecy, that "*tinkling cymbal* . . . sound in the ear," which would, it was said in 1665, "rather inchant the mind then inform it."[10]

Rather, in keeping with the understanding that the words of true prophecy "come without forcing,"[11] thus resembling the natural movements of the mind and the soul, Milton says of his "unpremeditated Verse" (8.24) that its "sense" will be "variously drawn out" from verse paragraph to verse paragraph and, by implication, from book to book of his poem. That is, his verse will burst the boundaries created by rhyme; and books, breaking through arbitrary barriers, will spill into one another. Milton's poetry, deriving from "nightly visitation[s] unimplor'd" (8.22), will find its closest resemblance in those scriptural works of "an exalted Imagination," in the very process putting on display what Milton's contemporary of 1665, John Spencer, claims was no longer evident in aspiring prophets, the gift of interpreting Scriptures anew, of snatching from them a new revelation. The scriptural revisionism evident in Milton's last poems (*Paradise Lost, Paradise Regain'd,* and *Samson Agonistes*) makes a contrary point, with thunder—and then one: that in the words of Spencer again, prophecy "doth raise in a man a more fine and exquisite power of perception";[12] it engenders *more and more perceiving.* Milton makes this point as early as *Areopagitica,* where "our apprehensions" are said to be "enlarg'd and lifted up . . . [by] degrees" (YP 2:559) and where God is said to enlighten by "steps"—"to dispense and deal out by degrees his beam, so as our earthly eyes may best sustain it" (YP 2:566).

Milton's titles for his epic prophecies remind us, moreover, that such captions are words about, and only sometimes words from, a poem until in the examples afforded by *Paradise Lost* and *Paradise Regain'd* both titles are encapsulated within words from the latter poem: "The Son of God . . . / . . . hast *regain'd lost Paradise*" (4.602, 608; my italics). Furthermore, whether the title imparts generic identity or denotes subject matter, it builds expectations, which may be met, surpassed, or broken, as when *Paradise Lost* becomes a poem equally about the recovery of paradise; or as when *Paradise Regain'd* dashes expectations for a poem about the Crucifixion, replacing the expected story of Christ's Passion with the wilderness temptations and declaring of them, "A fairer Paradise is founded *now*" (4.613; my italics). It seems as if the space of Milton's titles is continually being invaded by interrogations that challenge rather than meet expectations, which in *Paradise Lost* the poem surpasses and in *Paradise Regain'd* disappoints, even as the paired titles seem to promise that these poems will always echo each other's songs.

Indeed, Milton's revision of the initial five lines for what is now book 12, including "the world destroy'd and world restor'd" (12.3), establishes a neat juxtaposition and thereby reinforces the parallelism with the first five lines of the initial book of the poem: "Of Mans First Disobedience, and . . . / . . . loss of *Eden,* till one greater Man / Restore us, and regain the blissful Seat" (1.1–5). From 1671 onward, when *Paradise Regain'd* was published with *Samson Agonistes,* it is impossible for knowing readers of Milton not to think of his two epics in conjunction, as the twin halves of one vast design. In the Dublin edition of 1724, that linkage is secured when *Paradise Regain'd,* until now paired with *Samson Agonistes,* is published as a companion to *Paradise Lost.*[13] This new linkage is ballast for the irony harbored within the initial lines of *Paradise Regain'd*, their echo of Virgil's proclamation (probably written for the *Aeneid* but later excised from it) in which he bids farewell to pastoral poetry as he moves beyond it. Like Virgil, Milton pushes beyond his earlier poetry, including *Paradise Lost*, by establishing radically new norms for heroic deeds and epic heroism as he now sings of "deeds / *Above* Heroic" (1.14–15; my italics).

In the case of *Paradise Lost*, the first edition holds clues to an original horizon of expectations, and subsequent editions provide evidence of horizonal shifts, some of which are doubtless owing to Milton's recasting of epic and radicalizing of his theology in *Paradise Regain'd*, as well as the inevitable intertwinings of his epic poems with his earlier prose writings. Jonathan Richardson Sr. makes a crucial point with brutal honesty: "'tis Remembred *Paradise Lost* was not yet produc'd, and the Writings on which his Vast Reputation Stood were Now Accounted Criminal, Every One of them, and Those Most which were the Main Pillars of his Fame"[14]—that is, *Eikonoklastes* and the two defenses of the English people. The history of any one of Milton's works, but especially of *Paradise Lost*, harbors this or that "Secret History" (the phrase is Richardson's); and that history, once set forth, makes clear that *Paradise Lost* as a book is "less a product," in the words of Stephen Orgel, "than a process, part of an ongoing dialectic."[15]

Indeed, the history of Milton's diffuse epic includes stories of imitations, adaptations, and appropriations; of translations and of transposings of rhymeless into rhymed verse, of poetry into prose, with early maskings of Milton's poetic content inviting later unmaskings and, with them, the revival of old arguments over whether Milton was a heretic or whether, instead, all those seemingly heterodox moments in Milton's epic are, as Richardson conjectured, "very Capable of an Orthodox Construction."[16] It is tempting to quell any controversy over the authority of the editions of *Paradise Lost* in Milton's own lifetime: "So—*Go thy ways, the Flour and Quintessence of all Editors.* [T]he Edition of 1674 is the Finish'd, the Genuine, the Uncorrupted Work of *John Milton*"[17]—or so it seems, until the first two editions of *Paradise Lost* are allowed to interplay, and we witness a poem's symmetrical structure go into concealment even as other parallelisms, together with the poem's thematic core of Christocentric theology and heliocentric cosmology, each subtending the other, gather into steadily sharpening focus. Early editions of *Paradise Lost* interface intriguingly and complexly, engaging one another in an ongoing dialogue.

Between 1667 and 1674 we move from what Roy Flannagan describes as the relatively "austere aesthetic" of the first edition of *Paradise Lost*, its "economy of page," where there are no prefatory materials or "accessory ornaments," as if the poem were "designed like a Quaker table, on purpose," to a second edition with a frontispiece portrait, a significantly altered title page, Milton's own note on the verse, preliminary poems by others in advance of Milton's poem, and arguments now appended as headpieces to each book. Peter Lindenbaum puts a telling construction on such observations: "In a good number of seventeenth-century poetry volumes . . . , the poetry begins with signature B, implicitly leaving the poet space to gather encomia to himself [to be inserted later] while the printer proceeds ahead with his task. [The] 1667 *Paradise Lost* starts with signature A right after [the] title page, suggesting that from the start no prefatory material was intended."[18] Not from "the start . . . intended," perhaps, but very soon afterward, prefatory material was incorporated into the *first* edition. Thus, what appears in the edition of 1674 comes as an afterthought, fragments of which, however, turn up in later issues of the first edition, with the full formation not present until "A Poem in Twelve Books" is published in the year of Milton's death. The development of *Paradise Lost* by alteration and accretion, then, is equally the story of its first edition, encapsulated in issue 4 within a movement of signatures from "*A*" to "a" to "A" (this time in roman caps) as the poem proper commences.[19] It is a poem of false starts as its expanding front matter seems to indicate and as its proliferating proems within the poem proper also seem to testify.

The issue for Flannagan is "inexpensive book design" and subsequently the wish to give a fresh look to a book not selling well, but for others it is an initial thumbing of Milton's nose (immediately evident in his animadversions against rhyme) at "Restoration literary fashions." What Lindenbaum challenges in his shrewd response to Flannagan is the latter's presumptions, first, that there were additional materials available to the printer for inclusion or exclusion, affording Milton the opportunity to economize, and, second, that final decisions were being made by Samuel Simmons rather than (as Lindenbaum argues) by "Milton . . . himself." The task now before us, Joad Raymond chimes in, is to grasp "the cultural significance of the organisation of the page," and then to try "to 'read' typography and the paratext." In doing so, we should acknowledge immediately that the organization of *Paradise Lost,* from the very beginning, by book and line number, oftentimes with a numerological sophistication, gestures toward (so as to place the poem within) classical and sacred traditions of verse and then within the most refined, and often esoteric, systems of composition.[20]

II

As McGann acknowledges, to take account of such matters and to observe a poem's operations within a radial field, including its interactions with different contexts, affects our readings as well as our interpretations:

> For one thing, it forces us to realize that books involve a "reading" of their audiences which those audiences may or may not realize, and may or may not submit to. [Books] . . . interact with . . . audiences by absorbing and regularizing the possible modes of response. [The book may labor] . . . to minimize its own internal conflicts, as well as the possible conflicts its message might generate. In order for us to *read* . . . , then, rather than to be *read by* it, we have to explode the illusion of contextual seamlessness which the work projects. We have to "step outside" that fiction of a homogeneous context and read the work in a framework and point of view which it has not already absorbed and anticipated. This requires reading the work in those contexts which [it] . . . has tried either to forbid, or to declare nonexistent.[21]

In these remarks, McGann provides cues for a preliminary reading of *Paradise Lost* that commences with the title pages and continues with the front matter of the first edition, all the while contending with contexts, either forbidden or suppressed by Milton, his friends or his editors, as well as his translators, illustrators, imitators, and critics. McGann also gestures toward the recognition that, while books in themselves do not make revolutions, as Adrian Johns remarks, "the ways they are made, used, and read just might."[22] A poem published in the aftermath of the English revolution may still have *revolution* within its sights.

In its afterlife, the book called *Paradise Lost*, like the text of that poem in Milton's own lifetime, developed by accretion: with the addition of an epigram to the new frontispiece portrait as well as illustrations, and a subscription list (1688); then with the inclusion of explanatory notes promised for each book in 1695, the year of P. H.'s (Patrick Hume's) commentary of 321 pages, plus tables of descriptions, similes, and speeches. Those tables were greatly expanded in early eighteenth century editions until *Paradise Lost* was published with a full index in 1724. A dedicatory page, actually two pages, was included in 1705 and, 20 years later, in 1725, a catalog of emendations appeared (1725). Eventually, essays in criticism were added, such as those by Addison sometimes cited in advertisements and then eventually published in two different issues of the 1719 Tonson edition, plus lives of the poet, Elijah Fenton's "Life" (along with a postscript) being the first of them to appear as an accompaniment to Milton's poetry (1725). Finally, annotations by various hands accumulated, over time achieving the clout of a variorum edition (1749), at which time a book that had been published as one was usually bloated into two volumes. In this way, certainly, a look at the first edition of *Paradise Lost* in its various states forecasts a larger history.

Since Milton never specifies, we will never know the extent of his collusion with printers or their compositors concerning the makeup of his books, much less their title pages. Still, it is evident in *An Apology against a Pamphlet*, then *Areopagitica* and *Eikonoklastes*, and finally in his *Defense of Himself* that during the seventeenth century others as well as Milton scrutinized both titles and title pages (YP 1:876, 877; 3:343, 597; 4:733–34). As he worries over what is an apt title in *Areopagitica*, Milton notices how "Sometimes 5 *Imprimaturs* are seen together dialogue-wise in the Piatza of one Title page, complementing and ducking each to other" (YP 2:504) and, in the same work, speaks of "shrewd books, with dangerous Frontispices" (YP 2:524). In *Defense of Himself*, moreover, Milton admits to collusion concerning the frontispiece portrait to the 1645 *Poems of Mr. John Milton* as he explains that the picture "prefixed" to this volume is there "at the suggestion and solicitation of a bookseller" with whom he "suffered" to cooperate (YP 4:750–51), and then specifically praises the title page to his *Second Defense of the English People* as "veracious and in all respects proper to the book" (YP 4:734).[23]

Additionally, title pages, loose, as Adrian Johns reminds us, were often "set out as advertisements" in bookstores, in this way serving as announcements of a book's availability and as invitations to a preliminary reading.[24] The presentation of a book and of its author obviously affects how both are perceived: how books are made and displayed may afford evidence of sedition, blasphemy, or obscenity and may alienate a readership or, alternatively, entice it. Portraits were not the only way to create and control images of an author, for what eventually is rejected from the front matter of a book, for instance, may be as revelatory as what is initially included or what eventually appears there. Thus, emendations included in a first edition may engender errata lists in subsequent editions, Milton's initial gesture opening the way and functioning as a precedent, however tardily, for later editors.

The best surmise, when it comes to the title pages for *Paradise Lost*, is that, besides providing the poet with a way of mediating his work to a readership, they constitute part of a collaboration between poet and printer and hence should be regarded both as implicit commentary by Milton on his poem and as an early reception, indeed as a way of anticipating and shaping reception and thus as an integral part of this poem's reception history. These title pages, like seventeenth century title pages generally, are themselves (and imply that so too are the texts they accompany) sites for mediation between poet and printer and between both and a book's readership, often with the author taking the lead. Furthermore, if John Phillips (in his "Response") is a reliable guide (see YP 4:905), Milton was fully aware of the circumstances under which an author may publish anonymously, or nearly so, as Milton did with his poem "On Shakespear," the 1637 edition of *A Mask*, the 1638 publication of *Lycidas*, the first edition of *The Doctrine and Discipline of Divorce*, and two issues of *Paradise Lost*, each with a 1668 title page.

In Milton's case, the most striking evidence of literary collaboration and poetic competition comes early, in the Edward King memorial volume, *Justa Edovardo King Naufrago* (1638), where *Lycidas* seems to be in continuous dialogue with the poems it succeeds, in both halves of the volume, and in strident competition with some of those poets, most notably Henry King, Samson Briggs, and Thomas Norton. It is folly to forget that "typographically sophisticated" elements in texts, whether Spenser's or Milton's, whether *Lycidas* or the later *Paradise Lost* are, in the words of Mark Bland, "more likely to have come from an author or a party acting on the author's behalf, rather than the printer" and a mistake, too, to overly credit Flannagan's contention that "The blind Milton obviously exerted less control on the printing of what he wrote than the sighted Milton."[25] This first point is illustrated powerfully by the title page to *Areopagitica*. If the printer has suppressed his own name, Milton fearlessly showcases his identity, incorporating it into the subtitle of this work. The second point, earlier challenged (as we have seen) by Richardson, finds its best illustration in the expanding front matter for *Paradise Lost* as that poem moves through different issues and eventually into a second edition, this front matter implying that the two editions of Milton's poem are decidedly different from each other, perhaps exaggeratedly so, in this way warding off the presumption that different editions of a work are all the same. Indeed, in the instance of *Paradise Lost*, what may have seemed a taming of the first edition is, instead, a centering and highlighting of its revolutionary content, quite literally the moment of civil war and revolution, including the Copernican revolution, as each is focused in book 6 and what will eventually become books 7 and 8 of *Paradise Lost*. This strategy is evident as early as *Lycidas*, where an epigraph not printed with the first edition is added to the second, thus underscoring that this oracular poem, a monody, features a prophetic center.

Signatures of authorship become marks of honor for Milton as he complains, in his *Second Defense*, about engaging in polemic with those who, publishing "furtively and by stealth," choose to remain "nameless" and who, doing so, are neither "devoted enough . . . nor loyal enough" to their cause. By contrast, Milton says of himself, "I was so far from being ashamed either of myself or my cause that I considered it disgraceful to attack so great a theme without openly acknowledging my identity" (YP 4:561, 560–61). Anyone who argues that the later Milton is hiding out when he publishes nearly anonymously with initials only ("J. M.") the second edition of *The Readie and Easie Way*, as well as some early issues of *Paradise Lost*, needs to keep in mind that earlier titles of both works bear his full signature and that similarly anonymous works, like *A Treatise of Civil Power*, even if their title pages bear no more than an initialed signature, carry prefaces (in this instance, "To The Parlament") with a bold signature: **JOHN MILTON**. Or, in analogy with *Paradise Lost*, of the two issues of *Accedence Commenc't Grammar*, both published in 1668, on one title page Milton's name is spelled out; on the other, only his initials are given, as they are again on the title page for *Of True Religion* (1673). These arguments are not conclusive, but they are important checks on any explanation of Milton's anonymous— or nearly anonymous—publication, whether it is explained in terms of social pressure or political caution. And more: such arguments enjoy the pedigree of Milton's own thinking on such topics, as well as his literary practice.

If often not enough has been made of Milton's signatures, too much should not be made of them either. Trust invested in a book by its readership depends in a major way on both its prior knowledge and current opinion of the book's author. The very idea of authorship appears on the title pages to *Paradise Lost* at precisely the moment when "The Author," according to some, goes into hiding behind his initials. The designation of "The Author" from this time forward is a constant on title pages for the first and second editions of *Paradise Lost*. Furthermore, the appearance of this phrase on the title pages makes abundantly clear that here J[ohn] M[ilton] either claims, or is credited with, authorship; that there is no effort to shift the responsibility of authorship from the poet to the printer and every effort, in the second edition, to identify the poet as his own revisionist, enlarger, editor, and commentator: "The Second Edition / Revised and Augmented by the / *same* Author" (my italics). Indeed, the errata list present in some issues of the first edition includes the remark "Other literal faults the Reader of himself may Correct" [a4v]. Milton thus invites his readership to collaborate with him in the editorial job of proofreading even as, in comparison with Milton's note to the second edition—"Revised and Augmented by the / same Author"—restrictions seem to be imposed on a collaboration wherein we may proofread and correct but *not* revise and augment. We are not licensed to add—or to subtract—from his words. The Richard Bentleys of the world of Milton scholarship have been thus anticipated and admonished.

Some thought—and many continue to think—that the very name of "John Milton" ensures a resistant readership, some of whom, remembering Milton's prose writings and hence withholding their trust, would recoil from *Paradise Lost* in disgust if its author's identity were known. In this context, one must remember, further, that only Milton's initials, not his name, were given to the licenser of *Paradise Lost*. If politics were an issue as early as 1638 when *Lycidas* was published nearly anonymously (simply initialed "J. M."), it was probably first the politics of the poem's author, especially in view of the fact that other poets in the Edward King memorial volume reviled just the sort of critique of religion that Milton composed within his own poem. Relevant, too, is the fact that, as Peter Levi relates, "Dr Bastwick of Colchester, with the Revd Mr Burton of Friday Street, who had been railing against bishops since 1624, went to prison in 1637 and had their ears cut off in the pillory; Prynne," having already had his ears cut off, now "had the stumps . . . sawn off."[26] Prynne's punishment is a poignant reminder that authorial responsibility and culpability extended beyond what was actually written to interpretations inferred from or fixed upon a published text, especially if the medium was prose. With *Paradise Lost,* someone—either poet or printer—felt threatened, and thus sought a shield of protection, confirmed by the fact that, after Milton's signature was restored to the title page and the printer of the poem identified, only then (in edition 1, issue 4, dated 1669) was the title page announcement "Licensed and Entred according to Order" dropped. Only then, presumably, was the text also safe from the licenser's interference, which, had he been provoked, could have taken the form of either erasure or emendation. *Paradise Lost* had finally averted the eye of the censor.

It is certainly possible that the strategy implicit in the initialed signature, as David Masson remarks, was to save a poem like *Paradise Lost* by saving its reputation from that of its author. For it is likely that Milton's name, as well as any poem he produced, would be suspected of bearing political meanings and seems to have been thus suspected by friends and associates from John Phillips to Theodore Haak and H. L. Benthem and even, if only because he protests too much to the contrary, by Andrew Marvell.[27] On the other hand, it is possible that the two initialed title pages for *Paradise Lost* (edition 1, issues 3A and 3B, both dated 1668) reveal not a poet hiding from his prospective readers, but a printer concealing his associations with and wanting to avoid the same fate as the poem's beleaguered author, who admits to having "fall'n on evil dayes, / . . . and evil tongues" and, in fear of his life, complains of now being blind, "In darkness, and with dangers compast rouud [*sic*]" (7.25–26, 32–39, 27). After all, no printer's name is given on the title pages of *Paradise Lost* dated 1667, nor on those for two of three issues dated 1668.

Much earlier Adrian Vlacq complained that the printer of Milton's *First Defense of the English People,* "as is his wont, . . . was unwilling to have his name attached to it" (YP 4:1089). And Milton himself argues in *Defense of Himself* that, in the absence of an author's name, "he who published [the book] . . . must be considered its author" (YP 4:701). Printing houses were sometimes seen as sites of sedition, and the printers themselves (as well as booksellers) as engineers of rebellion. Thus, on the one hand, both could lend a book integrity and veracity but also, depending upon their reputations, could implicate a book in controversy, even conspiracy. Indeed, if as Adrian Johns contends, the names of printers and booksellers on title pages "could tell a prospective reader as much about the contents [of a book] as could that of the author," especially with radical books, then *Paradise Lost* seems to have been in double jeopardy and, as a poem, would deploy all the subterfuges of its art in order to deliver its message, even if in disguise.[28]

If after the fall of the Protectorate, as Nicholas von Maltzahn reports, "Milton went from publishing with the government printer to the Baptist bookseller Livewell Chapman, at the center of radical religious politics," he made a choice, which would not have gone unobserved and which thus might have consequences both for him and for the printers and booksellers of his later poems.[29] At some time, all were likely to be caught in a web of suspicion. From a family of dissenting printers and booksellers, Samuel Simmons—whose name appears on three (but *not the first three*) title pages for *Paradise Lost,* on ones dated 1668 and 1669, and whose signature (S. Simmons) is appended to the addition, "The Printer to the Reader"—already had one encounter with the government in the very year Milton's poem was published and, in consequence, had been arrested.[30] Simmons obviously would be leery of another encounter with the authorities and would want to avoid yet another arrest. Poet and printer are equally vulnerable and, evidently, similarly cautious; booksellers perhaps less so. Yet Robert Boulter, named as one of the booksellers on five of the seven title pages, had been hauled into court to explain 200 copies of a pirated almanac in his bookshop.[31] And such issues, not restricted to *Paradise Lost,* come to mind again with the publication of *Paradise Regain'd* and *Samson Agonistes.* John Starkey, for whom these poems were printed, is known to have participated in the tactic whereby multiple printing houses were deliberately involved in the production of risky texts as a way of neutralizing responsibility for a book, the contents of which any one printer knew only piecemeal.[32] Moreover, as Annabel Patterson reported to me in conversation, by 1671 Starkey was already an icon for radical publications.

From the sixteenth century onward, censorship was used as a check on political sedition and religious heresy, and anonymity, as Robert J. Griffin perceives, often "an officially tolerated form of sanctuary," was not only an author's safeguard against detection and sometimes assertion of humility but also evidence of "anxiety over public exposure, fear of prosecution, hope of an unprejudiced reception," as well as a "desire to deceive" (even to hide from) one's printer or publisher.[33] Milton had something to lose, then, but so too did Simmons, although poetry itself was an ideal mechanism that, because a convenient subterfuge, could hide discord in its basement while maintaining an impression of harmony on its surface. Nevertheless, to focus on just two of the seven title pages for *Paradise Lost* is, finally, to ignore the virtual parity established on all the other title pages for the first, as well as the second, edition of *Paradise Lost* between author and title, poet and poem, and thus to resist the clear implication from three of these title pages, also bearing the name of Simmons, that reading *Paradise Lost* is "reading" Milton.

It is abundantly evident from the printer's note to the reader in two issues of the first edition of *Paradise Lost* that printer collaborates with poet to produce both the note on "why the Poem Rimes not" (*A2*) and the arguments to its individual books, each reminding us that there is a poet behind this poem overseeing and orchestrating the whole performance even to the point of revising it. The nature of the revisions (especially with regard to structure) is revelatory,[34] no less so inclusions as well as exclusions (preliminary poems by S. B. [Samuel Barrow] and Andrew Marvell in the first instance, and in the second the absence of a dedicatory page). When *Paradise Lost* went into a second edition, this point was reinforced by the acknowledged revision of a ten-book poem into a twelve-book poem, then punctuated by the expansion of the front matter to include the preliminary—and mediatorial—poems by S. B. and Andrew Marvell. The arguments, once preliminary matter, were assimilated into the poem and printed as headpieces to the 12 books even as some 15 lines of new poetry, some of them carefully calibrated for their bracketing power, were silently added.

With the disappearance of the printer's note from the second edition, Milton himself, through his note on "The Verse," acted as mediator even as he seemed to enlist S. B. and Andrew Marvell, through their preliminary poems, as additional negotiators with his readers. Taken together, this front matter constitutes a negotiation strategy probably crafted by Milton, who is, in this way, seen at the portal to his poem quite apart from the frontispiece portrait added to this second edition. He is also seen in his revisions to poems (witness the title page acknowledgment for the second edition of *Paradise Lost*, previously cited), with the "Omissa" to *Samson Agonistes* further illustrating the point, as if flagging Milton's presence and thereby driving home Anne Middleton's proposition that "the author's labors as maker also situate the author himself within . . . [a poem's] reception history as reviser."[35] In the very act of mediating a poem to its audience, the author becomes a crucial player in the drama of its reception with Milton, in the second edition of *Paradise Lost*, usurping from his printer direct responsibility for mediating his verse form to the public, and, while acknowledging revisions, except for the shift from a ten- to a twelve-book poem, specifies none. (There was no errata sheet for this edition as there was for the first.)

Particularly remarkable about Milton's title pages, together with the accumulating front matter, is that poet and poem, poem and reader, are bound inextricably in a single compact in order to insist upon

the poet's presence in a poem that completes itself in the mind of
the reader, so as to establish outside the poem the dialectical relationship between poet and reader that is at its core. In "The Printer
to the Reader," Samuel Simmons addresses Milton's *"Courteous
Reader"*—an address occasioned by those "many" readers who have
enquired about the "reason . . . why the Poem Rimes not" (*A*2).
Through his own note, entitled "The Verse," and then through the
arguments for the individual books of the poem, Milton responds to
these concerns of his readership. As earlier remarked, the table
labeled "ERRATA" similarly prompts the reader: "Other literal faults
the Reader of himself may Correct" [a4v]—just as the errata sheet
for the 1673 *Poems, &c. upon Several Occasions* will similarly
instruct readers to correct errors. Yet in "The Verse," in the very
moment he acknowledges his readership, Milton differentiates
between "vulgar Readers," apt to construe the absence of rhyme as
"a defect" [a4], and those he eventually designates in his poem as a
"fit audience . . . though few" (7.31)—those alert to the politics
encoded in rhymelessness, a politics (as we have seen) that Milton
may have found enunciated by his contemporary John Spencer in the
very year, 1665, that Milton allegedly completed *Paradise Lost*. Yet
it is a politics Milton would, in other ways, rescind by presenting
Paradise Lost as a prophecy to a world from which Spencer would
rid such "Seditious" writings; and to a world from which, unlike
Milton, Spencer scuttled the idea of all the Lord's people becoming
prophets on the grounds that prophecy was not a gift bestowed upon
all, certainly not upon "ruder minds" or the "ignorant Multitude."[36]

As we proceed from some title pages to *Paradise Lost*—where
Milton's name (in initials only) is nearly anonymous to later ones
(still belonging to the first edition); where the poet's name, even if
muted by comparison with other elements of the title page, is nevertheless spelled out; and then onward to the second edition of
Paradise Lost, where the poet's image is flashed across the title
page by virtue of its frontispiece status—the conclusion seems obvious. In 1668, at any rate, Milton mutes his presence through a prac-
ticed self-effacement, as explained by John Phillips in his "Response"
to John Rowland as he perhaps borrows on Milton's wisdom. To
Rowland's remark, "it is by no means unusual for worthy men to

withhold their names [as does] St. Paul in the Epistle to the Hebrews,"
Phillips retorts. "He did, to be sure, write anonymously, but to a people bitterly hostile to his name about matters quite new and little
credited" (YP 4:905), the emphasis falling not so much on the author
as subject as on the subject matter of the author's discourse, which
itself requires a shield of protection. We may continue to look for
Milton in his writings and, in doing so, discover him as a disruptive
presence in the folds of a torn text. Such tears are first evident in con-
spicuous omissions, then in marked revisions, and finally in the discrepancies that exist between what some of the arguments to books
of *Paradise Lost* promise and what individual books, in contradistinction, then provide.

III

What seizes, then commands, the attention of Milton's first variorum editor is a silence, an omission: *Paradise Lost* has no patron,
no dedicatee—an oddity Thomas Newton explains away with the
observation that Milton "designed" his poem for no single person
but rather "for the wise and learned of all ages,"[37] but also an oddity
he then compounds with the acknowledgment that eighteenth century editors supplied a dedication for the very poem from which Milton
deliberately withheld one. Paradoxically, for Newton, the apparent
violation of Milton's intention actually accentuates both his aesthetic
commitments and his political gesture—"an essentially republican
gesture," says Peter Lindenbaum[38]—wherein the dedicatee "*John*
Lord *Sommers*, Baron of *Evesham*," because of his sponsorship of the
famous 1688 edition of *Paradise Lost*, is used to highlight, first, that
in the figure of Milton England has finally produced a model "in poetry
superior to any or all the nations in Europe" and, second, that, as
Newton goes on to say, Milton's life had been dedicated to a "long,
and glorious struggle in the cause of liberty,"[39] here symbolized by
a poet who, commencing his career within an aristocratic patronage
system, eventually springs free from it—so free that by 1688 *Paradise
Lost*, still without a patron, is published by subscription.

If Milton deliberately omitted a dedication from *Paradise Lost*, he
inadvertently left it to his editors and commentators to repair that

omission in more or less the spirit of *Paradise Lost*. Thus, it is no small irony that John Dryden—who walked with Milton in Cromwell's funeral procession and is later described by him as a rhymester but no poet—once he gets his hands on Milton's poem and tags it with rhyme—should then supplement it with a dedication, giving "new" meaning to "majesty," an attribute that in a decidedly different sense he will associate with Milton in his epigram for the 1688 edition. In 1677, however, Dryden's title page, inscribed with a dedication, reads: "The State of Innocence, And Fall of Man: An Opera. Written in Heroique Verse, and Dedicated to Her *Royal Highness*, The Dutchess. By *John Dryden*, Servant to His Majesty."

In "The Authors Apology for Heroique Poetry; and Poetique Licence," Dryden makes clear that he was neither long in choosing a topic nor long in writing his poem: "*at a Months warning, in which time 'twas wholly Written, and not since Revis'd,*" he says in lines that, effusive with praise for Milton, also hint at shortcomings: "*sublime Genius . . . sometimes erres*" yet, in the case of Milton, even if the poet is misguided at times, he should not be "*tax'd . . . for his choice of a supernatural Argument.*"[40] Dryden leaves it to Nathaniel Lee, in a dedicatory poem, to spell out differences between these poets; Dryden, knowing his place as it were, is more concerned with reforming poetry than with reforming the world. Yet Dryden is still addressed as "O mightiest of the inspir'd men," who with "new Theams" is emptying his pen in order that he may "The troubles of Majestick CHARLES set down." Unlike Milton, Dryden will not "affright" our eyes with heavenly spectacles involving Satan, nor will he cast his poetry as "rudely" or as "roughly" as Milton had done, Dryden thus re-creating, according to Lee, the "perfect World" that continues to elude Milton.[41]

If Dryden is here canceling Milton's vision with his own 11 years later, he is responsible for another substitution in which his lamely rhymed and otherwise vacuous epigram, just mentioned, displaces the provocative poems by S. B. and Andrew Marvell:

> *Three* Poets, *in Three distant Ages born,*
> Greece, Italy, *and* England *did adorn.*
> *The* First *in loftiness of thought Surpass'd,*

The Next *in Majesty; in both the* Last.
The force of Nature *cou'd no farther goe:*
To make a Third *she joynd the former two.*[42]

Dryden's larger project, it seems, is to turn Milton's own poetics and politics on end, thereby anesthetizing the politics that Milton brings out of concealment in his observations on the verse form of *Paradise Lost:* "ancient liberty . . . modern bondage" (a4). While Dryden records the king's "troubles," Milton writes, rather, of a world troubled by kingship and beset with its tyrannies. As Lindenbaum remarks, "the decision to publish *Paradise Lost* on the open market and without benefit of protection or support of some great man represents not simply a religious decision but a political one," especially evident in Milton's "desire to educate a whole nation" through his poem, and to do so from a posture of not just political but also moral independence.[43] Milton may thus be praised in the very terms used in his *Defense of Himself:* "he alone is to be called great who performs great deeds, or teaches how they may be done, or writes about them in terms becoming their greatness" (YP 4:774). Or: "Singular indeed is the favor of God toward me, that He has called me above all others to the defence of liberty" (YP 4:735).

If liberty is the master theme of Milton's prose works, by virtue of the note entitled "The Verse," it looms equally large at the entrance to *Paradise Lost,* only to be underscored by the generic definition Milton gives his poem (both in the arguments to books 1 and 2 and in the prologues to books 1, 3, and 4), first as epic, then as prophecy: "the Poem hasts into the midst of things" (*A2*), this epic formula standing out from the environing prose by virtue of its not being printed in italic; then comes Satan's recollection of *"an ancient Prophesie or report in Heaven"* and reference to his wish *"To find out the truth of this Prophesie"* [A2v]. The same point is reiterated in the argument to book 2 where Satan again is said to desire *"to search the truth of that Prophesie or Tradition in Heaven concerning another world and another kind of creation equall or not much less inferiour to themselves"* [A2v]. Lest the idea of prophecy be lost, it is hammered home through allusions to *"Tiresias* and *Phineus* Prophets old" (3.36), as well as Orpheus (3.17), in the prologue to book 3 and

through the citation of that "warning voice" (4.1) in the abridged prologue of the subsequent book. Prophecy is then showcased by Andrew
Marvell in his preliminary poem to the second edition: "Just
heaven . . . / Rewards with prophecy thy loss of sight."[44]

As *Paradise Lost* unfolds, however, it becomes increasingly evident that Milton's poem is a critique of the very genres, epic and
prophecy, with which it asserts identity. There is no surprise here.
As Heather Dubrow wisely observes, Milton's approach to genre, early
on, is "complicated" and "ambivalent," inasmuch as this poet was
so aware that "If the hope of creating reformed genres is potentially
imperiled by the fallen man who writes them, it is threatened as well
by the fallen reader liable to misinterpret them."[45] And the critique
itself, an extension into the poem of the one commenced in the note
on its verse, is a reminder of the originally subversive thrust of both
genres, each of them centered in the human mind and centering on—
anatomizing—its operations. With Milton (in what might well be
called a principal manifestation of Miltonic Romanticism), epic,
prophecy, and tragedy merge into a mental theater in *Paradise Lost*
and remain merged in the 1671 poetic volume including *Paradise
Regain'd* and *Samson Agonistes*. Genres, once tamed, are now
untamed by Milton and his Romantic heirs.

If it is true that illustrations accruing to Milton's poem "complement Milton's arguments,"[46] enabling a better grasp of his complex
plot, it is also the case that those arguments are among the earliest
critical commentaries on Milton's poem and that, like many later
illustrations, they often exhibit an asymmetrical relationship with
the poem they accompany. Like the note on Milton's verse, the arguments, appended initially as preliminary matter to the poem and only
in a second edition fixed to individual books, often exist in tension
with the poetry they would elucidate even as they shy away from
the controversies lurking within them. Never a polemic, the arguments are crafted by a wily poet, as headpieces to books, which are
an active complication of their claims and, on occasion, a subtle sub-
version of them. The arguments never announce an interpretation,
but they do nudge us toward an ampler understanding of *Paradise
Lost*. As improvements to his poem, those arguments, containing
generic markers, also act as generic signals, bringing Milton's poem

"more fully in line with the norms for presenting classical epic."[47] Just as important, however, as signatures of epic, those arguments sit in tension with (as genre to countergenre) a poem continually aspiring to the strains of prophecy.

By Milton's time, as Mark Bland allows, "Black-letter, roman, and italic were invested with new associations" and implied "newly assumed functions," with roman and italic often used to discriminate different strands and interwoven material, to layer meanings and even develop tensions among them.[48] If, by the seventeenth century, roman type had become the primary face for poetry, italic, in its developing associations with speech, hence with the orality of a text, was used sometimes for signaling the strong classical and continental influences on a text (*Lycidas* as distinct from the Nativity poem or "The Passion" in the 1645 *Poems*); other times for marking generic differences—to distinguish a play from a poem, as on the title page to the 1671 poetic volume; and still other times to create dialectical play between different components of a text, in the example of *Paradise Lost*, between the prose arguments (in italic) and the poetry (in roman type). By 1673, the huge caps accorded LYCIDAS in the table of contents to the volume bring a prophetic character into focus within a poem that is about formation, and the italicized epigraph, printed not just with the poem, put (in part) on the contents page, underscores the oracular character of this poem, a *"Monody,"* which *"foretells the ruine of our corrupted Clergie."*

In *Paradise Lost*, even as rhymeless verse signals prophecy, indeed declares Milton's poem to be a prophecy, the arguments to books 1 and 2 promptly call prophecy into question: is it *"ancient Prophesie or report,"* *"Prophesie"* or mere *"Tradition"* that Satan hears in heaven [A2v]; and, if the former, is there any "truth" to garner from searching "this Prophesie" [A2v]—or is it just crude forecasting? If Milton presses us to question whether the prophecy is true or false, Satan's actions within the poem make us consider both the uses and abuses of prophecy in the modern world. They are also a prelude to the poet-narrator's wondering if, "unrein'd," his own song wanders erroneously (7.17–20). If the poem is his invention rather than a gift from the heavenly muse (8.46–47), if it is thus "an empty dreame" (7.39), the poet-narrator wonders if he is not on surer ground when he "Sing[s] with mortal voice" (7.24). By the end of *Paradise Lost*, however, in its final book, prophecy, revived as the poem's principal mode and theme, is again subjected to scrutiny and renewed critique.

The poet knows that one consequence of the Fall, thus delineated in book 8, is that the mind has been "dark'nd" (8.1054) so that the poet himself, like Adam in the last book of *Paradise Lost*, is limited by fallen (hence sometimes false) consciousness. Thus, even if the poem is a vision emanating from a divine source, it is filtered through, its meaning subject to the quirks and distortions of, human consciousness. The last book, therefore, presses the questions: What is the efficacy of prophecy in the modern world? What are its limitations in and even perils to fallen existence? How is book 10 to be read then: as history (prophecy fulfilled) or as prophecy (history anticipated)? Such questions become self-answering with the emerging awareness that consciousness, awakened in book 9, sharpens perception in book 10, where the gates of understanding are gradually opened in an unending mental progress. It is not so much that Milton searches the past as prophets do the future. Rather, he wrings from the past a revelation of current history and of the possibilities for future history.

Alternatively, when we turn from the argument for book 1 to the one for book 2, we are made to square its claim, that "Satan *debates*" [A2v], with the poem itself, where Satan does not actually participate in the debate, the outcome of which he nevertheless determines. Probably with Daniel Defoe in mind, Coleridge once remarked, "Readers have learnt from Milton alone, that Satan & Beelzebub were different Persons (in the Scriptures they are different names of the same Evil Being),"[49] thus ignoring the prompt in the argument to book 2, *Satan debates*, and so forgetting not only Satan's later declaration, "Both waking we were one" (5.675), but also the emphasis here on the unity of the devils who, throughout book 2, "Firm concord" hold (2.497). The debate *is* Satan's in that it consists of alternative plans for action passing through and being weighed within his mind. The participating devils (Moloch, Belial, Mammon, and Beelzebub) can thus be seen as representing different angles of Satan's vision, various layers of his consciousness, diverse aspects of his evil, as well as alternative manipulations for achieving his wicked ends. In the end, though, these devils are all interchangeable; they are one with Satan, his different manifestations—all fragments of the same fallen angel.

Long before William Wordsworth, Milton created a poetry in which the mind was his "haunt, and the main region of . . . [his] song";[50] a poetry of consciousness, of process; of a mind-shattering, mind-transforming, mind-expanding drama that finds its chief expression in Milton's argument to book 9 of the first edition with its description of Adam's mind as *"more and more perceiving his fall'n condition"* [a2v], the climactic moment of which is registered in Adam's "O miserable of happie!" speech (9.720–850). Moreover, this description of Adam's mental enlargement, not unlike that attributed to Constantine in Milton's *The History of Britain*, a mind "contracted and shrunk up," but then "with a wak'n'd spirit . . . dilating" (YP 5:124), is an equally apt description for the process Milton's readership now experiences, in parallel with Adam, in the final books of *Paradise Lost*. It is a process capturing internal movements, the motions of a mind, darkened, as it moves toward enlightenment.

What becomes evident in a juxtaposition of the first and second editions of *Paradise Lost* is a general tendency through revisions in the second edition to highlight, or reinforce, inflections in the first edition. The mental drama, playing itself out in the last half of the first edition and, as we have just observed, inscribed within the argument to book 9, is (in the second edition) presented in quick epitome as Milton revises a line in old book 7, "To whom thus *Adam* gratefully repli'd" (7.641) to read: "Then as *new wak't* thus gratefully repli'd" (8.4; my italics). Recalling a whole parcel of lines, the italicized phrase, *new wak't*, when read fast-forward, anticipates Eve's awakening in the concluding book of *Paradise Lost:* "*Adam* to the bower where *Eve* / Lay sleeping ran . . . but found her wak't" (10.1499). Yet when read by winding backward through Milton's text, the same phrase recalls "When *Adam* wak't" (5.3), then when Eve "wak'd . . . but with startl'd eye / On *Adam*" (5.26–27), and when she gladly "wak'd" again, in contrast with John Keats's Adam, "To find this but a dream!" (5.93). The phrase, new to Milton's second edition, echoes one in the text of *Paradise Lost* from the very beginning: Adam "new wak't" after his creation (7.890) and then awakening to Eve's creation: "I wak'd, and found / Before mine Eyes all real" (7.946–47); "awake I stood" (7.1101), says Adam; "I wak'd / To find her" (7.1115–16).

Ironically, Eve's dream will become more and more the reality into which she and Adam will awaken, both like Samson "wak'd / Shorn of . . . [their] strength" (8.1061–62). Yet if Earth signals their fall by trembling, Earth also heralds their regeneration—"the Earth now wak'd" (9.94)—and eventually their resurrection. For while metaphorically sleeping, by the end of the poem both Adam and Eve are "found" newly "wak't" as they will finally be "Wak't in the renovation of the just" (10.65). "[B]ut not so wak'd / *Satan*" (5.654–55; my italics). Only Satan is exempt from the process in which first the Earth, then Adam and Eve, and eventually the poet-narrator and Milton's readers participate—a process within which comes the promise, threaded through *Paradise Lost,* of a new heaven and a new Earth. *New wak't:* an apocalypse of mind is a prelude to an apocalypse in history. Already there in *Lycidas,* the idea is now unfurled in *Paradise Lost.*

The mind, awakening to more and more reality, "*more and more perceiving,*" in the words of the argument to book 9 [a2v], has been the poet's haunt since book 1—"The mind is its own place, and in it self / Can make a Heav'n of Hell, a Hell of Heav'n" (1.254–55). It remains so in the argument to book 4, in its dwelling on "Satan . . . *fall*[ing] *into many doubts with himself*" [A3v] and in his then entering Eve's mind through dream, the "*troublesome*" [A4] character of which is accentuated at the beginning of the argument to book 5. This episode contrasts with Eve's "*gentle dreames*" [a3] noted in the argument to book 10, engendering in her a "*quietness of mind*" [a3] in anticipation of "A Paradise within thee, happier farr" (10.1478) promised to Adam by Michael in the finale to *Paradise Lost,* and even the "calm of mind" (1758) allegedly achieved by God's servants who, in *Samson Agonistes,* are witnesses to Samson's "horrid spectacle" (1542). As they proceed, the psychological interiority of Milton's last poems deepens; and with it, the sense of mental anguish, so movingly rendered, becomes acute in those lines strategically added to the second edition of *Paradise Lost:* "Dæmoniac Phrenzie, moaping Melancholie / And Moon-struck madness, pining Atrophie, /

Marasmus, and wide-wasting Pestilence" (11.485–87)—lines that instead of reconceiving or re-envisioning the poem underscore the inward turn of the first edition with all of the mental anguish that accompanies physical suffering and the fear of dissolution.

Moreover, the phrase now added to the second edition, *new wak't*, is crucial to thematizing Milton's larger project of showing a world awakening to new possibilities as its inhabitants become better angels of their own humanity. Margaret Fuller puts it best when she declares that Milton is one of "the Fathers of the Age, of that new Idea which agitates the sleep of Europe, and of . . . America."[51] As Blake and Shelley knew when each of them, independently, called Milton the Awakener, an awakener is in the process both of himself awakening and of awakening others. At its profoundest level, *Paradise Lost* would rouse an entire nation from sleep, even as it renews the earlier ambition of *Areopagitica*, of making "all the Lords people . . . [into] Prophets" (YP 2:556; compare 554), of turning England into a nation of visionaries in anticipation yet once more, as the argument to Book 9 announces, of "the renewing of all things" [a2v]. Prophecy is restored in the concluding book of *Paradise Lost*, "from . . . [our] eyes the Filme remov'd" (10.412), and in the moment of its restoration we are invited to dream again on the things to come as apocalyptic hope revives, most poignantly near the end of the poem when Adam and Eve wipe tears from their eyes: "Som natural tears they drop'd, but wip'd them soon" (10.1536), Milton thus invoking, as he had done so movingly in *Lycidas*, the apocalyptic promise that a time will come when "God shall wipe away all tears from their eyes; and there shall be no more death, neither sorrow, nor crying" (Rev. 21:4). The postlapsarian books of *Paradise Lost*, in an arc that reaches from the argument to book 9 into the last lines of book 10, are bracketed by apocalypse, and these books themselves are replete with apocalyptic murmurings.

Poets cannot rouse the faculties to act until the eyes have been cleared and the doors of perception opened again, in part by introducing to their poetry a collision of perspectives, sometimes through competing, often contradictory, formulations. The argument to book 2 invokes "Tradition" [A2v] almost as if to alert us that, like prophecy itself, *Paradise Lost* is a poem of traditions, often competing ones, as when the argument to book 6 ([*A4v*]-a) reminds us of the apocalyptic tradition of a celestial battle, including the different interpretive schools surrounding it, especially concerning the duration of the battle and the matter of whether the three-day battle is a veiling of the Crucifixion story, as well as of the rival interpretations concerning its triumphant protagonist, whether he be identified as Michael or as Christ. Lines unique to the second edition of the poem reinforce an alignment of Christ's battle at the end of time with his trials in the midst of time: "They eat, they drink, and with refection sweet" of the first edition (5.636) becomes "They eat, they drink, and in communion sweet / Quaff immortalitie and joy" in the second edition (5.637–38)—lines that with their now eucharistic overtones suggest the institution of Communion at the Last Supper and thereby reinforce the coding of the Crucifixion story into that of the celestial battle, an idea by no means unique to Milton.

Similarly, the argument for book 7 hints at other narrative complexities: Adam's memory, "*what he remember'd since his own Creation,*" what *he* remembers especially of "*his placing in Paradise, his talk with God concerning solitude and fit society*" (a), and the veracity of Adam's report when it is juxtaposed with an account of Creation by Raphael that, pointedly, according to the poem, derives not from memory—"I that Day was absent, as befell, / Bound on a voyage uncouth and obscure" (7.866–67)—but from prophetic inspiration, his "words with Grace Divine / Imbu'd" (7.852–53). We may think backward to the sharp distinction Milton draws in *The Reason of Church-Government* between the daughters of memory and those of inspiration (YP 1:820–21) or look forward in *Paradise Lost* to the moment in book 9 when God (or God in Christ) mocks Adam's words on solitude in the earlier book 7: "Where art thou *Adam* . . . / . . . I miss thee here, / Not pleas'd, thus entertaind with solitude" (9.103–05), God (or God in Christ) tells Adam in clear recollection of what Adam tells Raphael concerning his conversation with God: "In solitude / What happiness, who can enjoy alone, / . . . what contentment find?" (7.1001–03). In such moments, the arguments function as cue cards, alerting the reader to seemingly innocuous details that eventually become fraught with difficulty. Furthermore, these arguments give a supplementary voice to the poet different from the one, both lyrical and autobiographical, that he creates in various prologues to individual books; and different, too, from the voice of the commentator / interpreter sometimes interrupting the narrative, even challenging its drift as in book 2, when at the conclusion of Belial's speech we hear: "Thus *Belial* with words cloath'd in reasons garb / Counsel'd ignoble ease, and peaceful sloath, / Not peace" (2.226–28).

The arguments sometimes simplify what the poetry presents complexly and, in their tendency to simplify, especially concerning matters of theology, lead us into theological traps and metaphysical bramble bushes. Take, for instance, the argument to book 3, with its assertion that *"The Son freely offers himself a Ransome for Man"* [A3] and then its representation of Satan as not only mankind's deceiver but also the deceiver of angels as well [A3v]. In the first instance, the argument points not only to atonement theory, but also to what was made a contentious point within such thinking as early as Gregory Nazianzen and as recently as Hugo Grotius. In the second example, Satan's deception of Uriel alerts us to what God himself will say, that "Man falls deceiv'd" (3.130), a position Satan shares in *Paradise Regain'd*—"*Adam* and . . . *Eve* / Lost Paradise deceiv'd by me" (1.51–52), but which, later in *Paradise Lost*, Milton's (unreliable?) narrator will challenge: that Adam falls, "not deceav'd, / But fondly overcome with Femal charm" (8.998–99). Or, as other examples, take book 9 where the prose argument relates what Adam teaches Eve in contrast to the poetry of that book, which, arguably, tells the story of what Eve teaches Adam. Or take, again, the argument to book 10, which signals the arrival of a "denounc[ing]" angel [a2v] who, if stern in his edict, is nonetheless "milde" in his address and also "benigne" in his demeanor (10.286, 334) and whose platitudes emphasize Eve's "submission" [a3] in contradistinction to the poetry in which Eve eventually rivals Adam in her heroism. If Adam supposed Eve to be sleeping, he "found her wak't" (10.1499).

The poetry, then, is not only an active complication of the prose arguments but also, occasionally, challenges positions or platitudes that the arguments inscribe. Sometimes, as in book 9, when not the Father but the Son journeys to the garden of Eden for the judgment of Adam and Eve, an argument may revise Scripture by contradicting it (Gen. 3:8–24) and then complicate the contradiction by shifting in 1669 from "Son" to "Angels,"[52] perhaps flirting with Socinian heresy, which denies the Son membership in the Trinity by sometimes according him the status of a mere angel.[53] In the absence of certainties, two possibilities present themselves. The shift from "Son" to "Angels" (a2) may be no more than a compositor's error, a trick of the eye or slip of the hand, which transfers "Angels" from line 1 of the argument to line 4. Or just possibly the shift may be more a sleight of hand, an example of heresy flickering in *Paradise Lost,* its author or printer (for just a moment) teasing the reader with Socinianism by demoting the Son to a position, in the world of *Paradise Lost,* even inferior to Satan, who is described as "of the first, / If not the first Arch-Angel" (5.656–57).

Throughout, but especially here, Milton's poem has been altogether slippery in establishing a knit of identity between the Father and Son only then to force distinction (or vice versa). In the argument to book 9, as we have seen, a distinction is drawn ("*He sends his Son*"). In the poem proper, the Father addresses "Assembl'd Angels" (34), then sends his Son in judgment (55–56), "both Judge and Saviour sent" (209). At the same time, though, the Father and the Son blur into one:

> unfoulding bright
> Toward the right hand his Glorie, on the Son
> Blaz'd forth unclouded Deitie; he full
> Resplendent all his Father manifest
> Express'd.   (9.63–67)

The Son is thereupon perceived as God: "the voice of God they heard / Now walking in the Garden" (9.97–98), and is so represented by the poem's narrator: "God / Approaching, thus to *Adam* call'd aloud" (9.101–02); and again: "the Lord God heard" (9.163). Does the argument, then, hint at a heresy the poem erases? Or are we rather left with the question of whether the Son is one with the Father or, alternatively, exalted from among the angels and still holding on to his identity as one of those fragments of deity, which are as much emanations and revelations of the Son as he is of the Father?

What these features, including the few (seemingly inconsequential) revisions of the first edition, highlight, the preliminary poems

to the second edition underscore, first, through the perplexing contradictions each poem inscribes and, second, through each poem's
contrary relationship to its counterpart. Each poem seems to sub-
vert its own chief claim: S. B. seeing a secret history folded into
Milton's epic narrative and attributing a poetics of discovery to a poem
whose epic character promises what E. M. W. Tillyard calls "communal or choric quality";[54] Marvell hollowing the radical ideology
and revisionary thrust from a poem that he thereupon declares to be
a prophecy. In contradicting themselves and one another, these
poems imply that *Paradise Lost* is itself a poem imbued with and
inspired by contradiction and, even more, that it submits to the very
kinds of readings against which especially Marvell protests. The
contexts forbidden, or seemingly declared nonexistent, are finally the
ones that really matter.

The contradiction at the heart of each poem opens upon various
contradictions between the two poems: the countergenres they
invoke, together with their contending traditions (now classical and
epic, and now scriptural and prophetic); the different aesthetic experiences the poems forecast, the one promising a disclosure of hidden
truths and the other an unperplexing conveyance of received interpretation of the Genesis story. And not just their contestatory relationship with one another but the mediatorial functions these poems
perform for *Paradise Lost* require attention: their flirtations with the
political implications and disclosures of Milton's poem, their eyes
fixed on *Paradise Lost,* to be sure (in the case of S. B., that poem's
sixth book), but with (in the instance of Marvell) a darting glance at
Samson Agonistes; indeed, their apparent cognizance of the politics
of *both* these poems, the militarism of the one and vengeful violence
of the other; their respective imaginings—and negotiations—of different horizons of expectations involving both national and sexual
politics. Especially in the example of Marvell, we witness the fash-
ioning of an *apologia* for Milton, from Milton's own defenses of
himself in both prose writings and poetic prologues to *Paradise Lost*
in the face of virulent attacks upon Milton, earlier by Roger L'Estrange
and more recently by Samuel Parker and Richard Leigh (or more
probably Samuel Butler). Those attacks reveal just the kind of threat
Milton was thought to be. As Sharon Achinstein explains, "he

represented . . . literary enthusiasm, a powerful force that embodied the most dangerous aspects of revolutionary energy: the conviction that one's ideas were divinely inspired and the belief that individual choice and experience could guide moral actions."[55] No wonder Dryden's own project should involve hiding the contexts and taming the problems that S. B. and Andrew Marvell had identified, that a chief item on his agenda should involve contradicting Milton out of his contradictions.[56]

Simmons's Shell Game
The Six Title Pages of *Paradise Lost*

STEPHEN B. DOBRANSKI

*[C]an you not tell water from air? My dear sir, in this world
it is not so easy to settle these plain things. I have ever found
your plain things the knottiest of all.*
—Herman Melville, *Moby-Dick*

Readers who purchased *Paradise Lost* between 1667 and 1674
would have encountered one of six different title pages that the publisher Samuel Simmons had printed with the first edition of the
poem (see figs. 1–6).[1] These title pages contain varying degrees of detail
about the work's provenance: three of the pages announce "Printed
by *S. Simmons*," for example, while the other three note instead that
the book was "Licensed and Entred according to Order"; five title
pages include John Milton's full name, while one refers more discreetly
to "The Author *J. M.*" The differences among these title pages have
prompted much speculation, especially over the past 150 years, as
modern critics have devised sometimes subtle theories to account
for Milton's changing attribution. Did Simmons and / or Milton
manipulate the title page's design so as to cloak the poet's identity?
Or can other factors account for the epic's inconsistent appearance?
In this essay I wish to examine the origin and implication of *Paradise
Lost*'s various title pages in the context of the seventeenth century
book trade. Analyzing the poem's first edition in relationship with
other early modern texts printed in multiple issues helps to explain

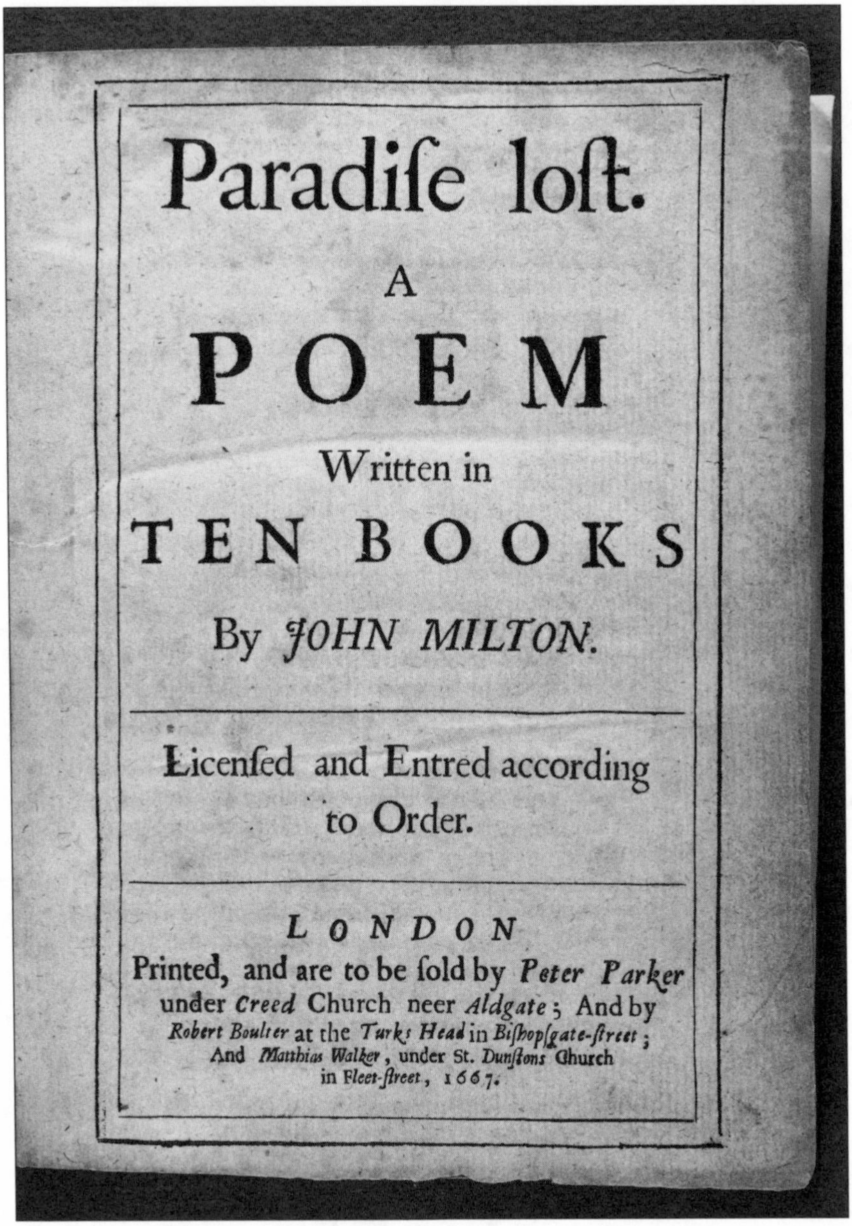

Fig. 1. First edition, 1667 (with larger authorial attribution)

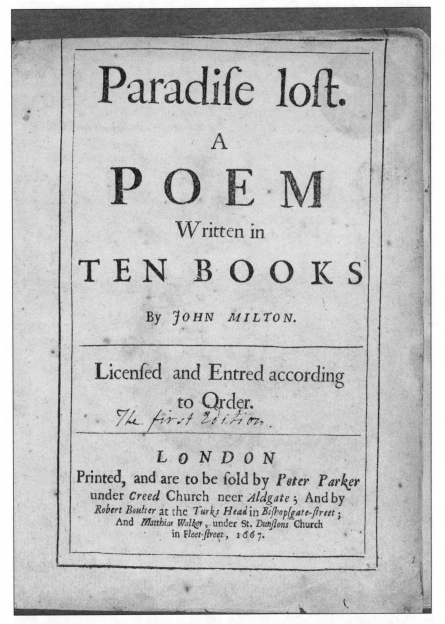

Fig. 2. First edition, 1667 (with smaller authorial attribution)

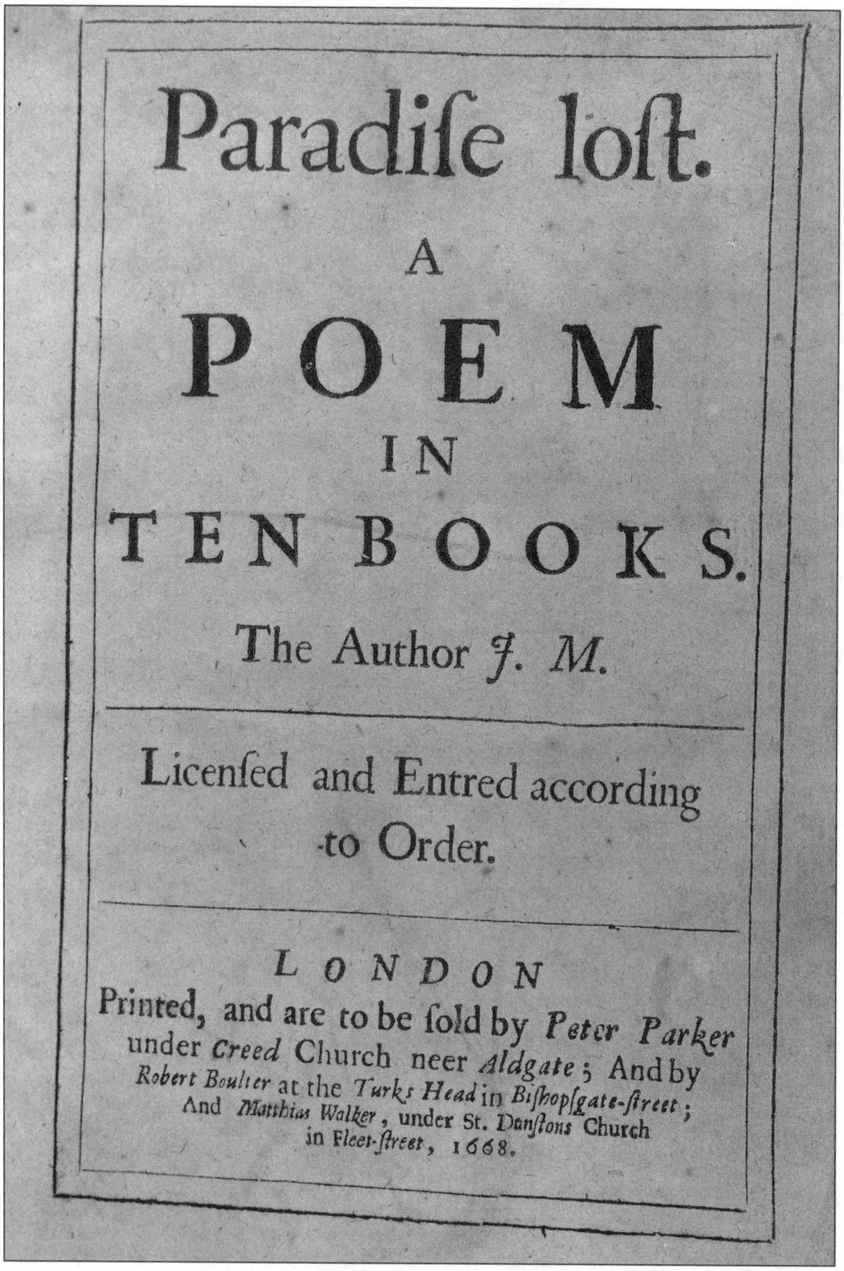

Paradiſe loſt.

A

POEM

IN

TEN BOOKS.

The Author *J. M.*

Licenſed and Entred according to Order.

LONDON

Printed, and are to be ſold by *Peter Parker* under *Creed* Church neer *Aldgate*; And by *Robert Boulter* at the *Turks Head* in *Biſhopſgate-ſtreet*; And *Matthias Walker*, under St. *Dunſtons* Church in *Fleet-ſtreet*, 1668.

Fig. 3. First edition, 1668 (wihout Simmons's name)

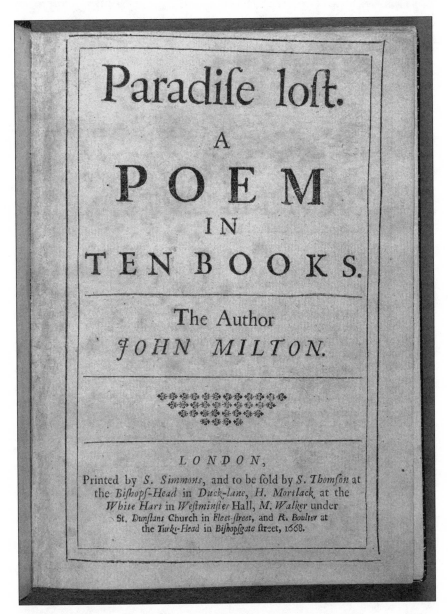

Fig. 4. First edition, 1668 (with Simmons's name)

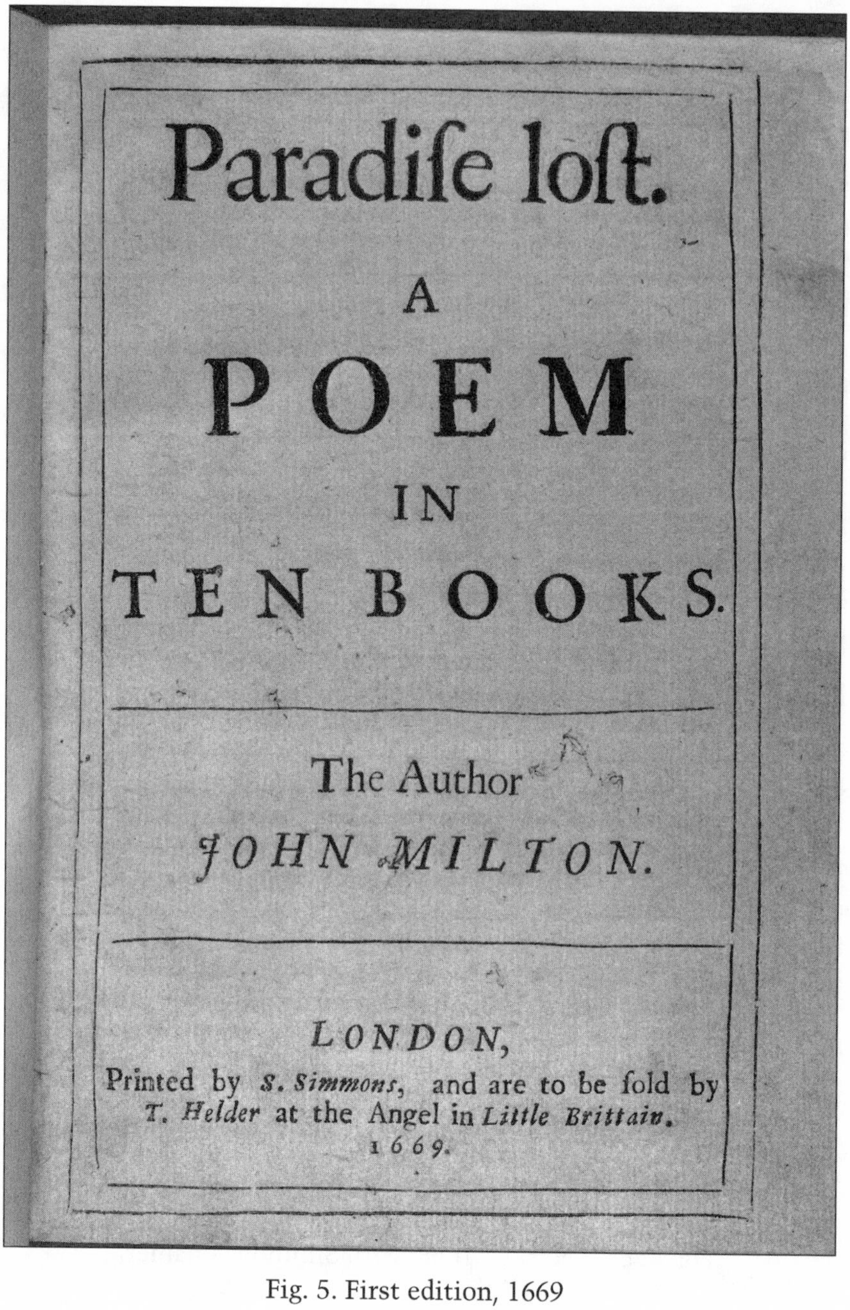

Paradise lost.

A
POEM
IN
TEN BOOKS.

The Author
JOHN MILTON.

LONDON,
Printed by *S. Simmons,* and are to be sold by
T. Helder at the Angel in *Little Brittain.*
1669.

Fig. 5. First edition, 1669

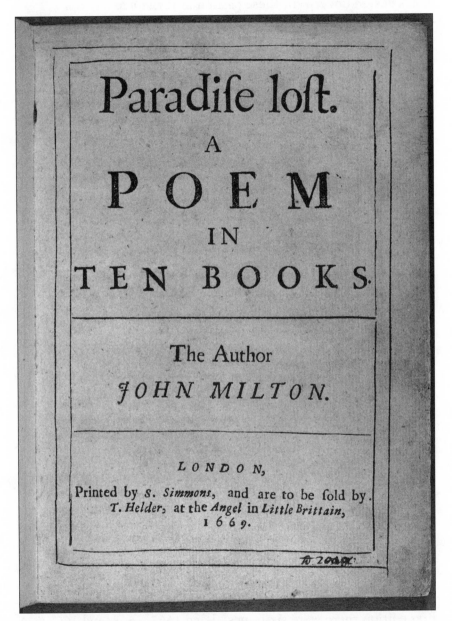

Fig. 6. First edition, 1669 (with altered punctuation)

why Milton's epic required so many title pages and why the first edition's design underwent these particular revisions.

The first step, however, is establishing how many title pages were actually printed for the epic's first edition, a task not as straightforward as we might suppose. Critics have counted as many as nine and as few as four issues for the first edition of *Paradise Lost*. The term "edition," we may recall, refers to all the copies of a book printed from one setting-up of type, while "issue" designates a special version of a book produced at one time, comprising mostly the original printed sheets but differing from the earlier form in some substantial way, often by the addition of new material. A "variant" or "state," by comparison, broadly refers to an alteration in a printed text made during the original printing, before the text is offered publicly for sale.[2]

For *Paradise Lost,* the confusion over the number of the first edition's issues and title pages stems in part from disagreements about what constitutes a separate title page (and thus a likely reissue) and what instead ought to be deemed merely a variant. I arrive at six as the number of *Paradise Lost*'s title pages by, first, setting aside nineteenth century claims for two unique title pages whose existence has never been proven. Henry G. Bohn in 1864 first referred to an unsubstantiated eighth title page, dated 1668, with Milton's name printed between two groups of asterisks, and, some 20 years later, David Masson claimed to have come across another unique title page in Scotland whose design and ownership he never divulged.[3] Of the seven substantiated designs that have been found bound with *Paradise Lost*'s first edition, two are virtually identical—the single difference is a period after the word "BOOKS" in the phrase "A POEM IN TEN BOOKS" (see fig. 3)—so that both pages were evidently produced during the same printing, and the version with the additional period can be classified as a variant.[4]

The remaining six title pages, then, contain significant enough distinguishing marks as to be counted separately. But we should not conclude, as does Douglas Bush in *A Milton Encyclopedia,* that "Of this first edition there were six issues, dated 1667, 1668, and 1669."[5] A new title page does not necessarily designate a separate issue. More probably, as K. A. Coleridge and R. G. Moyles have shown, there were only five issues of *Paradise Lost*'s first edition, and one of the title pages dated 1667 should be deemed another variant: the most striking feature on this page is the smaller type used for the words "By *JOHN MILTON*", a minor change presumably made before Simmons had the book distributed for public sale (see fig. 2).[6] Still, because critics have found this difference significant for tracking Milton's contemporary reputation—and because, as I will discuss, the border rules also appear to have been reset—I wish to discuss this title page separately without claiming that it signifies a separate issue.

The final point to establish near the start involves the relationship between these title pages and the epic's internal variants. Simply put, there is no relationship. We cannot trace a decreasing quantity of errors from those copies bound with the earliest title page to a more authoritative version bound with the later title pages. Based on Harris Francis Fletcher's examination of 151 copies of the first edition, approximately 100 variants occur in 16 of the book's 43 sheets.[7] Because these variants—minor stop-press corrections, mostly in spelling, case, and punctuation—are found in various combinations with all of the title pages, we can infer that the gatherer took sheets from formes in both their corrected and uncorrected states when collecting them into a complete copy of the book. The title pages were evidently printed later, as was customary, and then attached to different versions of the finished text.

The question then becomes why would Simmons have bothered to use so many different title pages with the same edition—and why this particular, fluctuating design. Title pages during the seventeenth century, we need to remember, were not an incidental mode of adorning printed books but served instead as the primary means of advertising. In addition to hoping that the information on a title page might catch the eye of a prospective customer visiting a bookshop, printers regularly included where a publication could be purchased, both the bookseller's name and the shop's exact location. Extra copies were then posted as fliers—in the "Windows also, and the *Balcone's*" where books were "set to sale," as Milton notes in *Areopagitica*.[8] Joseph Hall specifically describes walking across St. Paul's Churchyard and encountering the title leaf for a book of poems, "Nayl'd to an hundreth postes," while Ben Jonson suggests that such leaves were often dispersed even more widely, "on posts, or walls, / Or in cleft-sticks, advanced to make calls."[9] Jonson's specific use of "advanced" points up the practice of posting the titles for books that had not yet been published; according to another contemporary account, title leaves were placed every Saturday night on posts and doors around London for books that would go on sale in the coming week.[10]

Because the title page represented a crucial marketing tool, authors during the seventeenth century apparently had little control over the layout and wording. In *Mechanick Exercises of the Whole Art of Printing* (1683–1684), Joseph Moxon describes how a "good *Compositer . . .* reads his *Copy* with consideration" so as "to make the meaning of his *Author* intelligent to the *Reader*" and "to make his Work shew graceful to the Eye, and pleasant in Reading." The compositor's job, according to Moxon, should begin with designing an effective title page: the compositor "judiciously reads his *Title Page*, and considers what *Word* or *Words* have the greatest Emphasis in it"; he then selects the appropriate style of type, "*Lower Case*, or . . . *Capitals, Roman, Italick* or *English*, or a proper *Body*, which best pleases his fancy, or is in present mode." Because, Moxon adds, a "Lasting Rule cannot be given" for "ordering" title pages, compositors have license to decide on their own which lines to indent, where to insert line breaks, and where to incorporate extra word spacing or line spacing.[11]

Other accounts suggest that a member of the printing house also would determine a title page's wording. As George Wither notes in *The Schollers Purgatory* (1624), a stationer might even rename an author's manuscript, "according to his owne pleasure: which is the reason, so many good Bookes come forth imperfect, and with foolish titles. Nay, he oftentymes gives bookes such names as in his opinion will make them saleable, when there is litle or nothing in the whole volume sutable to such a Tytle."[12] While Wither may be exaggerating in claiming that this practice of renaming occurred "oftentimes" and with "many" books, the use of double titles during the seventeenth century may represent stationers' attempts at least to supplement what they deemed to be less marketable titles. Customers not immediately attracted to *Londons Dove* (1612), for example, would also read on the title page, "OR | A Memoriall of the life and | death of Maister *Robert Dove*, Citizen and | Marchant-Taylor of LON-DON"; in like manner, the ironically named *When You See Me, You Know Me* (1613) disproves its own claim to obviousness with the sub-title, "Or the famous Chronicle Historie of king | *Henrie* the Eight, with the birth and vertuous life | of EDWARD *Prince of Wales.*"[13] Among the various explanatory tags printed on Milton's publications, the title page of *Colasterion* (1645) emphasizes the appositive, "A | REPLY TO | A | NAMELES ANSWER | AGAINST | *The Doctrine and Discipline of Divorce,*" while the title page of *Tetrachordon* (1645) also helpfully reads, "EXPOSITIONS | UPON | The foure chiefe places in Scripture, | which treat of Mariage, or nullities in Mariage," and then lists the four passages that Milton examines in the tract.[14] It was during the late seventeenth century that printers began pro-moting authors by citing their other works—the title page for *The Holy War* (1682; Wing B5538), for example, reads, "By *JOHN BUN-YAN*, the Author of the *Pilgrims Progress*"—and the laudatory remarks regularly printed on early modern title pages also sound as if they were written in the bookseller's shop, not the poet's study. Thus, in a typical rhetorical gesture, Arthur Golding's translation of Ovid's *Metamorphosis* (1612; STC 18962) is described as "A Worke very pleasant and delectable"; Thomas Heywood's *The Wise-Woman of Hogsdon* (1638; STC 13370) is identified as a play "sundry times Acted with great Applause"; and Richard Hooker's *Of the Lawes of Ecclesiastical Polity* (1682; Wing H2633) is presented as part of "The Works Of that Learned and Judicious Divine, Mr. Richard Hooker." Nor were stationers, as Wither's earlier complaint suggests, overly fastidious about applying their terms consistently. We can gauge the popularity of historical publications during the sixteenth and sev-enteenth centuries in part because the label "history" occurs on so many early modern title pages, not only for books that clearly treat historical subjects, such as Shakespeare's *1 Henry IV*, but also for imag-inative texts such as Robert Greene's *Orlando Furioso* and Shakespeare's *Taming of the Shrew* and *Merchant of Venice.*[15]

In the particular case of *Paradise Lost*'s first edition, Samuel Simmons's family had a long-term relationship with Milton and, if the author had any ideas for the title page's layout, Simmons would likely have taken these recommendations seriously. Milton by 1667 had gained an international reputation with his prose works on behalf of the commonwealth, and he may have felt especially comfortable giving directions to the younger Simmons. Milton, for his earlier publications, seems to have helped compose at least some of the title pages, presumably supplying, for example, the passages from Matthew, Euripides, and Proverbs on, respectively, the title pages of *The Doctrine and Discipline of Divorce, Areopagitica*, and *Eikonoklastes*.

But Simmons, we should remember, had his own considerable stake in *Paradise Lost*'s presentation. Having purchased the text outright, the Stationer had the legal right to produce the book as he saw fit; also, having put up the capital to print the poem, he would not likely have depended on a blind poet to supervise the marketing.[16] And, while we should not overemphasize an absence of evidence, the surviving manuscript of the first book of *Paradise Lost* includes the licenser's imprimatur but lacks a title page, suggesting that members of the printing house may have created the first published title page entirely according to their own preferences.[17] Whereas modern scholarship sometimes overstates Milton's authorial authority and grants him exclusive control over all aspects of his publications, *Paradise Lost*'s title pages remind us that Milton, like other early modern writers, participated in a collaborative process of material production.[18]

Simmons should have especially taken pains with *Paradise Lost*'s title page because it constitutes the first issue's only front matter. Readers would turn from the title page, announcing "Paradise lost. | A | POEM | Written in | TEN BOOKS", to the start of Milton's epic: the next page repeats the words "PARADISE LOST" below a row of ornaments and adds the head-title "Book I" between single horizontal rules. The epic then begins immediately, "Of Mans First Disobedience, and the Fruit / Of that Forbidden Tree, whose mortal tast / Brought Death into the World, and all our woe."[19] As opposed to the elaborate appearance of other seventeenth century poetic works, the first edition of *Paradise Lost* has a simple design: no epigraph, no epistles, no portrait, no prefaces. The second edition in 1674, by comparison, includes a frontispiece portrait and introductory encomiastic poems by the court physician Samuel Barrow and Milton's protégé,

Andrew Marvell; the fourth edition, a beautiful folio published in 1688 by Richard Bentley and Jacob Tonson, also contains a frontispiece portrait as well as 12 engraved plates, a list of subscribers, and a prefatory epigram by John Dryden.[20]

In 1667, however, readers are hardly prepared at the start for "Things unattempted yet in Prose or Rhime."[21] Not only is the title printed as a sentence with lowercase type, but the page also contains no laudatory remarks, and the work is identified with the modest appositive, "A Poem," instead of with the more ambitious modifiers "epic" or "heroic." The description "Heroic Poem," in contrast, had appeared on the title page of William D'Avenant's *Gondibert* (1651; Wing D325) as well as on the title pages of later ten-book, poetic works—Richard Blackmore's *Prince Arthur* (1695; Wing B3080), Edward Howard's *Caroloiades, of the Rebellion of Forty-One* (1689; Wing H2967), and Samuel Wesley's *The Life of Our Blessed Lord & Saviour Jesus Christ* (1693; Wing W1371).

The other books published by Simmons that I examined also have more elaborate title pages than the plain design that introduces *Paradise Lost*. Each of the commentaries on the Book of Job that Simmons published with his mother Mary between 1666 and 1671, for example, includes an epigraph on the title page and a terse explanation of the author Joseph Caryl's office.[22] Milton's own *Accedence Commenc't Grammar*, published by Simmons in 1669, similarly seems designed to entice buyers. It begins with an epistle "To the Reader," highlighting the book's purpose and content, and contains a detailed sales pitch on the title page, explaining the book's intended audience: "For the use of such as, | Younger or Elder, are desi- | rous, without more trouble | then needs, to attain the *Latin* | *Tongue;* the elder sort especi- | ally, with little teaching, and | thir own industry."[23]

Milton's earlier poetic publications, produced by stationers other than Simmons, are also more forthcoming than the first edition of *Paradise Lost*. Milton's masque, as we read on its title page in 1637, was "PRESENTED | At Ludlow Castle, | 1634: | *On Michaelmasse night, before the* | RIGHT HONORABLE, | IOHN *Earle of Bridgewater, Vicount* BRACKLY, | *Lord Præsident* of WALES, And one of | His MAIESTIES most honorable | Privie Counsell."[24] The author's 1645 *Poems* begins even more elaborately: following Milton's portrait on the frontispiece (π1v), the title page bears his full name, includes an epigraph from Virgil's *Eclogues*, and announces, between two horizontal rules, that the collection has been *"Printed by his true Copies."*[25] Here, too, the publisher highlights Milton's distinguished connections; "The SONGS were set in Musick by | Mr. HENRY LAWES Gentleman of | the KINGS Chappel, and one | of His MAIESTIES | Private Musick."

We have to judge, then, whether Simmons's simpler design for the first edition of *Paradise Lost* is half empty or half full. Does the relative plainness of the six title pages reveal Simmons's confidence that Milton's name is sufficient to win over prospective customers, or does the book's unassuming appearance indicate that the publisher was hesitant after the Restoration to bring out a heterodox poem by the notorious John Milton?

Modern critics have favored this latter interpretation largely because of the title pages' changing authorial attributions.[26] On one of the two title pages dated 1667, Milton's name is printed in upper-case letters, "By *JOHN MILTON*" (see fig. 1); the other title page dated 1667 also reads "By *JOHN MILTON*" in all capitals but in a slightly smaller type (see fig. 2). The next title page, this one dated 1668, names only "The Author *J. M.*" (see fig. 3), while the fourth (dated 1668), fifth (dated 1669), and sixth (also 1669) more confidently announce between single horizontal rules, "The Author *JOHN MILTON*" (see figs. 4–6). David Masson and Harris Francis Fletcher were among the first to suggest that the diminution and omission of Milton's name, though temporary, reflect the publisher's efforts to prevent the author's political reputation from impeding sales.[27] This hypothesis may be supported by the surviving, licensed manuscript of book 1, which does not include Milton's name, and the entry of the epic in the Stationers' *Register*, which conceals Milton's identity as "I. M."[28]

But as tempting as such interpretations may seem, it is doubtful that Simmons printed Milton's name with smaller type in an attempt, as one recent biographer suggests, "to avoid calling attention to it."[29] With so little information on the 1667 title page, even the most casual readers must have noticed that *Paradise Lost* was written by John Milton, and only comparing the first two title pages side by side would have revealed the difference of a few millimeters in type size between the two versions: on one, Milton's name is printed in small capitals, and on the other it appears in uppercase letters. Rather than a deliberate marketing strategy, printing Milton's name in smaller type probably occurred because the compositor was trying to accommodate a more subtle alteration in the page's border rules. Measuring the space between the inner top border rule and the rule under Milton's name, James Pershing first discovered one-quarter of an inch less space on the second 1667 title page.[30] According to the simplest explanation, the border rules were damaged and reset while the first title page was being printed. For the second title page, Milton's name was printed in a slightly smaller type size because there was slightly less space available for it.

Also doubtful is the related argument that Simmons used only Milton's initials for the next title page, dated 1668, because he wished to hide the poet's identity. It makes little sense for Simmons to have published *Paradise Lost* with Milton's full name for a year—on two different title pages—and then to have switched to the author's initials so as to disguise Milton's authorship. The veil had already been lifted. And if Simmons intended to hide Milton's name on this one title page, as Hugh Amory reasons, surely he could have devised a better disguise than "J. M."[31]

Amory goes on to argue that Simmons had intended to market *Paradise Lost* with one of the title pages, dated 1667, that bears Milton's full name, but "For whatever reason, Simons' [*sic*] courage drained away as the day of publication approached, and Milton's prominence on the title-page shrank."[32] For the first issue, Simmons would thus have chosen the 1668 title page with its more cryptic attribution, "J. M.", and waited until he felt confident about the book's sales before he started drawing from the stockpile of earlier printed (and earlier dated) title pages.

Once again, such a narrative sounds plausible, but before accusing Simmons of a sudden loss of courage, we need to remember that in 1667 he had little to fear in terms of the text's legality: the Reverend Thomas Tomkins had already licensed Milton's poem, and the Stationer Richard Royston had approved its entry in the *Register*.[33] If Simmons were truly concerned about the repercussions of publishing *Paradise Lost*, he should have suppressed the names of the three booksellers that are printed on the 1668 title page, especially Peter Parker, who together with Simmons had experienced some legal difficulty around this time. According to the *Calendar of State Papers*, Parker and Simmons petitioned in 1668 to be "discharge[d] from restraint" for printing *Christ's Famous Titles* without a license.[34]

The argument for the 1668 title page's priority and Simmons's sudden loss of courage also rests on the similarity between the entry for *Paradise Lost* in the Stationers' *Register* and the wording on the 1668 title page. But given how often only initials are used in the *Register*, this similarity seems coincidental rather than purposeful. Given, too, the various differences between the entry and the title page—the entry states "by I. M." while the 1668 title page reads "The Author *J. M.*", Simmons's name appears in the entry but not on the title page, and the entry and title page differ dramatically in various spellings—it is difficult to accept that such a comparison reveals anything about the Stationer's motives.

Nor did Simmons have reason to fear that his author's reputation as a regicide would diminish the book's popularity. That the first edition sold at least 1,300 copies within 17 months certainly seems a respectable success, and during this same period Milton himself may have given away an additional 200 complimentary copies to friends and acquaintances.[35] The discovery of a copy of *Paradise Lost* owned by Charles II and bearing the fourth title page (which reads "The Author *JOHN MILTON.*" [fig. 4]) also indicates that the poet's reputation would not have prevented even the king's most loyal supporters from reading Milton's epic.[36] In fact, Milton's notoriety would more likely have helped Simmons attract customers: on five of the title pages associated with *Paradise Lost*'s first edition, Milton's name is featured in uppercase letters and constitutes almost the only reason offered for readers to purchase the poem.

I would suggest instead that the differences in Milton's attributions on the title pages of *Paradise Lost*, although they may seem extraordinary by our modern standards, are not inconsistent with the variants we find in the successive title pages of other seventeenth century texts. While booksellers depended on a title page's layout for marketing purposes, compositors adopted a more casual attitude with subsequent issues; as we saw with Moxon's description of a compositor's duties, the page's design and diction might be freely altered "to humour the Eye" and attract new readers.[37] The second edition of Robert Howard's *Five New Plays*, to take one example, was published with four different title pages between 1692 and 1700 so as to record the collection's changing booksellers.[38] But at the same time that compositors updated this pertinent information, they emended various other details for no apparent reason than personal preference or practical convenience. The line spacing surrounding the author's name is reduced and expanded; the swash letter "R" in "Robert" is sometimes replaced with a less dramatic, italic "R"; and on one page the publication year is changed from roman to arabic numerals. A change from roman to arabic numerals is the only revision made, for no apparent reason, to the title page of Dryden's *Annus Mirabilis* (Wing D2238, D2239), published successively in 1667 and 1668. On the earlier title page, the "year of wonders" is identified as "1666," and on the latter it is printed as "MDCLXVI." If we return to Milton's Latin grammar, published by Simmons, we find a more striking difference in the first edition's two title pages, both from 1669: while updating important information about the bookseller, the compositor has also expanded the author's name from "*J. M.*" to "JOHN MILTON" and reset the description of the book's function and audience so that the words "*LATIN TONGUE*" are printed in italic, uppercase type.

The nine editions and five issues of Abraham Cowley's *Works*, published between 1669 and 1700, perhaps best illustrate the alterations compositors commonly made to the design of their texts.[39] The title pages contain mostly the same information and follow closely the same layout; even the names of the booksellers between 1669 and 1672 remain unchanged on five successive title pages. Still, the compositors have made other, seemingly unnecessary revisions—perhaps most notably changing the type used for the words "Original Copies" in the clause "Now Published out of the Authors Original Copies." In 1669, these letters are emphasized with heavy leading and italic type. In 1672, by comparison, the type is crowded together, and now R, G, N, and P are swash letters; in 1680, the compositor used instead a slightly larger roman type. Among this book's other changes in 1681, the words "Original Copies" are again printed in heavily leaded, italic type; a new ornament is added; and the horizontal rules that sectioned off the page's information are removed.[40]

Based on these and other variations in other seventeenth century title pages, we ought not to infer too much about the reason for Milton's inconsistent attribution for the first edition of *Paradise Lost*—just as we would not overinterpret why only a few of the title pages include Simmons's name, why some read "Written in TEN BOOKS" while others happen to read "IN TEN BOOKS", why some read "The Author" while others read "By", and why the size of type used to print "*LONDON*" shrinks between two issues. Whether the title page reads "*J. M.*" or "*JOHN MILTON*" (in larger or smaller type) probably represents not a calculated rhetorical maneuver but more likely a compositor's preference, a decision based in part, if not exclusively, on the changing availability of type.[41]

The point to take away from *Paradise Lost*'s six title pages is, I think, that there were six title pages. By changing the year of publication from 1667 to 1668 and then to 1669, Simmons was working to make Milton's epic look more current and thus appeal to new audiences; and by partnering with so many booksellers and updating their names and locations—the main reason, after all, for revising the title page—Simmons was also striving to reach a larger audience. The first three title pages identify the book's vendors as Peter Parker, Robert Boulter, and Matthias Walker; the fourth drops Parker and adds two new booksellers, Samuel Thompson and Henry Morlock; the fifth and sixth title pages, both dated 1669, name only Thomas Helder. Plotting these six stationers' shops on a map of London, we find that Simmons had developed a relatively shrewd plan for marketing Milton's epic: Boulter's shop in Bishopsgate Street and Parker's shop in Leadenhall were located, respectively, in the north and northeast parts of London; Thompson's shop was situated northwest, near Smithfield, while Walker's shop was due west in Fleet Street and Morlock's shop was further southwest, actually in Westminster Hall. Simmons, in other words, was distributing *Paradise Lost*, at least for its first two years, in a series of shops across the city. When in 1669 only one bookseller's name is printed on the title page, these other shops may have continued to sell Milton's epic. But by then the word was out, the fliers had been posted, and Simmons could settle on

Thomas Helder presumably because his shop in north London "at the Angel, in Little Brittain" was in an important center for booksellers and was more conveniently located near both Milton's home in Artillery Walk and Simmons's own Aldersgate printing house.

Simmons also developed an inventive marketing technique for another of his publications, Joseph Caryl's commentaries on Job. Advertising these books in *The Term Catalogues,* Simmons tried to solicit early subscribers by charging a reduced rate—a £4 value for 50 s.—provided readers paid for their copies up front, before the volumes were printed and bound.[42] But prior to *Paradise Lost,* we should recall, Simmons had worked mostly as a printer; Milton's epic was the first book entered in the Stationers' *Register* as his own copy. That Milton had worked with Simmons's parents also must have motivated the young publisher. If Caryl's commentaries suggest Simmons's entrepreneurial spirit, the extra care he took with *Paradise Lost* may have also been personal. Surely Simmons would have wanted both to succeed with his first major publishing venture and to assist his father's longtime collaborator, the 59-year-old poet and statesman who had helped his father become a printer for the Council of State.[43]

Simmons's frequent updating of the poem's title page reflects his enthusiasm, as do the 14 pages of front matter that he added to a reissue of the first edition. Given that the surviving contract granted the Stationer exclusive rights to publish Milton's poem, Simmons did not have to undertake this considerable extra investment. Yet beginning in 1668, he added a list of errata, a defense of the verse, and the arguments that summarize each book. In some copies, Simmons also composed a brief note, preceding the arguments, explaining these addenda:

> *Courteous Reader,* There was no Argument at first intended to the Book, but for the satisfaction of many that have desired it, I have procur'd it, and withal a reason of that which stumbled many others, why the Poem Rimes not. *S. Simmons.* (A2r)[44]

This announcement gives us perhaps our best glimpse of Simmons as the first publisher of *Paradise Lost*—both his opportunism and zeal. He added these extra materials, as he explains, to help satisfy customers who requested them. And while he did not exploit this new issue by proclaiming on the title page that the text was revised and enlarged—a claim that other stationers would have made to boost sales—Simmons still bothered to announce the addition of these materials. This note, which itself was printed in two versions, suggests both his eagerness to please readers and perhaps, once again, the personal interest he took in Milton's publication.[45]

The occasion of these extra leaves also allowed Simmons to have a new title page printed (the fourth): the added front matter comprised seven leaves, which left one remaining to complete the two quarto sheets. The first edition's final title page was similarly created because Simmons made the most of necessity. Reprinting extra copies of signatures Z and Vv, which apparently had been produced in an insufficient quantity for the complete edition to be sold, Simmons took this opportunity to print more of the 1669 title page, most likely because of its more current date and publication information.[46]

Certainly Simmons's marketing strategy for *Paradise Lost* does not qualify him as a "sharper," the name, as Peter Lindenbaum observes, that Dryden used to disparage booksellers when he felt Jacob Tonson had cheated him out of his profits.[47] But with *Paradise Lost*, Simmons showed industry and persistence—in working with an unusually large number of booksellers for a poem, in adding an editorial apparatus to assist readers, and in repeatedly updating the title page's appearance.

Simmons and perhaps Milton also seem to have understood that the first issue's simple design—the terse title page and absence of preliminary matter—put pressure on the poem's opening lines. Readers trying to interpret the title and determine whether they were holding an allegory, say, a Christian poem, or a political satire could have quickly discovered the answer: "Of Mans First Disobedience, and | the Fruit | Of that Forbidden Tree, whose | mortal tast | Brought Death into the World, | and all our woe." By breaking these lines after "and," "whose," and "World" and by centering the resulting fragments—"the Fruit," "mortal tast," "and all our woe"—Simmons was helping readers discern at a glance that this poem does indeed address the loss of *that* paradise.[48]

Ultimately, we do not know whether the simple appellation of "A Poem" on *Paradise Lost*'s title pages reflects Milton's or Simmons's preference, or both. Milton similarly titled his court drama *A Mask* in the Trinity Manuscript, and, despite modern critics' preference for calling the drama *Comus*, it appeared as simply *A Mask Presented at Ludlow Castle* when it was printed in 1637, 1645, and 1673. The second edition of *Paradise Lost* in 1674, also published by Simmons, was printed with a similarly designed title page, "Paradise Lost. | A | POEM | IN | TWELVE BOOKS. | [single rule] | The Author| *JOHN MILTON*. | [single rule]".[49] And the title page for *Paradise Regain'd . . . Samson Agonistes*, published in 1671 by the bookseller John Starkey, also identifies the work as simply, "A | POEM. | In IV *BOOKS*", although, in contrast, the separate title page for *Samson Agonistes* within the text contains the more specific label, "A | DRAMATIC POEM."[50] Regardless of who supervised the composition of these later pages—one of Milton's amanuenses, a member of the printing house, and / or the poet himself—their design may have been motivated in part by an attempt to mimic *Paradise Lost*'s first edition. With the demise of patronage and the rise of a market system, authors were gaining increased importance during the seventeenth century; by the early 1700s, as Roger Chartier observes, the originality and thus value of a work would be predicated on the existence of an identifiable writer.[51] *Paradise Lost*'s six title pages, emphasizing Milton's name as "The Author" and excluding other marketing rhetoric, seem designed above all to foreground the poet's authority, creating brand recognition through their reiterated layout and wording.

The realities of editing a modern edition of Milton's works do not permit the kind of fidelity that would preserve such bibliographical details. Nor, admittedly, will the specific subject of *Paradise Lost*'s six title pages likely affect literary interpretations. But the poem's original title pages would have influenced its first readers—just as the editorial apparatus in a modern edition can, subtly and not so subtly, shape our own readings of Milton's works. Piecing together the bibliographical context of *Paradise Lost*'s first edition helps us to understand how the poem came into material existence. If we are inclined to bracket off the six title pages of *Paradise Lost* as containing merely extratextual information, the front matter that Simmons added to some of the poem's reissues shows how such distinctions are problematic. When for the poem's second edition Simmons moved the arguments summarizing each book from their initial position, at the beginning of the text, to their current position, at the start of each of the epic's respective books, he became more than *Paradise Lost's* first publisher; he became its first editor. It remains for current readers to read beyond our modern editions and return to Milton's original publications, discovering, perhaps for the first time, the author's intentions, but always, as *Paradise Lost* suggests, in dynamic relationship with his audience and printers.

Milton's 1667 *Paradise Lost* in Its Historical and Literary Contexts

ACHSAH GUIBBORY

The following essay attempts to recover how *Paradise Lost* appeared—and might be read—in the context of 1667, when Milton's epic first was published. My concern is not with the difference between the ten- and twelve-book versions, but rather with the ways in which the 1667 *Paradise Lost* was part of the cultural conversation in the decade immediately following the restoration of Charles II.

Materially, the 1667 volume looked different from the later ones. The fourth issue, in 1668, added an address of the printer to the reader, the arguments for each book, and Milton's remarks about the verse. In the 1674 edition, commendatory verses and an engraved portrait made the now twelve-book epic seem more formally polished, more traditional. By 1674, John Dryden—the poetic apologist for the Restoration and monarchy—had turned Milton's poem into an opera, *The State of Innocence* (though it was not published until 1677), in an act that arguably did not so much pay tribute to Milton as to colonize, tame, and civilize the epic of Dryden's literary rival, the defender of regicide. In 1688, the magnificent fourth edition of *Paradise Lost* in folio—with gorgeous full-page engravings illustrating each of the 12 books—made Milton's epic into a work that reflected glory on England through the achievement of her poet. Under the portrait of Milton that formed the frontispiece of this edition was an epigram by Dryden linking Milton to Homer and Virgil, whose respective virtues of "loftiness of thought" and "Majesty" were now united in England's epic poet. Visually and materially, the 1688 *Paradise Lost* seemed to model the refinement that Dryden had long been celebrating in his poems and prefaces as characterizing this new Augustan age. It would not be long before Milton's poem would be canonized in scholarly editions—first in 1732 by Richard Bentley and then in 1749 by Thomas Newton—replete with explanatory learned footnotes, which on some pages took up more space than the text itself.

But in 1667, Milton's poem appeared unadorned, its plain title page simply announcing "Paradise lost," its notable lack of prefatory material refusing any gestures of praise either toward a dedicatee or toward the author. Milton offered no formal address to the reader, no reverence toward potential earthly patrons, but simply began the poem, invoking his divine, heavenly muse. That Milton's 1667 epic represented an alternative, counterculture discourse and ideology becomes even clearer when we look at some of the events and published books in that first decade after the Restoration.

Milton's poem was substantially completed by 1665, though it was not published until 1667, when, Hugh Wilson suggests, Milton and his publisher may have felt it safe to take advantage of the temporary relaxation of censorship.[1] By 1667, the exhilaration many felt at the restoration had been dampened by the traumas of the 1665 plague, the 1666 Great Fire in London, and a humiliating Dutch naval victory over the English in the Thames. As Wilson puts it, "the royalist fairy tale" was over (32). Yet we need to realize that the optimistic royalist discourse was hardly silenced. Indeed, 1667 might seem a banner year. It saw the publication of Dryden's heroic poem *Annus Mirabilis* and Thomas Sprat's *History of the Royal Society*. Both Dryden's and Sprat's texts celebrated the accomplishments and bright future of England under the reigning Stuart monarch, expressing a celebratory, progressive view of history that was aligned with the Restoration establishment, and against which Milton's 1667 poem offered a dissident counterdiscourse, for those fit though few who could rightly read.[2]

In May 1660, Charles II had returned to England from France. Milton's *Ready and Easy Way*, published twice only a few months before, envisioned the imminent Restoration as a national catastrophe, analogous to the biblical Israelites' defection from God. A modern-day Moses or Jeremiah, Milton complained that the English people, ungrateful for their miraculous delivery from the Egyptian bondage of monarchy and prelacy, were "now choosing them a captain back for Egypt."[3] Royalist clergy and poets like Abraham Cowley, Edmund Waller, and John Dryden, however, greeted Charles as a Davidic ruler, returned by God's favor to an Israelite England that was only now coming into its national glory. Such hyperbolic praise confirmed Milton's belief that the English people idolized kings, making them their gods. Edmund Waller's poem *To the King Upon His Majesties Happy Return* had described Charles's "*full MAJESTY*" as like the Sun, "break[ing] forth / In the Meridian of your Reign."[4] It was poems like these that the licenser of *Paradise Lost*, sensitive to the poem's subversive potential, probably had in mind when he objected to Milton's depiction of Satan as the eclipsed sun.

Competing interpretations of history and appropriations of Israelite analogies were at work as England moved into the Restoration. Where Milton's *Ready and Easy Way* had warned that to bring back Charles would be to return to the bondage of Egypt, Abraham Cowley's *Ode, upon the Blesssed Restoration and Returne of His Sacred Majestie, Charls the Second* figured the king's return as deliverance from Egypt and the "fatall *Wilderness*." God was "Conduct[ing] them," like their Israelite predecessors, "To their *own Promis'd Land*." The Restoration was also deliverance from "the *Bonds* of *Long Captivitie*" in Babylon, and General Monck was their heroic "*Zerubabel*" (the leader of the ancient Jews when they returned to Jerusalem from Babylon), who would return the English to "*rebuild* their *Temple* and their *City*." Cowley implied that London was Jerusalem, the Church of England their temple, destroyed by an English Nebuchadnezzar. In a particularly bizarre analogy, presumably meant to confirm the Israelite identification of England (or at least the loyalist part), Cowley suggested that the blood shed during the civil wars was "the *Bleeding Mark* of Grace, / The *Circumcision* of the *Chosen* race," England.[5]

The language of such royalist poems suggested that, with Charles, England was not (as Milton had warned) returning to Egypt, but entering Canaan, being delivered from bondage, from Babylonian captivity under the Protectorate, entering into a promised land that resonated not only with the biblical David's kingdom but also with the restored Israelite kingdom the Hebrew prophets spoke of—a kingdom that would be ruled by a Davidic king (the reign having been interrupted), and would see unprecedented prosperity and terrestrial happiness. Such a vision of the present and a prophetic rewriting of history are clearly at odds with the vision of history and prophetic stance of Milton's 1667 *Paradise Lost*, which sharply countered these royalist celebrations of the restored monarchy. Milton placed Satan, at the beginning of book 2, "High on a Throne of Royal State," and in the final book he explicitly identified earthly kingship with tyranny, tracing its genealogy not to the Israelite kings but to Nimrod (10.915–35)—a bold move that Nicholas von Maltzahn shows was recognized by an early reader as evidence that Milton "holds to his old [republican] principles."[6]

In 1660, *Britannia Rediviva*—Oxford University's collection of poems—proclaimed the "rebirth" of England with the return of Charles. Oxford's learning poured out in tribute to the king, mostly poems in Latin or English, but also a few in Greek, Hebrew, even Arabic. Among the poems was one by the young John Wilmot, Earl of Rochester. The royalist printer Leonard Lichfield, in a poem appended to the volume, insisted that Charles's very "Name" "Inspire's us all with a Poetique flame."[7] But Milton's epic announced that God was his only inspiration and proclaimed the loss rather than regaining of paradise. As Laura Lunger Knoppers argues, *Paradise Lost*, in telling its "story of woe, . . . challenges a central tenet of royalist ideology in Restoration England, the return of the golden age on earth, the restoration of joy."[8]

With Charles on the throne, the Church of England, which had been disestablished by parliamentary ordinances in the 1640s, was now being reestablished in all its prelatical power and ceremonial glory. The Laudian style of worship that Milton had denounced as idolatry had returned. The Book of Common Prayer, its use prohibited by Parliament's ordinance in 1645, came out of hiding. Whereas the prayer book virtually ceased to be published in the 1640s and 1650s, in 1660 there were "nine issues in various formats, followed by another three in 1661."[9] A revised 1662 Book of Common Prayer was accompanied by the Act of Uniformity requiring its use. The new prayer book revised the prayer for the anniversary of the Gunpowder Plot (November 5) and added special set forms of prayer to be used on January 30 (the "martyrdom" of Charles I), and May 29 (the birthday and restoration of Charles II in 1660).[10]

Part of the reconstruction of the national Church of England involved the publication of other books seen as foundational to the official Anglican church. In 1661, Peter Heylyn published *Ecclesia restaurata*. While its title might seem to refer to the Restoration church, Heylyn's book was actually a history of the "reformation of the Church of England" from Henry VIII to its establishment under Elizabeth I. Heylyn, formerly chaplain to Charles I and now chaplain to Charles II, implied the continuity of the Restoration church with the earlier reformed one, countering Presbyterian and radical puritan objections to the reestablished Church of England while glossing over the fact that there would be no reform of the Laudian abuses that had developed in the reign of Charles I. In 1668, Heylyn's *Cyprianus anglicanus* appeared. It was a hagiographical biography of William Laud, who had been executed by Parliament as a traitor in January 1644/5 but now was being resurrected and canonized in print.[11]

The fifth edition of Launcelot Andrewes's *XCVI Sermons* was published in 1661, first edited and published by Laud and John Buckeridge in 1629. The 1661 title page declared that Andrewes's sermons were being published "by his Majesties speciall command." Which Charles had commanded its publication? The first or the second? The ambiguity served to emphasize the continuity of the Restoration and the earlier Laudian church. In 1662 and again in 1666 *The Works of Mr. Richard Hooker . . . in 8 books of ecclesiastical polity, completed out of his own manuscripts; never before published* appeared. It was Hooker that Andrewes and, then, Laud had looked back to as they wrote their apologia for the episcopal ceremonial English church that Milton so hated. This quarto edition of Hooker's *Lawes of Ecclesiastical Politie* was beautiful and stately. When readers opened it, they saw an elaborate, engraved title page featuring an architectural structure with columns, statuelike figures, a radiant sun with the Hebrew tetragrammaton at the top, and beneath that an arch with a picture of a cathedral or temple inside (perhaps St. Paul's). Dedicating the volume to Charles II, John Gauden (who had had a hand in *Eikon Basilike*) mentioned how Charles I, a few days before his "Martyrdom, commended to his dearest Children, the diligent Reading of Mr. Hookers Ecclesiastical Polity, even next the Bible."[12]

In 1667 George Herbert's *The Temple* was republished together with Christopher Harvey's high-church supplement, *The Synagogue*. Though Herbert's poetry was indeed of broad ecumenical appeal, still in 1657 and 1661 *The Temple* had been linked with Harvey's *The Synagogue* by their shared publisher, Philemon Stephens, who presented the two collections as paired voices of the Anglican church, in exile in 1657 but repatriated by 1661. This 1667 edition of Herbert's *Temple* seems yet another publication intended to confirm the antipuritan order of the established church, no longer a synagogue in hiding or exile but the religious institution of the kingdom.

Print as well as parliamentary acts and the restored practices of worship were resurrecting the established church and its high-church apologists in this first decade after the Restoration. These publications constructed a line of continuity between the Restoration church and the earlier Laudian one, which had adopted Hooker as its apologist. In the 1660s, Andrewes, Laud, and Hooker were presented in the marketplace of print as the pillars of a temple that Milton believed was idolatrous. We do not need to wait for the 1671 *Samson Agonistes* to see Milton's response, for Milton's 1667 *Paradise Lost*, from its first lines through the end of that last, tenth book, implicitly yet relentlessly opposes this reestablished English church and its ideology. Claiming the inspiration of God, Milton rejects "Temples" (1.18) in the opening invocation, reminding the reader that God prefers the temple of the heart to any one erected by human hands. He locates corruption and idolatry in temples (for example, 1.399–403) and in institutionalized religion. He identifies Satan and the fallen angels as "Architects" (1.732) of the "Temple"-like structure of Pandaemonium (1.713). The first and last books detail the origin and persistence of idolatry in human history, and Milton laments the attendant suffering (even martyrdom) of the faithful in the sweeping history of book 10, which brings the reader up to the present.[13]

From reading Milton's poem, one would never guess that England seemed to be embarking on a period of progress and glory. Nowhere did this national optimism seem more apparent than in the field of the new experimental science, which its practitioners and apologists described as promising to regain Eden and restore human power. The Royal Society was established by royal charter in 1662, and books published by its associates began to appear. Robert Boyle—one of the founding members of the society and an important natural philosopher and chemist who promoted the "corpuscular" philosophy—published his experiments. His *New Experiments, Physico-mechanical* appeared in 1662 and 1665; *Some Considerations touching the usefulnesse of experimental Natural philosophy* in 1663 and 1664; and *The Origine of formes and Qualities* in 1666 and 1667. In 1666 and again in 1667, Robert Hooke published *Micrographia; or, Some Physiological Descriptions of Minute Bodies Made by Magnifying Glasses*, a beautiful book with fascinating engravings showing small things (such as a flea) as they might look under a microscope.

Modern scholars have made us aware of Milton's interest in contemporary sciences. Karen Edwards shows that Milton's description of the flora and fauna of Eden shares the experimental scientists' fascination with knowing *"what things looked like"*; Stephen Fallon places Milton's "animist materialism" in the context of mid-seventeenth-century philosophy. John Rogers shows how "monistic vitalism" offered a new, politically radical "concept of material bodies and the body politic."[14] The experimental science—and particularly corpuscular philosophy—had a leveling potential that might have appealed to Milton. As Boyle stated, the "matter" of all bodies is "the same common Matter"[15]—a sentiment echoed by Raphael in his "one first matter" speech to Adam (5.472). But we should be wary of concluding that Milton was enthusiastic about the goods of the new science. Ken Hiltner argues that Milton, by representing the Fall as the wounding of the earth and the beginning of human separation from earth and place, was a prophetic, prescient ancestor of modern environmentalists—a sharp critic of man's efforts to dominate the earth through science.[16] In order to understand the complexity of Milton's attitude toward the new science, we also need to realize that, in the later seventeenth century, the institution of scientific inquiry and experimental philosophy was not apolitical but specifically linked to Charles II, monarchy, and the king's restoration.

Hooke's *Micrographia*, which was registered to be printed in November 1664 but did not appear until the notable date of 1667, was dedicated to "The King": "Amidst the many *felicities* that have accompani'd *your Majesties* happy *Restauration* and *Government*, it is none of the least considerable, that *Philosophy* and *Experimental* Learning have *prosper'd* under your *Royal Patronage*."[17] Hooke praised Charles II as the "Great Founder and Patron" of the Royal Society.[18] Echoing Francis Bacon's vision that the new science would regain paradise and restore man's dominion over nature lost at the Fall, Hooke's preface to his readers announced man's "great prerogative . . . above other Creatures." The monarchical analogy was significant. Insisting that humans "have the power of . . . *altering* . . . them [the Creatures?] to various uses," Hooke asserted that by "*artificial Instruments* and *methods*, there may be, in some manner, a reparation made for the mischiefs, and imperfection, mankind has drawn upon it self." "Remedies" for our postlapsarian condition can only "proceed from the *real*, the *mechanical*, the *experimental* Philosophy."[19]

Milton's treatment of the invention of gunpowder (6.498) or the disemboweling of the earth for gold (1.688–90), his location of experiments, dangerous inventions, or building bridges (1.1027–30) in demonic impulses and hell, demand to be read in the specific context of the 1660s, when the Royal Society, founded and patronized by Charles II, was being lauded as a means for recovering paradise. Although atomistic philosophy could provide a scientific model for populist or revolutionary politics, Milton's 1667 poem insistently places itself at odds with the experimental new science of the Restoration—and indeed with many of the arts of "civilization," which were associated with the fallen angels who invent them in hell. Scientific invention originated as the rebel angels invented gunpowder in an attempt to destroy heaven. Experimental science in *Paradise Lost* seems yet one more example of fallenness, not an instrument for restoring paradise. Might we not hear in Michael's advice to Adam to seek a "Paradise within" (10.1478) Milton's retort to the ideology of the Royal Society (patronized by a false king), which was part of the Restoration establishment's quest for power and glory?

Interestingly, Milton's skeptical treatment of science—along with his clear fascination with it—is similar to Margaret Cavendish's position, published at about the same time. Exhibiting satirical contempt for the workings of the Royal Society that she had once visited, Cavendish published her *Observations upon Experimental Philosophy. To which is added, The Description of a New Blazing World* in 1666. Her mocking attack on "our Modern Microscopical or Dioptrical Writers" was aimed at Hooke. Cavendish and her husband were ardent royalists, ideologically conservative and politically at odds with Milton, and her royalist politics are evident as she compares those "Naturall Philosophers" who would "pull down the learning of Ancient Authors" to the "unconscionable men in Civil Wars" who ruin palaces and churches. Nevertheless, her contempt for those who "busie themselves more with other Worlds, then with this they live in" sounds a lot like Raphael's advice when Adam asks about the secrets of the heavens: "be lowly wise: / Think only what concerns thee and thy being; / Dream not of other Worlds" (7.810–12).[20] Adam dutifully acquiesces, "not to know at large of things remote / From use, obscure and subtle, but to know / That which before us lies in daily life, / Is the prime Wisdom" (7.828–31).

The institutions of science, the monarchy, and the English church were all intertwined, as becomes clear when we look at the figure of Thomas Sprat, author of the monumental *History of the Royal-Society* (1667). Sprat was ordained a priest in the Church of England in 1661, and he became dean of Westminster and bishop of Rochester in 1683 and 1684, respectively. The frontispiece of his *History of the Royal Society* displays a bust of Charles II (crowned with a wreath) on a pillar decorated with an inscription describing the king as "AUTHOR & PATRONUS." Dedicating the work "To the King," Sprat praises Charles for freeing people from "the bondage of Errors," as if the restoration of English monarchy were a liberation from Egyptian bondage that facilitated the analogous scientific liberation of people from philosophical error. Sprat praises the *"Vulgar Arts"* (the province of the Royal Society) as valued by God—and points out that "in the whole *History* of the first *Monarchs* of the World, from *Adam* to

Noah," what the Bible records is that they taught *"posterity"* to "build *Cities,* to play on the *Harp* and *Organs,* and to work in *Brass* and *Iron."*[21] Milton, however, identifies these very things—cities, organs, works of brass and iron—with the satanic in the first and last books of the 1667 *Paradise Lost* (1.670–709; 10.552–72). In book 1, we see Mammon and his crew first "wound" one of the hills in hell and rifle it for golden "Ore," which they transform through "wondrous Art" into the "Fabrick" of Pandaemonium (1.688–710). In book 10, Michael's history lesson shows Adam the progeny of Cain, dwelling in the "tents of wickedness":

> whence the sound
> Of Instruments that made melodious chime
> Was heard, of Harp and Organ; and who moov'd
> Thir stops and chords was seen: his volant touch
> Instinct through all proportions low and high
> Fled and pursu'd transverse the resonant fugue.
> In other part stood one who at the Forge
> Labouring, two massie clods of Iron and Brass
> Had melted.
>   . . . .
>   the liquid Ore he drein'd
> Into fit moulds prepar'd, from which he formd
> First his own Tooles.   (554–62, 566–68)

Milton presents the inventors of arts as those who turned away from God. As Michael tells Adam,

> studious they appere
> Of Arts that polish Life, Inventers rare,
> Unmindful of thir Maker, though his Spirit
> Taught them, but they his gifts acknowledg'd none.   (10.605–08)

At pains to distinguish his art and his poem from ungodly art and satanic invention, Milton is as skeptical about "inventors" as about earthly monarchs—both perpetuate the diabolical in the world, rather than restoring paradise.

Sprat's dedication of his *History of the Royal-Society* "To the King" concluded by praising Charles for establishing "a perpetuall Succession of *Inventors."* It was as if scientific progress were analogous to royal succession—and dependent upon it. For Sprat, civilization and monarchy went together, and the progression of civilization depended upon monarchical stability. Abraham Cowley's "Ode to The Royal Society" follows Sprat's dedicatory epistle, and further extols the redemptive possibilities of science, emphasizing its religious dimension. Cowley invokes the image of the restoration of paradise: with the establishment of the Royal Society, the "Orchard" has been liberated, and all can "enter" "that will" and "gather" the "ripen'd fruit." Cowley announces how he expects these "Great Champions" (the Royal Society scientists)—"Gideon's little Band"—to conquer Canaan and destroy the "idols," bringing about the glorious endtimes, making England into a new Jerusalem, where we'll see "New Scenes of Heaven." Hyperbole, analogies from the Hebrew Bible, and Revelation combine in Cowley's vision of England's royalist and scientific progress.

Puritan millenarian hopes seemed dangerous to those who embraced monarchy and the Restoration. Nevertheless, the millenarian discourse and biblical Israelite analogies were appropriated by royalists like Cowley and placed firmly under the patronage of Charles II. The reestablished order was represented as ushering in a kind of utopian "new age"—secularized, but still absorbing and retaining some religious power and resonance. A kind of religious patriotic fervor is evident in Sprat's first section of his *History*. Speaking of the "greatness of the Design" of the society and its amazing "progress," Sprat announces that "the zeal which I have for the Honour of our Nation" has made him write this history. He is proud to be "an *Englishman.*" At one time Milton was, too, but no longer in 1667 did he sign himself, "John Milton, Englishman." Whereas Milton believed that the English had shown their truly base, ignoble spirit, Sprat praises their "invincible and heroick Genius" (122); grateful that England has recovered from her "miseries" (3)—that is, the period of the civil wars—he looks forward to her progress.[22]

That same year, Dryden published his similarly jingoistic *Annus Mirabilis*. The events of 1665 and 1666—the terrible plague, humiliating defeat by the Dutch, the Great Fire—had challenged the sense of England as a blessed nation, thriving under Charles, making strides in experimental science. Like Sprat, however, Dryden rejected the view that these were God's punishments for England having restored the monarchy and national church. Instead, he proclaimed England's favor and offered a vision of England's progress. Where Milton's 1667 epic was notably austere, lacking any images, Dryden's much shorter heroic poem featured an engraved frontispiece representing the poet. Where Milton disdained dedications, Dryden prefaced his poem with addresses to the city of London, Sir Robert Howard, and the Duchess of Albemarle. Milton's and Dryden's poems constitute rival heroic efforts, authorial presentations, and visions in 1667.

Hugh Wilson quite rightly observes "the contrast" between "Dryden, on the one hand, and Marvell and Milton on the other."[23] But we need to think further about Milton in relation to Dryden, about the fascinating oppositions and intersections between them. Not only did Dryden probably work briefly in the same office as Milton and Marvell in the late protectorate; he also marched with them in Oliver Cromwell's state funeral in 1658. Dryden's modern biographer, James Winn, notes with frustration our lack of knowledge about Dryden's relation with Milton, which Winn suggests was probably formal and distant, though Winn remarks that Dryden always later referred to Milton with respect, whereas he engaged Marvell in controversy.[24] Not only did Dryden adapt *Paradise Lost* for the stage, but evidence of Milton's influence is also obvious in *Absalom and Achitophel*, despite the poem's anti-Whig, antirepublican politics.

It is worth further examining Dryden's *Annus Mirabilis* as we think about the context for Milton's 1667 poem. *Paradise Lost* is written in blank verse. Dryden wrote *Annus Mirabilis* in "quatrains or stanzas of four in alternate rhyme," as he explains in his prefatory "Account," "because I have ever judg'd them more noble, and of greater dignity . . . then any other in Verse in use among us." Dryden admits the "advantage" of the "learned languages," which are not "tied to the slavery of any rhyme." Dryden's image was echoed the next year when Milton defended his blank verse as a liberation from "the troublesom and modern bondage of Rimeing." Still, Dryden chose rhyme and declared his subject the "most heroick"—"the beginning, progress, and successes of a most just and necessary war."[25] I think it likely that Milton's redefinitions and revisions of heroism (for example, 10.685–93), and his treatment of satanic military strategy in book 6, are engaging not just with earlier epic but also with contemporary English heroic writing such as Dryden's *Annus Mirabilis*.

Dryden's "heroick" poem, *Annus Mirabilis: The Year of Wonders, 1666*, celebrates England's defeat of Holland (her Protestant rival to trade and empire), despite a humiliating setback. He acknowledges the traumatic losses brought about by the plague and the destruction of London by the Great Fire. Describing the raging fire as a "usurper," Dryden represents the catastrophe as an embodiment of the ravages of civil war and England's condition under the usurper Oliver Cromwell. Dryden was clearly distancing himself from the regicide, the protectorate, everything with which Milton was associated. Having detached himself from an unsavory past and memorialized a plague and fire that had destroyed London but had, in a sense, wiped the city clean, Dryden ends with a startling vision of progress as he predicts London's resurrection to greater glory.

Dryden has a keen sense of the uniqueness of his work, a sense that he has done something as yet "unattempted . . . in Prose or Rhyme"— as Milton says of himself at the beginning of *Paradise Lost*, 1.16. In dedicating his poem to "the Metropolis of Great Britain . . . the city of London," Dryden remarks, "Perhaps I am the first who ever presented a work of this nature to the Metropolis of any Nation" (sig. A2r). We might think of Milton's frequent self-promotions in his earlier prose. In "An Account of the ensuing Poem," Dryden pays tribute to the prince and the general, whose military valor "inspir'd me with thoughts above my ordinary level" (one can imagine what Milton would say). He thinks of "Invention" (a word with satanic associations throughout *Paradise Lost*) as "the first happiness of the poet's imagination."

Whereas Milton's epic is insistently *not* a celebration of his nation, a strong nationalistic, imperial stance shapes Dryden's poem, which criticizes Holland for having usurped the colonial trade that seems by divine right to belong to England. In the war with Holland, God and "Heav'n" are described as being on "Britain's side" (st. 19–20). Even in the devastating fire, God intervenes, sending "the cherub with the flaming Sword." The odd echo of Genesis 3:24 turns London, even in her devastation, into Eden—the place from which Adam and Eve are expelled in the Bible and at the end of Milton's poem.

Having established England as God's chosen, *Annus Mirabilis* moves to a final prophetic description of a newly risen London, which embodies the glories Dryden anticipates for Restoration England:

> Me-thinks already; from this Chymick flame,
> I see a City of more precious mold:
> Rich as the Town which gives the Indies name,
> With silver pav'd, and all divine with Gold.   (294)

Dryden's dedication of the poem to London had promised that his "History of your destruction" would be followed by "a Prophecy of your restoration" (sig. A4v). Might we not hear in Dryden's impassioned lines an echo of Milton's prophetic vision of England in *Areopagitica* (1644)? "Methinks I see in my mind a noble and puissant nation rousing herself like a strong man after sleep. . . . Methinks I see her as an eagle muing her mighty youth, and kindling her undazzled eyes at the full midday beam."[26] Milton's bird of choice in *Areopagitica* is the eagle (associated in Exodus 19:4 with God, who was said to bear his children "on eagles' wings"; compare Deuteronomy 32:11), where Dryden's is the "Phoenix in her ashes," an emblem of "the suffering Deity"[27]—and an image that will, strangely, reappear at the end of Milton's *Samson Agonistes* as the Semichorus describes Samson (1699–1707).

Critics usually read Dryden's prophecy of England's glorious future near the end of the poem as an imitation of Virgil's prophecy about Augustan Rome, and Dryden as insisting on England's Augustan identity. But it is crucial to recognize that Dryden's language is also indebted to Isaiah's vision of the restored Israel / Jerusalem (also latent in Milton's analogy), which in Dryden's verse melds with Revelation's description of the New Jerusalem, whose "city was pure gold" (Rev. 21:18). Dryden compares Londoners, returning after the disastrous fire, to the "Jews of old" who, coming back from Babylonian exile, "Their Royal City did in dust behold" (st. 291). London is Jerusalem, and the effort of rebuilding England's principal city recalls the divinely supported effort of the Jews, who with "constancy" and "vigor" went to "rebuild it" (st. 291) when they returned from captivity. The apocalyptic, heavenly, otherworldly aspect of the vision of Revelation recedes as Dryden envisions a future England that will enjoy the quiet, earthly peace and material prosperity Isaiah promised to Israel:

Now, like a Maiden Queen, she will behold,
From her high Turrets, hourly Sutors come:
The East with Incense, and the West with Gold,
Will stand, like Suppliants, to receive her doom.   (St. 298)

Although Dryden's vision is markedly contemporary as he looks toward expansion of trade with the East and with the Americas, his description recalls a particularly significant past—the biblical description of Solomon's empire, centered in Jerusalem, at the height of its glory:

> And all king Solomon's drinking vessels were of gold, and all the vessels of the house of the forest of Lebanon were of pure gold; none were of silver: it was nothing accounted of in the days of Solomon.
>
> For the king had at sea a navy of Tharshish with the navy of Hiram; once in three years came the navy of Tharshish, bringing gold, and silver, ivory, and apes and peacocks.
>
> So king Solomon exceeded all the kings of the earth for riches and for wisdom. And all the earth sought to Solomon, to hear his wisdom, which God had put in his heart.
>
> And they brought every man his present, vessels of silver, and vessels of gold, and garments, and armour, and spices, horses, and mules, a rate year by year.   (1 Kings 10:21–25)

Dryden's lines also invoke Isaiah's prophecy, in chapter 60, that when Israel is finally restored in those latter days, a Davidic king will once again sit on the throne as in the days of Solomon, and the metropolis Jerusalem will again be the center to which nations come to receive the wisdom of God and to bear tribute. "The abundance of the seas shall be converted unto thee" (Isa. 60:5); "all they from Sheba shall come: they shall bring gold and incense, and they shall shew forth the praises of the Lord" (Isa. 60:6); "For the nation and kingdom that will not serve thee shall perish" (Isa. 60:12); "The sons also of them that afflicted thee shall come bending unto thee, and all they that despised thee shall bow themselves down at the soles of thy feet" (Isa. 60:14).

Isaiah had expressed both utopian hope and nostalgia for the wealth, justice, peace, and prosperity of the biblical Solomon's kingdom. With Charles II safely on the throne, Dryden appropriates the Hebrew Bible to sanction England's imperial and trade ambitions, as he imagines the "vent'rous Merchant" unloading in London (a place of "splendour") and "depart[ing] no more" (st. 301). He ends envisioning an England with a monopoly on world trade:

Thus to the Eastern wealth through storms we go
But now, the Cape once doubled, fear no more;
A constant Trade-wind will securely blow,
And gently lay us on the Spicy shore   (st. 305)

—as if arriving in the spicy East is coming home, regaining paradise. Earlier in the poem, Dryden had accused the Dutch (England's Protestant rival) of having "Stop't" the "flow" of "Trade," which he compares to the circulation of the blood recently discovered by William Harvey (st. 2). This circulation of trade is thus naturalized, and science is made to support political and mercantile desires. England sits at the center of the circle. Trade will flow to her; peoples and nations will come to her with their tribute and for "doom" or judgment. Trade, commerce, and mercantile competition assume a greater role in Dryden's poem than in the Bible, which is here used to legitimate England's imperial ambitions.

Milton, at the end of the *Ready and Easy Way*, had denounced his fellow citizens' belief that a restored monarchy would improve England's trade and economic condition. He ridiculed their "vain and groundless apprehension that nothing but kingship can restore trade"[28]—such avarice was clear evidence of the failure of spirit, a decline into the luxury that destroyed the liberty of Rome. The very trade that Milton denounced, Dryden celebrates in his vision of England and London as the metropolis and center of trade. The contrast with Milton—in the two poets' reading of history and their concluding visions of England's future—could not be stronger.

Both poets claim in their 1667 poems a prophetic power. In the Bible, the prophet invariably speaks *against* kings and institutionalized power. Milton—with his repeated diatribes against idolatry—is the more authentic, traditional prophetic voice, warning against doom, berating the defection of the nation's leaders from God. But Dryden's is the voice of a new, secular prophet, a visionary who is now part of the system and celebrates the nation's potential and achievements, even as he invests them with biblical rhetoric.

Dryden would soon become the voice of the Restoration establishment. Though ten years earlier he had worked with Milton for the protectorate and written "Heroic Stanzas" on the death of Oliver Cromwell, in 1668 Dryden became Charles's (and England's) official poet laureate, while Milton continued to live in obscurity. Twenty years later in 1688, when the magnificent illustrated folio of *Paradise Lost* was printed "by *Miles Flesher,* for *Jacob Tonson,* at the Judge's-Head in *Chancery-lane* near *Fleet-street," Annus Mirabilis* (bound with Dryden's poems on Charles's restoration and coronation) was "Printed for Henry Herringman, and sold by Jacob Tonson," as the title page declares.[29] How curious to imagine Milton's and Dryden's books keeping company in the bookseller's shop.

Surely Milton, had he known this, would have turned over in his grave, for his *Paradise Lost* had firmly set itself against the Restoration establishment discourse. It is in this Restoration context—not just the failure of the earlier revolution—that we need to read Milton's refusal to include in his epic any praise of his nation. We have seen in Dryden, and the books about science, a patriotic discourse of progress, of triumph, a progressive view of history and of the English nation's future that contrasts so sharply with the vision of history that Milton presents in *Paradise Lost,* particularly in that last book, whose relentless record of the earthly triumph of evil, sin, and persecution is perhaps more powerful in its concentrated ten-book form. The world that survives after the flood (analogous to the London plague and fire) is not redeemed, even by Christ's death. Instead, Michael tells Adam in that last book, with its revisionist, antiprogressive history, "so shal the World goe on, / To good malignant, to bad men benigne, / Under her own waight groaning" (10.1429–31). Where Dryden and the Royal Society men put their hopes in a perfected earthly state and English nation, toward which the present institutions were confidently progressing, Milton in 1667 abjured all hopes of a perfected nation, all earthly monarchies and kingdoms and religious institutions, looking instead at the end of book 10 to the day of justice, when "New Heav'ns, new Earth" will be raised from "the conflagrant mass, purg'd and refin'd" (10.1440–41). Although his epic is far from hopeless, its hopes and faith are not placed in this world, and in this way the poem clearly marks its moral distance from the late Stuart establishment as the first decade of the Restoration was drawing to a close.

The Emperor's New Clothes
The Royal Fashion of Satan and Charles II

Richard J. DuRocher

> Lear. [To Edgar, dressed as Poor Tom] You, sir, I entertain for
> one of my hundred; only I do not like the fashion of your gar-
> ments. You will say they are Persian; but let them be chang'd.
> —*King Lear*, 3.6.77–80

An anecdote, probably apocryphal but repeated in several eighteenth century sources and included in J. Milton French's *Life Records of John Milton*, recounts a spirited exchange between King Charles II and Milton during the early Restoration. According to the *Gospel Magazine; or, Treasury of Divine Knowledge* for October 1776, Charles verbally accosted the blind poet upon their chance meeting in St. James Park. But Milton gave the king a sharp retort. The anecdote, recounted in a brief article entitled "Bon Mot of Mr. John Milton," goes as follows:

> King Charles II once said to this great man, "Milton, don't you think that your blindness is a judgment upon you, for having written in defense of my father's murder?"—"*Sir,*" answer'd the poet, "'*tis true,* I have lost my EYES: but, if all calamitous Providences are to be consider'd as Judgments, your Majesty should remember that your royal father lost his HEAD."[1]

The origin of the anecdote—unless the encounter actually took place—probably lies in the autobiographical passages of the *Defensio*

Secunda, or *Second Defense,* in which Milton denies that his blindness resulted from divine punishment for any wrongdoings, as Salmasius had charged.[2] In that tract, the monarch whom Milton was disputing was the previous King Charles, and contrary to the anecdote, the dispute—at least in Milton's mind—was not personal but principled. His aim was not to slander Charles but to oppose tyranny. As Milton insisted: "Iconi Iconoclasten opposui; non *regiis minibus insultans,* ut insimulor, sed reginam veritatem regi Carolo anteponendam arbitratus" ("I opposed to the *Eikon [Basilike]* the *Eikonoklastes,* not, as I am falsely charged, 'insulting the departed spirit of the king,' but thinking that Queen Truth should be preferred to King Charles"). Robert Fellowes best captures the tone of Milton's Latin retort in his translation, first published in Symmons's edition of Milton's prose in 1806: "I did not insult over fallen majesty, as is pretended; I only preferred queen Truth to king Charles."[3]

In recounting this supposed encounter between Milton and Charles II in Restoration London, I am not arguing for its strict historical veracity but suggesting the likelihood of a relationship between the two men. As the anecdote indicates, this relationship was antagonistic and sustained by verbal means. In his prose tracts, Milton refers repeatedly and scornfully to the younger Charles. My chief concern in this essay is to explore the possibility that Milton composed a subtle yet scathing representation of Charles II in *Paradise Lost.* A variety of evidence—historical, visual, and literary—indicates that the portrait of Satan in *Paradise Lost* displays a number of striking similarities to King Charles II, as he was known to appear in person and as he was represented in several media during the early Restoration. Charles II was known among his contemporaries as the "Black Man," chiefly for his dark hair and eyes, though this was also a nickname for the devil.[4] The portrait of Charles II painted circa 1665 by an unknown artist, National Portrait Gallery no. 1313, illustrates these dark features (fig. 1). In general terms, Satan is cast as a tyrant in *Paradise Lost,* and his rule reflects aspects of Charles's reign. Because accusations of tyranny both in the poem and in the day were widespread, however, with Oliver Cromwell and God the Father receiving the same label, I will also present more detailed contextual evidence associating Charles II with Milton's Satan.

Fig. 1. King Charles II, ca. 1665, artist unknown.
Courtesy of National Portrait Gallery, London.

Perhaps the most specific links between Satan and Charles II arise from their shared mode of dress and imperial styles. In particular, as I will show, Milton's references to Satan as a "great Sultan," or Muslim tyrant, ominously reflect the king's chosen style of dress between 1666 and 1670–72, specifically his brief adoption of the so-called Persian vest as a distinguishing feature of his court. Thanks to Milton's friendship with Andrew Marvell, Milton would have been well informed of the king's change of style. Moreover, Restoration verse satire that mocked the king's new fashion may have prompted Milton to treat the topic poetically. Given the timing of the publication of the first edition of *Paradise Lost* in 1667, Milton was in a position to incorporate references to the king's style of dress and government in books 1 and 2 of *Paradise Lost*, particularly as these references appear in sections of the poem that are believed to be among the last completed parts of the epic.[5] In a notorious epic simile in book 1, lines 594 to 604, Milton dared to compare Satan to doomed monarchs who appear as "the Sun new ris'n" (594) amid "misty Air," or emerging "in dim Eclipse" from behind the moon. The royal censor rightly read Charles II as this new risen sun or son, and interpreted these lines as an incitement to sedition.[6] Milton's imaginative link between the style of Satan and Charles II risked the same charge. Hence, I shall consider Milton's subtle attack on Charles II in the 1667 epic as a case of writing under censorship, along the lines Annabel Patterson has so richly explored.[7] Since the king's adoption of the "Persian" style can be securely dated as beginning in 1666 and ending no later than 1672, this attack must have struck readers of the first edition of *Paradise Lost*—and of its several reissues and variants before the second edition of 1674—as a timely literary intervention on Milton's part. By the same token, we need to reconstruct Milton's likely rationale for retaining the details depicting Satan as an "Oriental" tyrant in the poem's second edition of 1674. While published under the royal censor's eye, the 1667 *Paradise Lost* pointedly reflects and discredits the iconography of the contemporary Caroline court, exposing in particular the flawed figure at its center, while pursuing its larger, diachronic project of "assert[ing] eternal providence."

I

Milton's references to the younger Charles Stuart in his prose works from the 1650s set a contemptuous, scoffing tone toward the man who would be king. In the *Pro Populo Anglicano Defensio* (1651), or *First Defense*, Milton's attack is directly aimed at Claude Salmasius; the young Charles comes in for criticism only indirectly, as a measure of the opponent's weakness. In the first of these assaults, Milton attacks Salmasius as an effete, ineffective academic whose rhetorical force is insufficient to move even a "boy-king" or to reach the low standard of mock-epic combat: "But what impudence could have led you from playing the part of a prattling orator in your class-room to think that by sounding an attack you could rouse even a boy-king with your voice so foul and quavering that surely its trumpeting could never have moved even Homer's mice to fight the frogs" (YP 4:322–23). As a former schoolmaster, Milton launches an attack on Salmasius the unworldly educator, an attack that could have been leveled upon himself. In addition to noting its dismissive reference to Charles as a "boy-king," I draw attention to this passage because of Milton's move of satirizing his opponents through the ancient literary genre of mock epic. Recalling the putatively Homeric battle of the mice and frogs, Milton treats Salmasius and the "boy-king" as would-be promoters of just such a miniature battle. In brief, they are laughable and unworthy opponents, beneath the serious concern of a full-scale, epic antagonist like Milton. Something of this mock-epic strategy of diminishing the monarch and his champion survives in Milton's eventual depiction of Charles II through the epic medium of *Paradise Lost*.

In later references to Charles in the *First Defense*, Milton essentially makes two points: that the younger Charles embodies the same despicable values as his father; and that a base crew of attendants surrounds the young man. Throughout the 1650s, Charles held court in France, since he had been declared king of England upon his father's execution. Retreating to France, his mother's homeland, was a natural move, but even the king's ardent sympathizers in England were aware that young Charles II was attended to and influenced by a number of French courtiers. Inevitably, Charles would be picking up French habits, tastes, and ways, English readers realized. Proleptically, Milton aims in his tract to deny the expatriate prince sympathy, even legitimacy, should monarchy be restored in England. Milton warns his fellow Englishmen in 1651, and again in 1658, when the tract was reissued, "what sort of king you will have if he should return" (YP 4:531). Like his father, young Charles is already committed to the divine right of kings, Milton tells readers. Either Charles or his courtiers, Milton surmises, must have prompted Salmasius to claim that Parliament could be charged with treason against the king when that body is no more than the king's "vassal." Salmasius is too stupid, and too foreign, to have come up with this clever but narrow reading of English law: "Never would it have occurred to this wretched foreign grammarian to write, or to think he could write, about the laws concerning the king of England, had not that exile Charles, who is steeped in his father's teachings, and his profligate advisers been so careful to tell him what they wanted written on this subject" (YP 4:531–32). "Steeped in his father's teachings" and steered by a band of immoral and self-serving courtiers exiled in France, the younger Charles in Milton's formulation is destined to mimic his father's views on statecraft. Likewise, in the tract's peroration, Milton challenges Salmasius's claim to have written his *Regia* in response to the prompting of his conscience. Who called upon you, Salmasius, a foreigner, to deal with this English matter? Milton asks. Was it your wife? Or was it, Milton wonders, a second King Balak (Charles II) who found a second Balaam for his defender? Adapting an Old Testament narrative, Milton constructs an allegory that castigates the prince, his court, and Salmasius as well:

> Or was it the younger Charles and his damned crew of emigrant courtiers who called upon you, a second Balaam summoned by a second King Balak, to deign to restore by your slanders the king's cause when it was already hopelessly lost by its poor defence? (YP 4:534)

The identification of Charles as a second King Balak and his champion as a second Balaam fits Milton's rhetorical purposes in the tract in several ways. In the Book of Numbers, chapters 22–24, the Moabite King Balak is afraid of the many Israelites who have pitched their tents in the plains of Moab. Therefore, Balak speaks with the elders of Midian (22:4), and they decide to offer riches to Balaam if he will curse Israel and drive the people out of the land, for the king has observed Balaam's verbal power: "whom thou blessest is blessed, and whom thou cursest is cursed" (22:6). The champion Balaam takes up the king's offer, but instead of cursing the Israelites, he unexpectedly delivers a terrible prophecy against the Moabites:

> There shall come a Star out of Jacob, and a Sceptre shall rise out of Israel, and shall smite the corners of Moab, and destroy all the children Of Sheth.
>
> And Edom shall be a possession, and Seir also shall be a possession for his enemies; and Israel shall do valiantly. (24:17–18)

Whether read as a fable of divine retribution or rhetorical power, the story of Balak and Balaam in Milton's retelling casts young Charles and Salmasius as villains opposed to God's chosen people. During the Restoration, of course, Milton's adoption of Balaam's prophecy to predict the success of the English people against a scheming, fearful tyrant would itself seem to have proven ironic: Even if Salmasius weakened the king's cause, young Charles was restored to the throne and the puritan sympathizers, the encamped Israelites in Milton's application of the narrative, found themselves once again under King Charles's dominion.

Considered within Milton's development as a writer, however, this episode of contesting Charles II's authority by associating him with a biblical tyrant opposed to God's chosen people amounts to a watershed. Milton would take the same approach in *Paradise Lost*, in seeking to serve the same cause that he upholds at the end of the *First Defense:* "to maintain the common rights of our people against the unrighteous tyranny of kings, doing so not because I hated kings, but only tyrants" (YP 4:535). History would offer Milton another opportunity to serve this goal in the mid-1660s, through the rather unlikely means of the king's adoption of a new garment.

II

On October 7, 1666, Charles II declared in Council, or more probably the Committee for Foreign Affairs, his intention to adopt and maintain a new fashion.[8] Samuel Pepys notes the king's declaration, giving several particulars, in his diary entry for October 8: "The

King hath yesterday in Council declared his resolution of setting a new fashion for clothes, which he will never alter. It will be a vest, I know not well how; but it is to teach the nobility thrift, and will do good."[9] Other sources corroborate several points of the king's declaration in Pepys's account, particularly Charles's intention never to give up the new vest, and the notion that the change is intended to promote economy at court. In addition to contributing to moral and economic reform, the new fashion marks a break from French ways, an English newsletter of October 11 observes: "Our Nation having for severall years especially at this season too much used themselves to ape the French in their fashions, his Ma[ty] for avoiding the like vanity in the future has been pleased to signify that he himselfe will weare a vest & not alter that mode."[10]

The newsletter *Mercurius Politicus Redivivus* describes the first public appearance of the vest on October 14, 1666:

> In this month his majestie and whole Court changed the ffashion of their Cloathes: viz: a Close Coat of Cloath pinkt wth a white taffety vnder the cutts this [which?] in length reachd to the calf of the legg and vpon that a Sercoat: cutt att the brest which hung loose and shorter then the Vest six Inches the breeches the Spanish cutt and buskins, some of Cloath and some of leather but of the same Colour as the Vest or Garment, of neuer the like fashion since William the Conquest which was in the yeare 1066 he begane his Reigne in October, the 14 day and o[r] new standing faishion [*sic*] begane 14 day of October 1666.[11]

In an October 17 entry Pepys records a quip by the king about the pink-on-white color of the vest ("The King says the pinking upon white makes them too much like magpies"), and thus points to a shift to black or plain velvet colors that shortly followed. The *OED* credits King Charles II with introducing the vest, which the dictionary defines, citing Pepys's diary, as "a sleeveless garment of some length worn by men under the coat" (3.a.). Edward Montague, the First Earl of Sandwich, includes a rough sketch of the new fashion in his journal (fig. 2). His caption for the sketch reads: "The habitt taken up by y[e] King & Court of England Nouemb[r] 1666, w[ch] They Call a vest."[12] The earl uses the term "vest" as a synecdoche for the entire outfit, a usage followed in this essay. A full-length portrait of Lord Baltimore painted by Gerard Soest around 1670 depicts the vest in intricate detail

The habitt taken up by y^e King & Cerut of England
Novemb^r 1666. wch They Call a Vest.

Fig. 2. Sketch of the vest from the manuscript journal of Edward
Montagu, First Earl of Sandwich. From Francis M. Kelly, "A Comely
Vest After the Persian Mode," *The Connoisseur* 88 (1931): 98.

Fig. 3. Lord Baltimore, by Gerard Soest. (Messrs. Duveen Bros.)
From Tancred Borenius, in *The Burlington Magazine for
Connoisseurs* 63, no. 368 (November 1933): 192–93.

(fig. 3). As these illustrations show, the vest is worn as a kind of cassock that extends to the knees, with buttons running its length; it is gathered at the waist by a belt or sash. An open coat or tunic with short sleeves completes the ensemble.

The newsletter's claim that Charles's vest returns to William the Conqueror's style is a curious one that I have not seen confirmed elsewhere. If true, it would mean that Charles's "new" fashion of 1666 actually reverts to a pattern worn by the invading Norman of the eleventh century. The fact that the vest amounts to a revolt against current French fashion, however, is certain. Clearly one of Charles II's motives in making the change was to distinguish the English royal style from that of the French court. In summarizing this fashion event, Esmond de Beer explains it as a barometer of Anglo-French relations: "[The fashion] came into existence in the period of Charles II's reign when this country and France were most widely divergent in their policies; nominally we were at war with France; there was however no important engagement between the forces of the two countries."[13] As a sign that the French understood the political point of Charles's adoption of the vest, Pepys tells the story in his diary entry of November 22, 1666, that Louis XIV had all his footmen dressed in vests in order to ridicule the English outfit.[14] If clothing style may be used as a political weapon, it is apparently a double-edged one.

Like many a New Year's resolution, however, within a brief span both of the king's announced aims—that the vest would contribute to English economy and that he would never abandon it—came to naught. A month after the vest first appeared, Pepys notes its metamorphosis into a luxury item displayed by the beau monde. At a court ball for the queen's birthday in November, Pepys saw rich, elaborate versions of the vest everywhere: "The King in his rich vest of some rich silke and silver trimming, as the Duke of York and all the dancers were, some of cloth of silver, and others of other sorts exceeding rich" (November 15, 1666). Other observers of this ball estimated that the nobility's new vests cost at least 100 pounds each, and some vests ornamented with jewels ran over a thousand.[15] Given Charles II's attempt to promote economy through court dress, the enduring plain style of Oliver Cromwell's portraiture, Laura Knoppers has argued, haunted Charles II during the 1660s.[16] Contemporary observers, including Edward Chamberlayne and John Evelyn, note that the fashion disappeared from court between 1670 and 1672; that is, within two years of the unofficial Treaty of Dover (May 22, 1670), when Charles's sister Henriette paid a visit to Dover and thus helped bring about a closer alliance between England and France.[17] Chamberlayne's *Anglia Notitia* had recorded the first appearance of the vest in the English court; in its sixth edition, published in 1672, it explains "but that is now left."[18] Confirming the view of the vest as reflecting a political difference with France, seventeenth century observers describe the king's eventual abandonment of the article as a capitulation to French dominance. As Evelyn writes, "It was a comely and manly habit, too good to hold, it being impossible for us in good earnest to leave ye Monsieurs vanities long" (October 30, 1666).

It is less the vest's difference from the French mode than its similarity to "Persian" or more generally Middle Eastern or "Oriental" patterns, however, that I wish to emphasize. John Evelyn is justly credited with characterizing the king's choice as the adoption of the Persian vest. Evelyn had given the king a copy of his pamphlet *Tyrannus; or, The Mode,* published in 1661, which recommends the style. In his journal entry for October 18, 1666, Evelyn describes the king's new fashion as "Eastern" and "after the Persian mode":

> To Court. It being ye first time his Ma^{ty} put himself solemnly into the Eastern fashion of vest, changing doublet, stiff collar, bands and Cloake, etc.: into a comely vest, after ye Persian mode, with girdle or shash, [*sic*] and Shoe strings and Garters, into bouckles, of which some were set with precious stones, resolving never to alter it, and to leave the French mode, which had hitherto obtain'd to our greate expense and reproach. . . . I had sometime before presented an invective against that unconstancy, and our so much affecting the French fashion, to his Ma^{ty}, in which I tooke occasion to describe the comelinesse and usefulnesse of the Persian clothing, in ye very same manner his Ma^{ty} now clad himselfe. This pamphlet I intitl'd "Tyrannus, or the Mode" and gave it to his Ma^{ty} to reade. I do not impute to this discourse the change which soone happen'd, but it was an identity that I could not but take notice of.

Evelyn's Janus-faced account—pointing out his role in recommending the Persian fashion but denying that his encouragement caused the king's change—may owe something to a courtier's expected humility before the monarch. Even though Evelyn, on a trip to Italy in 1645, had seen several Persians wearing vests, de Beer seems eager to discount the Persian origin of the vest, claiming, "its only definite association with the Persian fashion comes from Evelyn."[19] If we take Evelyn's term "Persian" as referring broadly to a Middle Eastern or Asian style, however, then multiple eyewitnesses can be produced to support the identification. This distinction is worth noting, for it is the broader recognition of the vest as a Middle Eastern or, in seventeenth century parlance, "Oriental" model that is crucial to my argument linking Charles's fashion with the depiction of Satan in *Paradise Lost*. For example, Chamberlayne's *Angliae Notitia* (1669) recognized the fashion as both a rejection of the French mode and a turn to the East: "Since our late breach with *France*, the English Men (though not the Women) have quitted the French Mode, and taken a grave Wear, much according with the Oriental Nations."[20]

Whatever its advantages, Charles II's turn to the Persian or Eastern style of clothing would carry for his subjects a potentially treacherous, even sacrilegious message. Stevie Davies aptly summarizes the attitude of most Europeans to the East in Charles's day: "The East stood in a permanently aggressive posture toward Christendom: together with the Egyptians, Babylonians, and Persians of antiquity, these races confronted the West intending only outrage, and, being pure autocracies, they could speak and act with one mind in a way that the fragmented European world, split between Catholic and Protestant, nation and nation, party and party, could never do."[21] In his prose work, *A Brief History of Moscovia*, written before the poet's total blindness of the 1650s, Milton had described in detail one colorful form of the autocratic Eastern ruler. "The Emperour" of Moscow, Milton writes, "exerciseth absolute power. . . . The Revenues of the Emperour are what he list, and what his Subjects are able; and he omits not the coursest means to raise them" (YP 8:487, 498). For Charles to don the apparel of an Eastern autocrat provoked speculation about how far he was inclined to take on the ways of such an absolute monarch. Both Milton and Marvell, as we shall see, read Charles's adoption of the Persian vest as a desire for the pure autocracy that an Oriental tyrant—as opposed to a Christian monarch—enjoyed.

One aspect of Restoration culture that may have led to Charles's adoption of the vest was the theater, which was focused upon and intimately bound up with the court. Diane De Marly documents a particular vogue for Oriental subjects in plays, some of them based on events in Turkish history, produced at court during the 1660s. Among these plays she includes the lavish production of William Davenant's operatic *The Siege of Rhodes* in 1662, and Lord Orrery's *The Tragedy of Mustapha, the Son of Solyman the Magnificent* in 1665. "Thus," De Marly writes, "the court was used to seeing the oriental vest upon the English stage."[22] Soon they would become used to seeing it upon their monarch. According to Evelyn (3.216), the king first appeared in the new vest at a production of "Lord Brahals Tragedy cal'd *Mustapha*" at Whitehall Palace on October 18, 1666— a case of life imitating art. Dressed in his new vest, the king would thus have looked upon a play presenting actors, one of whom represented the Ottoman sultan Mustapha, dressed in similar garb. Charles's costume unmistakably draws attention to its Middle Eastern provenance. While no portrait of Charles in his vest survives, Greenhill's portrait of the actor Thomas Betterton in the costume of Bajazet, the Ottoman sultan (fig. 4), shows him in a vest in 1663. Betterton's vest is worn under the coat, and it has a sash and a row of buttons down the front, like those worn by English noblemen in other portraits.

The link between the so-called Persian vest and the personal style of Charles II during the 1660s, then, seems to be well established. Before turning to poetic evidence linking Charles's Oriental vest to *Paradise Lost*, however, one might reasonably doubt whether Milton would even have been aware of the king's fashion. Granted that the court and its followers were keenly attuned to Charles's sartorial preferences, would the blind poet, in relative seclusion and reduced circumstances since the Restoration, have had access to the latest developments at court? One constant in Milton's life during the Restoration was Andrew Marvell, who as a member of Parliament for Hull had interceded on Milton's behalf concerning the Act of Oblivion I in 1660, and who wrote his commendatory poem, "On Mr. Milton's *Paradise Lost*," for the epic's second, 1674 edition. Sometime between those verbal interventions Marvell wrote a series of satires on the reign of Charles II, among them his contribution of verses to a *jeu d'esprit* entitled "The Kings Vowes." Apparently the work of multiple authors including Marvell, the poem exists in several different versions, including a manuscript version dated 1667.[23]

Fig. 4. A theatrical vest. From De Marly, "King Charles II's
Own Fashion," in *The Journal of the Warburg and Courtauld
Institute* 37 (1974): 381.

I suggest that Marvell and Milton discussed this satire, which would have told the blind poet everything he needed to know about the king's new fashion. The master conceit in the satire is to imagine Charles II, at a low point in his fortunes during his exile in France, making a series of vows "to his Maker—If ever I see England againe" (5–6). Marvell is thus able to reflect sharply upon events of the 1650s and 1660s, as the king replaces the troublesome particulars of history with his own fantasies. The vows begin, for instance, with this doggerel couplet: "I will have a Religion then all of my owne, / Where Papist from Protestant shall not be knowne" (7–8). In stanza 15 the king imagines the style of clothing he will wear upon his return, which Marvell significantly associates with his preferred style of rule:

> I will have a fine Tunick a Sash and a Vest,
> Tho' not rule like the Turk yet I will be so drest,
> And who knows but the Mode may soon bring in the rest?(49–51)

The first thing to note is that the poet is well aware—and acts as though his readers are, too—of the king's preferred ensemble of tunic, sash, and vest. The point of Marvell's satiric barb is that, despite the king's protestations to the contrary, Charles is indeed happy to "rule like the Turk." The king's fashion will soon "bring in the rest," that is, carry with it the autocratic power of the Turkish ruler he appears. In Marvell's poem, Charles's costume, like the rest of his fanciful vows, reveals his true desire for unlimited power. In the view of the alert English citizenry, as Milton put it in his *Observations upon the Articles of Peace* in 1649, it expresses the king's desire "to endeavor the introducing of a plain Turkish Tyranny" (YP 3:313).[24]

III

Perhaps the major rhetorical battle early in *Paradise Lost* is the struggle between the followers of Satan and God to associate their opponents with the label of tyranny. Satan concludes his first speech, for example, by vowing to Beelzebub to wage "eternal War" against God, whom he styles "our grand Foe," who "[s]ole reigning holds the Tyranny of Heav'n" (1.122, 124). Contributing to that struggle is Milton's association of Satan with a Turkish or broadly Eastern tyranny—a style of leadership reflecting the monarch on the English throne at the time of the epic's first publication. At the beginning of the epic's plot, as soon as Satan rallies the fallen angels, who had been scattered on the burning sea of hell, Milton begins to discredit their leader. Milton's approach is subtle and indirect, befitting the poem's composition under state censorship. Satan's followers are compared to "a pitchy cloud / Of *Locusts*, warping on the Eastern Wind, / That o'er the Realm of impious *Pharoah* hung like Night" (1.340–42). In this Egyptian setting, the depiction of the devils as locusts is certainly unflattering. At the same time, as a threat to "impious *Pharoah*" they might be seen as doing God's work, and Milton specifically describes them as arising in response to the "potent Rod" of Moses (338–39). Immediately, however, Milton shifts the metaphor of Moses' rod to the "Spear" of "thir great Sultan." With this image the theme of Oriental tyranny is introduced:

> Till, as a signal giv'n, th' uplifted Spear
> Of thir great Sultan waving to direct
> Thir course, in even balance down they light
> On the firm brimstone, and fill all the Plain.   (347–50)

No longer the servants of Moses, the fallen angels now obey "thir great Sultan." Readers in 1667 would have understood a sultan to name "the sovereign or chief ruler of a Mohammedan country" (*OED* 1) and, in quality, to be "an absolute ruler; *gen.* a despot, tyrant" (*OED* 2). Supporting the second, qualitative sense, Milton's description has the devils reassume their previous form as locusts or insects: "down they *light*" (my italics). Politically, this horde of absolutely obedient, dangerous though tiny followers is the perfect match for their "great Sultan."

This description of Satan as a "great Sultan" or Eastern tyrant is further developed in Milton's description of the debate in Pandemonium, which opens book 2. Here the references to the Oriental tyrant glance unmistakably at Charles II. The book begins:

> High on a Throne of Royal State, which far
> Outshone the wealth of Ormus and of Ind,
> Or where the gorgeous East with richest hand
> Show'rs on her Kings *Barbaric* Pearl and Gold,
> Satan exalted sat.   (2.1–5)

The excessive opulence alone of this monarch's throne serves as a tip-off to its occupant's dubious morality and politics. Milton's comparison of Satan's throne to "the wealth of Ormus" specifically refers to the island port of Ormus or Hormoz between the Persian Gulf and the Gulf of Oman. The lucrative port city of Ormus had been captured from the Portuguese by Shah Abbas I with the aid of an English fleet in 1622.[25] The wealth of Satan's throne is said to exceed ("outshone") this luxurious Persian trading center, but in Milton's poem excessive wealth is not a virtue. In describing the building of Pandemonium a few lines earlier the Miltonic narrator delivers a severe moral judgment on riches: "Let none admire / That riches grow in Hell; that soil may best / Deserve the precious bane" (690–92). Moreover, in the 1667 edition, "*Barbaric*" in the passage from book 2 is italicized, which suggests that it is a place name, referring to the North African Barbary Coast.[26] To a seventeenth century English reader, "*Barbaric* Pearl and Gold" would inevitably suggest riches stolen by Muslim pirates of that region. Overall, Satan's association with the "gorgeous East" is highly pejorative, serving to cast in doubt his real worth and authority. The effect of Milton's comparison is to link Satan with a wealthy and, at the very least, morally suspect Persian leader. For readers aware of King Charles II's adoption of the Persian style of dress, however, the comparison would carry a further point. Knowing that the king chose to appear in Persian garb, readers in 1667 could easily substitute Charles's face for that of the Persian ruler or Satan described by Milton's lines.

Beyond Charles's new Persian vest, other contextual evidence from the early Restoration period links the king with English fascination with the East. Blair Hoxby has traced the imagery celebrating Charles's promotion of Eastern trade that fills the spectacle and poetry of the king's royal entry into London in 1661. Most of our knowledge of that royal progress depends upon John Ogilby's *The Relation of His Majesties Entertainment* (1661), greatly expanded and illustrated in *The Entertainment of His Most Excellent Majestie Charles II* (1662).[27] One brief episode from the royal entry particularly supports Milton's poetic link among Persia, Satan, and Charles. One of the royal procession's stops along its passage through London was at East India House on Leaden-Hall Street. There, a poem was read to Charles celebrating his exceptional patronage of the East India Company's trade:

> For you have outdone Solomon, and made
> Provision for more than Ophir Trade[28]

In 1 Kings and 1 and 2 Chronicles, the ships of Solomon travel to Ophir—understood variously to lie in Arabia, India, or North Africa—and return with fine gold. The East India Company's procedure was the opposite: exporting gold bullion to the East in exchange for the luxury items it brought back to England. Hoxby explains that, because it could lead to debasement of the national currency, the export of bullion was generally illegal. Thus, Charles's support for an exemption for the Company's illegal procedure—which Hoxby reads as the narrow meaning of "the more than Ophir Trade" which the poem alludes to—was by far the most controversial aspect of the East India trade. Certainly it was an ambitious enterprise, one promising to make London the center of a global economy and Charles its "universal monarch."

In *Paradise Lost*, however, as J. Martin Evans and David Quint have shown, such global capitalism is presented as the devil's work. In short, Quint writes, "the Satanic plot of *Paradise Lost*" is "the devil's conquest of the earth for Sin and Death."[29] Quint discusses an epic simile in book 2 that depicts Satan not merely as a global wanderer but especially as a merchant adventurer:

> As when far off at sea, a fleet descri'd
> Hangs in the Clouds, by *Equinoctial* Winds
> Close sailing from *Bengala*, or the Isles
> Of *Ternate* and *Tidore*, whence Merchants bring
> Their spicy Drugs: they on the Trading Flood
> Through the wide *Ethiopian* to the Cape
> Ply stemming nightly toward the Pole. So seem'd
> Far off the flying Fiend.   (2.636–43)

In addition to depicting Satan as a commercial trader, this simile also builds upon Milton's presentation of Satan as a "great Sultan" or Oriental figure. Ternate and Tidore are two of the Moluccas or Spice Islands that Europeans increasingly traded with in Milton's day. Ternate in particular was an important Muslim center whose sultan had granted the spice concession to the Dutch in 1607. As Milton readied *Paradise Lost* for publication in 1667, England was involved in a war with the Dutch that centered on the two nations' rival trade empires. Overall, Satan aims to create a "nether empire" to God's, an empire built on colonialism and trade.[30] For this empire to grow, Satan, like the merchant, depends on fortune, speculation, and ultimately on deception. As Charles was promoting English trade with the East, he would find an ally in merchant adventurers of Satan's kind. In Milton's epic, then, Satan and Charles are economic partners as well as iconographic counterparts.

Satan's journey through *Paradise Lost* culminates in book 9 of the 1667 edition in a return to his throne in hell described in book 2. This return, I suggest, might be seen as Satan's equivalent of Charles II's restoration. Stevie Davies has brilliantly described not only the cluster of Asiatic allusions with which Milton introduces the scene but also their accompanying political themes of disorder, dissension, and self-consumption.[31] Unlike the glorious return of Charles II, Satan returns to his throne uncelebrated and unseen—perhaps in order to spy upon his minions. As they await the return of "thir great adventurer," the fallen angels are described in a simile comparing them either to "the Tartar" or "the Bactrian sophy," that is, either to Mongolian Sunni Muslims or Persian shahs (10.431–40 [1674 ed.]). When they finally notice the return of their ruler, the devils are said to be "rais'd from thir dark *Divan*" (10.457 [1674 ed.]). This account recalls the raising of the fallen angels from the burning lake by Satan's voice, which Milton describes in book 1, lines 330–38, immediately preceding the identification of Satan as "thir great Sultan." In 1667 a divan denoted "an Oriental council of state; specifically in Turkey, the privy council of the Porte, presided over by the Sultan, or in his absence, by the grand vizier" (*OED* 1). One implication of "divan" in this sense would be that the demons in council, perhaps led by Satan's lieutenant, Beelzebub, have been conspiring against their absentee leader during his travels. Could Milton be pointing to English royalists who looked to other princes or powers during Charles's exile yet were forced, upon his return, to acknowledge Charles as their monarch? In any case, after his victory speech, Satan unexpectedly finds himself hissed and his followers humiliated.

Even at this moment of triumph and restoration to his throne, Satan's empire is beginning to unravel.

IV

Stepping back from Satan's characterization in *Paradise Lost,* one senses that the issue of dress in the poem may convey something beyond its literal significance as clothing. Dress and clothing in the epic partake of a larger Miltonic project: the mingling of corporeality and spirituality in all created beings. As is the case with Milton's reading of Jacob's dream of a ladder to heaven in book 3, lines 499–525, in which "Each stair mysteriously was meant" (516), clothing worn by angels contributes to Milton's mysterious mingling of matter and spirit. Admittedly, Milton's discussion of clothing worn by angels may strike some readers as merely evidence of the poet's confusion. Samuel Johnson upbraided Milton for "unhappily confusing his poetry with his philosophy," particularly in his depictions of the angels. C. S. Lewis came to Milton's defense, arguing that his angelology is not only based on seventeenth century pneumatology but also successful as a poetic experiment. Instructed by the work of Stephen Fallon and others, readers have recently come to see Milton's stance of monist materialism as a serious and consistent philosophical position that accounts for the apparent confusion Johnson upbraided.[32] The relevance of Milton's ideas about matter to dress may require some elucidation. For example, Johnson and others considered the wearing of armor by Michael's faithful angels unreasonable, a laughable mistake the poet was forced to rectify by having Michael's band remove their armor. For material angels such as Milton presents, however, not only is armor appropriate as a protective casing, but it also serves the decorous purpose of marking out or signifying the faithful service these angels embody. Material angels wisely remove the armor when it becomes an impediment. In a similar way, the "bright harnessed angels" whom Milton describes at the end of the Nativity poem display in that harness an emblem or badge of their appropriate service to their newborn king.[33]

Whether fallen or standing, warfaring or wayfaring, angels are always spirits, however, and as such they require no dress. By the same logic, Satan is never described as being dressed in a vest or other clothing in *Paradise Lost*. Nonetheless, readers are well aware of the several "disguises" that Satan adopts in order to deceive those who rely, too trustingly in the event, on appearances. In book 3, when Satan, traveling in the region of light on his journey toward Earth, sees a glorious angel, he quickly changes his appearance from his "proper shape" to put on the appearance of "a stripling Cherub" (634–36), the better to gather information without arousing suspicion. In order to effect the temptation of Adam and Eve, of course, Satan "dresses" as a serpent. When Eve momentarily resists his seduction, Satan "puts on" the "new part" or role of an impassioned orator akin to those in Athens or Rome, and Satan completes the act by putting on a show, using gestures and shape to complete the disguise (9.664–78 [1674 ed.]). When Adam and Eve lie down together in their bower in Eden, the Miltonic narrator is pleased to observe that they were unencumbered by "These troublesome disguises which wee wear" (4.740). Eden, the narrator implies, can well do without disguises, without pretenses, without clothing. One recalls the moment from book 5 at which Milton says that Eve appears before the angel Raphael "Undeckt, save with herself," and that "no veil / She needed" (383–84).

Such celebrations of unlibidinous nakedness, however, are a far cry from saying that the language of clothing along with its many rich connotations has no place in *Paradise Lost*. Clothing has its own decorum in human culture, and Milton observes this decorum in his grand masterpiece. To prove the point, one has only to return to Raphael's appearance in the Edenic bower. When directed by God to visit Adam and Eve, Raphael—unlike Eve some 100 lines later—is presented as being "veiled":

> Nor delay'd the winged Saint
> After his charge receiv'd; but from among
> Thousand Celestial Ardors, where he stood
> Veil'd with his gorgeous wings, up springing light
> Flew through the midst of Heav'n.   (5.247–51)

Milton's reiterated use of the word "veiled" in these two cases is revealing. Both observe decorum. In her innocent state, Eve needs no supererogatory veil such as Roman Catholic statuary provides for its subjects. Raphael is veiled with what is appropriate to his angelic nature, his wings. One might take this as a Miltonic joke, another spin on the tale of the emperor's new clothes, in which such veiling, rather than an attempt to hide, reveals by identifying its wearer. Playfulness abounds in this passage, as in the pun on "light." Milton continues the play on Raphael's changes in appearance as he approaches Eden: one moment he seems to be a Phoenix (272), the next he returns to "his proper shape," in which "six wings he wore" (275–76). The last change is likewise motivated by decorum, so that his "lineaments Divine" do not dazzle human eyes. My point is that this angel is depicted as being dressed appropriately—yet revealingly, without deception, without pretense—before a variety of onlookers.

When fallen Adam and Eve encounter the next unfallen angel, they are themselves fallen, and here the discussion of dress comes full circle. In book 10 God sends Michael to Eden to prepare Adam and Eve for their new life. If Raphael is the quintessentially "sociable" spirit, Michael in book 10 is a "solemn and sublime" one, Adam realizes, for "such Majesty / Invests him coming" (11.232–33 [1674 ed.]). In light of what we have seen previously about Milton's questioning of Charles II's presumptuous authority and Satan's dubious kingship, Michael with his proper "majesty" stands as a counterweight. Adam's recognition of Michael's "Majesty" revives the political argument surrounding Satan in his appearance as "great Sultan." Unlike that of Satan and Charles in the poet's vision, Michael's majesty, his authority, is God-given (11.99–125 [1674 ed.]). Significantly, Michael appears wearing a vest:

> Not in his shape Celestial, but as Man
> Clad to meet Man; over his lucid Arms
> A military Vest of purple flow'd
> Livelier than *Meliboean,* or the grain
> Of *Sarra,* worn by Kings and Heroes old
> In time of Truce.   (11.239–44 [1674 ed.])

Though unsettling, Michael's mission is ultimately comedic in a Dantesque sense. He comes to bring hope to the fallen Adam and Eve. He comes as a kind of ambassador between offending and offended parties, and appropriately, though an angel, he appears "as Man / Clad to meet Man." Fowler notes that he appears without wings because, in contrast to Raphael's spiritual instruction, his mission is to accommodate Adam to the "mundane," terrestrial matters of human history.[34] But the purple in the vest is more than merely mundane. With its allusion to "*purpura Meliboea*," the description recalls Virgil's *Aeneid* 5.251, where a gold and purple cape, emblematic of kingship, goes to the victor in one of the funeral observances for Anchises. The same phrase appears in Lucretius's *De Rerum Natura* 2.500, where the color stands for the embodiment of the best among sensible things. Within the Christian tradition, the purple vest reflects the penitential vestments of Lent. According to Mark 15:17, the soldiers clothed Christ before his scourging with purple and made him wear a crown of thorns. The "military" vest Michael wears connects and interfuses these associations, for he has been a soldier and he comes bearing that insignia of his office. A modest though magisterial spirit, Michael comes with news of the Redeemer to come. He comes humbly, on a mission to humble sinful humankind. As the 1660s unfolded, with their new cycle of insults and executions in the reestablished monarchy of England, such a divine ambassador as Michael would have been welcome again, Milton suggests. Whether he would have been welcome in Charles's court, despite his purple vest, is another matter.

V

In the 1688 edition of *Paradise Lost*, Henry Aldrich's plates for books 1 and 2 depict Satan in Roman breastplate and skirt. Moreover, Aldrich's Roman Satan bears an uncanny resemblance to royally commissioned statues of the 1680s by Grinling Gibbons showing Charles II and his brother James II in similar clothing and poses. The publisher of the 1688 edition, Jacob Tonson, and many of his financial underwriters were committed anti-Jacobites, who would certainly have been pleased to see illustrations in the 1688 edition that discredited the Stuart line.[35] All in all, the illustrations of the 1688 text directly challenge the myth of Charles's return as the dawn of a new Augustan age, a myth Charles had promoted as the official story of his reign.

The 1667 edition of *Paradise Lost*, in contrast, was completely lacking in illustrations, and some critics might take this fact as evidence against my case for a connection between Satan and Charles based on the Persian vest. While the lack of visual evidence in the 1667 text does not add particular details presenting Satan as a Turkish tyrant or Roman emperor, I maintain that it serves the more important purpose of keeping these and other imaginative possibilities alive. Milton's poetic approach rules neither view out of the reader's imagination. Merritt Hughes warned in 1964 of the folly of reducing *Paradise Lost* to a *roman à clef*, and my argument should not be taken as proof that Milton's portrait of Satan points always and everywhere to Charles II. While rejecting readings of the epic as historical allegory, however, Hughes nonetheless recognized that Milton "encouraged [Satan's] identification with figures on his immediate political scene."[36] Focusing his antagonism on the current English king was hardly a new occupation for Milton when Charles was restored to the English throne. Moreover, beyond the first edition of *Paradise Lost*, Milton continued to probe questions of what defined true kingship in *Paradise Regained* (1671).

If we grant that Milton wanted readers in 1667 to associate Charles II with Satan, however, a further question remains. Books 1 and 2 of *Paradise Lost*, on which my argument is primarily based, show no substantive changes between the 1667 and the 1674 editions. Likewise, despite the redistribution of the poem into 12 books for the second edition, the passage on Michael's vest remains unchanged in the later edition. As I have shown, certainly Charles abandoned the Persian vest by 1672. Why should references to the king's now discarded fashion remain in the later authorial edition? Was this inclusion the result of forgetfulness—or worse, of spite—on Milton's part?

Such assumptions, however, show a misunderstanding of the associative and polysemous nature of Milton's poetry. The kaleidoscopic, encompassing narrative of *Paradise Lost* makes glancing references to various stories and events, as it unfolds its tale of cosmic disobedience and eventual restoration. Milton's epic argument rehearses biblical and classical tales, while it reminds seventeenth century readers of recent history including Galileo's telescope, the burglarizing of rich burghers' homes, and "all our woe"—all topics Milton directly associates with Satan. This associative style serves a political as well as a spiritual agenda. At the same time, the 1667 *Paradise Lost* reflects on recent events while avoiding slander, and thus denies to the royal licenser definite grounds on which to censor the poem. Given Milton's approach, readers in 1667—and those in 1674 or 2007—might see in Satan a fleeting, cunning resemblance to King Charles II. If, in the "darkness visible" of hell, readers see—or think they see—in the figure of Satan the current ruler wearing his favorite vest, then Milton's poem would have succeeded in providing exactly the right blend of suggestiveness, doubt, and illumination.

"Now let us play"

Paradise Lost and Pleasure Gardens in Restoration London

LAURA LUNGER KNOPPERS

[28 May 1667.] Presently comes Creed, and he and I by water to Fox hall and there walked in Spring-garden; a great deal of company, and the weather and garden pleasant . . . it is very pleasant and cheap going thither, for a man may go to spend what he will, or nothing, all as one—but to hear the nightingale and other birds, and here fiddles and there a harp, and here a jews trump, and here laughing, and there fine people walking, is mighty divertising.[1]

For Samuel Pepys, as for many Londoners in the 1660s, the new or newly restored gardens and royal parks were a place of many pleasures: taking in the fresh air, walking in the groves, listening to the birds, admiring the natural beauty, and enjoying music, food, drink, and sexual dalliance.[2] Pleasure gardens were part of what historians have termed the commercialization of leisure in the late seventeenth and early eighteenth century.[3] Largely closed or restricted over the Interregnum, gardens and royal parks, along with such urban spaces as theaters and coffeehouses, marked a new leisured and pleasure-seeking society in the 1660s.[4] Yet we will also see that Pepys is torn between work and pleasure, a tension that marks his accounts of Charles II and resonates more broadly in Restoration London.

The 1667 edition of *Paradise Lost* emerges precisely at the time when pleasure gardens had become a visible—and increasingly notorious—part of the actual and imagined urban landscape in London.[5] While classical and biblical gardens undeniably shape Milton's depiction of the archetypal pleasure garden, Eden, and while scholars have looked at links with Italian gardens and with English gardening techniques, this contemporary context of pleasure gardens in Restoration London has not been explored.[6] In sharp contrast to the spaces set aside for leisure and play, Milton's depiction of gardening labor is both precise and daring.[7] While Milton shows multiple pleasures of the garden, he uniquely links pleasure with Adam and Eve's joint and unremitting labor.[8] Adam and Eve fall when they separate labor and pleasure, when they turn to "play" apart from discipline and obedience, the obedience that is the main product of their gardening.

References to Vauxhall, Mulberry Garden, Barn Elms, Cherry Garden, Hyde Park, and St. James's Park recur in diaries and other accounts of Restoration London, most notably in the chatty pages of Samuel Pepys. On May 29, 1662, Pepys goes with his wife, two maids, and his boy to Old Spring Garden at Vauxhall: "And there walked long and the wenches gathered pinks" (3:95). But, given that they "could not have anything to eat but very dear and with long stay," the party makes its way to the New Spring Gardens, "where I never was before, which much exceeds the other" (95). Here, Pepys walks with his wife and maids "while the boy creeps through the hedge, and gather[s] abundance of roses" (95). Exiting the gardens, they dine on cakes, powdered beef, and ale at an ordinary house, before returning home by boat "with much pleasure" (95). Similarly, on June 23, 1665, Pepys recounts that "[Creed] and I took boat and to Fox hall, where we spent two or three hours, talking of several matters very soberly and contentfully to me—which, with the ayre and pleasure of the garden, was a great refreshment to me, and methinkes that which we ought to Joy ourselfs in" (6:136). Pepys also frequents Barn Elms to read, walk, or gaze upon the other company, as on May 26, 1667, when having taken the boat to the gardens, he "walked the length of the Elmes, and with great pleasure saw some gallant ladies and people, come with their bottles and basket[s] and chairs and form[s] to sup under the trees by the waterside, which was mighty pleasant" (8:236).

Part of the pleasures of the gardens were the planned landscapes, including flowers, fruits, wildernesses, trees, arbors, groves, alleys, and, in some cases, elaborate garden beds or "knots." A detailed account of the physical setting of Vauxhall in 1663 is provided by a Frenchman, Monsieur de Monconys, who made a trip to England and published an account of his travels on his return to France. Monconys admired the grass walks and the gardens laid out in 20- to 30-foot squares enclosed with hedges of gooseberries. Within the squares were raspberry bushes, rose bushes, and other shrubs as well as herbs, vegetables, and fruit, including peas, beans, asparagus, and strawberries. Walks bordered with jonquils, gillyflowers, or lilies led to numerous private arbors.[9]

In addition to the natural beauty, fresh air, and exercise, the pleasure gardens offered food, drink, song, and other merriment. On May 11, 1668, Pepys goes to New Spring Garden (Vauxhall) after enjoying another London pleasure, the theater: "After the play done, I took Mercer by water to Spring-garden and there with great pleasure walked and eat and drank and sang, making people come about us to hear us, and two little children <of one of> our neighbours that happened to be there did come into our Arbour and we made them dance prettily" (9:196). Although he sometimes forgoes the food as too dear, Pepys does enjoy a good dish in the gardens, such as the Spanish *Oleo*, "endeed a very noble dish, such as I never saw better, or any more of," which he ordered in Mulberry Gardens on April 5, 1669 (9:509).

Although he notes (and enjoys) the food and drink, music, and diversions in the gardens, Pepys's pleasure, as is well known to any reader of his famous diary, often took one particular form. Hence, several of his accounts of pleasure gardens are linked with his own sexual imaginings or escapades. On May 18, 1668, Pepys takes a boat to Vauxhall, "where we walked and eat and drank and sang, and very merry; but I find Mrs. Horsfield one of the veriest citizen's wifes in the world, so full of little silly talk, and now and then a little sillily bawdy, that I believe if you had her sola, a man might hazer algo [try something] with her" (9:204). On April 23, 1668, after an evening of drinking, eating lobster, and singing at Cocke Ale-house, Pepys takes the boat to Vauxhall with the actress Mrs. Knepp, and "there she and I drank; and yo did tocar her corps [touch her body] all over and besar sans fin her [kiss her without end], but did not offer algo mas [anything more]; and so back and led her home, it being now 10 at night . . . and to bed, weary but pleased at my days pleasure—but yet displeased at my expense and time I lose" (9:172–73).

The final words in this description are telling. Pepys is troubled not about the sexual dalliance with Mrs. Elizabeth Knepp, an actress at the King's House whom he elsewhere describes as "the most excellent mad-hum[ou]red thing; and sings the noblest that ever I heard in my life" (6:321), but about the expense of the garden *and* about neglecting business for pleasure. An extended entry on May 29, 1666, reveals the same tension. As Pepys works in his office, "thither my wife comes to me to tell me that if I would see the handsomest woman in England, I shall come home presently. . . . And so I home, and there found Creed also come to me; so there I spent most of the afternoon with them; and endeed, she is a pretty black woman—her name, Mrs. Horesely" (7:135–36). The afternoon's leisure only whets Pepys's appetite for further pleasures, a dilemma that he describes in significantly moral terms: "But Lord, to see how my nature could not refrain from the temptation, but I must invite them to go to Fox hall to Spring Garden, though I had freshly received minutes of a great deal of extraordinary business" (136). Torn between the work "freshly received" and the allure of the pleasure garden, Pepys avows that "I could not help it; but sent [the ladies] before with Creed, and I did some of my business, and so after them and find them there in an Arbour. . . . So here I spent 20s upon them, and were pretty merry. Among other things, had a fellow that imitated all manner of birds and dogs and hogs with his voice, which was mighty pleasant" (136). Although the pleasures of listening to these imitations may seem innocent enough, the neglect of business prompts more guilt in Pepys than any number of instances of illicit gazing, dreaming, kissing, touching, or groping.

Underlying several of Pepys's accounts of the gardens, then, is a worry about neglecting work for pleasure, an inclination for which Pepys elsewhere berates himself: "God forgive me, I do still see that my nature is not to be quite conquered, but will esteem pleasure above all things; though, yet in the middle of it, it hath reluctancy after my business, which is neglected by my fallowing my pleasure. However, music and women I cannot but give way to, whatever my business is" (7:69–70).

This neglect of business is something for which Pepys also critiques the new king, Charles II, whose pleasures were on display not only in the court but also in pleasure gardens and royal parks. The restoration and enhancement of St. James's Park, which began almost immediately after Charles's return to England, stressed pleasure and play as part of the king's new image, and Charles frequented the park with his queen and royal mistresses.[10] On July 13, 1663, hearing that "the King and Queene are rode abroad with the Ladies of Honour to [St. James's Park] and seeing a great croude of gallants staying here to see their return," Pepys also stayed, "walking up and down" (4:229). His efforts were soon rewarded: "By and by, the King and Queene, who looked in this dress, a white laced waistcoat and a crimson short petty-coate and her hair dressed *a la negligence,* mighty pretty; and the King rode hand in hand with her" (230). Not surprisingly, the party also included the king's long-term mistress, Barbara Castlemaine, but Pepys observes that "the King took methought no notice of her; nor when they light did anybody press (as she seemed to expect, and stayed for it) to take her down, but was taken down by her own gentleman. She looked mighty out of humour, and had a Yellow plume in her hat" (230).

Although here and elsewhere, Pepys gazes upon Castlemaine, glutting himself with looking upon her and dreaming of sleeping with her, he also sees her as a dangerous lure away from business. Pepys confides to his diary as early as May 15, 1663, the court gossip that "the King doth mind nothing but pleasures and hates the very sight or thoughts of business . . . my Lady Castlemayne rules him; who he says hath all the tricks of Aretin that are to be practised to give plea-sure—in which he is too able, having a large ——" (4:136–37). On February 26, 1666, Pepys records that another acquaintance "cries against my Lady Castlemayne, that makes the King neglect his busi-ness; and seems much to fear that all will go to wrack, and I fear with great reason" (7:57).

Other ladies of pleasure—whether in the park or the court—represented a similar danger. John Evelyn gives a March 1671 account of walking with the king "thro St. *James's* Parke to the *Garden,* where I both saw and heard a very familiar discourse betweene —— & *Mrs. Nellie* [Nell Gwynne] as they cal'd an impudent Comedian, she looking out of her Garden on a Tarrace at the top of the Wall, & —— standing on the green Walke under it; I was heartily sorry at this scene: Thence the King walked to the *Dutches* of *Cleavelands,* another Lady of Pleasure & curse of our nation."[11]

Removed from the work-a-day world, often quite literally by the need to take a boat ride to the outskirts of the City, the pleasure gardens and royal parks in Restoration London became potent spaces of leisure and play. Yet contrasted with and detached from labor and responsibility—sometimes guiltily—such pleasures threatened to turn profligate. While seemingly oblivious to his own peccadilloes, Pepys is attuned to some of the sexual threats that, by the late 1660s, made the gardens and parks increasingly risqué and associated with sexual profligacy. On May 28, 1667, walking in Spring Gardens, Pepys notices "two pretty women alone, that walked a great while; which [being] discovered by some idle gentlemen, they would needs take them up" (8:240). Observing how the "poor ladies . . . were put to it to run from them, and they after them; and sometimes the ladies put themselfs along with other company, then the others drew back," Pepys is relieved to see the ladies finally make their escape and take a boat, as he is "troubled to see them abused so" (240–41). Similarly, walking in Vauxhall in July 1668, Pepys observes "how rude some of the young gallants of the town are become, to go into people's arbors where there are not men, and almost force the women—which troubled me, to see the confidence of the vice of the age" (9:268).

Pepys, then, worried about the effects of the pleasure-seeking society in which he himself participated, including the habits of what one recent scholar has termed the "priapic" monarch at its head.[12] As for the merry monarch himself, Charles blandly observed to Bishop Gilbert Burnet that "God would not damn a man for a little irregular pleasure."[13] But, as we shall see in our exploration of *Paradise Lost,* Milton was not so sure.

An avid walker, who lived during the Interregnum in a house in Petty France that had a back garden gate opening onto St. James's

Park, Milton would undoubtedly have been keenly attuned to the transformations in the royal parks and pleasure gardens in Restoration London.[14] In linking the pleasure of *Paradise Lost* with chaste and disciplined garden labor, Milton provides a counter to the dalliances and diversions, the leisure of the pleasure gardens. While Milton draws upon classical and biblical gardens, his Eden is also informed by— and responsive to—contemporary gardens, including the urban spaces frequented by Pepys and by the king himself. The resonant and con- tested spaces of Restoration pleasure gardens illumine the dangers of separating pleasure and labor in the marital dialogue preceding the Fall. Once Adam and Eve are separated from their joint labor, Eve is susceptible to the predatory Satan who lies in wait, and Adam and Eve's own pleasure becomes lustful and parodic, leading to and mark- ing the Fall.

As the reader is introduced to Milton's garden, in part through the voyeuristic eyes of Satan, *Paradise Lost* highlights its natural pleasures: perfumed air, the song of birds, walks and alleys, bowers, fountains, flowers, and luscious fruit. Satan himself takes the air and pleasure of the garden as "of pure now purer aire / Meets his approach, and to the heart inspires / Vernal delight and joy" (4.153–55).[15] But, of course, such air, "able to drive / All sadness but despair" (4.155–56), cannot soothe the tormented Satan. Paradoxically, Satan's exclu- sion only heightens for him the pleasures of the garden, in which he views

> To all delight of human sense expos'd
> In narrow room Natures whole wealth, yea more,
> A Heaven on Earth: for blissful Paradise
> Of God the Garden was.   (4.206–09)

Milton's language—"in this pleasant soile / His farr more pleasant Garden God ordaind" (4.214–15)—reminds the reader that the Hebrew word for "Eden" means pleasure.

In addition to the profusion of natural beauty—"All Trees of noblest kind for sight, smell, taste" (4.217) and "Flours worthy of Paradise which not nice Art / In Beds and curious Knots, but Nature boon / Powrd forth profuse on Hill and Dale and Plaine" (4.241–43)— Milton's garden of Eden holds the pleasures of love and dalliance. Adam and Eve are first seen as innocent lovers walking in the garden:

> So hand in hand they passd, the lovliest pair
> That ever since in loves imbraces met,
> *Adam* the goodliest man of men since borne
> His Sons, the fairest of her Daughters *Eve.*   (4.321–24)

The two sit down to an idyllic meal: "to thir Supper Fruits they fell, /
Nectarine Fruits which the compliant boughes / Yeilded them"
(4.331–33). The envious and voyeuristic Satan highlights, among
Eden's delights, sexual pleasures for Adam and Eve, "Imparadis't in
one anothers arms / The happier *Eden*" (4.506–07).[16] But this couple
is distinctively, chastely, and safely married:

> Nor gentle purpose, nor endearing smiles
> Wanted, nor youthful dalliance as beseems
> Fair couple, linkt in happie nuptial League,
> Alone as they.   (4.337–40)

Yet in striking contrast to other gardens (classical, biblical, and contemporary), pleasure in *Paradise Lost* is linked not with pastoral ease
(*otium*) but with labor. Initially, such gardening labor seems to be
simply another uncomplicated pleasure in the garden of pleasures,
"sweet Gardning labour" (4.328) that "made ease / More easie, whol-
som thirst and appetite / More grateful" (4.329–31). But the profusion of Milton's garden also calls for a profusion of labor. Hence, even
Adam's early adjuration to Eve extolling their "delightful task"
proves more complicated than first may seem:

> But let us ever praise him, and extoll
> His bountie, following our delightful task
> To prune these growing Plants, & tend these Flours,
> Which were it toilsom, yet with thee were sweet.   (4.436–39)

Adam's final line here is troubling. Why add "were it toilsom"? Is
the gardening possibly toilsome? Why mention—in conjunction
with toil—how much he enjoys their gardening *together?*

Labor in *Paradise Lost* is, then, not a simple contrast to the gardens of leisure, but a more complex task and challenge. Adam's
ensuing commendation of "pleasant labor," for instance, is countered
by eight lines indicating the overwhelming nature of the task:

> To morrow ere fresh Morning streak the East
> With first approach of light, we must be ris'n,

> And at our pleasant labour, to reform
> Yon flourie Arbors, yonder Allies green,
> Our walks at noon, with branches overgrown,
> That mock our scant manuring, and require
> More hands then ours to lop thir wanton growth:
> Those Blossoms also, and those dropping Gumms,
> That lie bestrowne unsightly and unsmooth,
> Ask riddance, if we mean to tread with ease.   (4.623–32)

By detailing how much work needs to be done in the garden, Adam underscores the importance of working together, a stress not found in the original mandate to till and keep the garden. Branches and blossoms are "overgrown," "dropping," "unsightly," "unsmooth." They "mock" their gardening efforts. Everything is couched in terms of joint labor: "we" must be risen and at "our" pleasant labor; "our" walks, "our" manuring, more hands than "ours." More gardening help is needed. Even the final bedtime prayer contains a reminder of incomplete work, as the garden, this "delicious place" (4.729), is "For us too large, where thy abundance wants / Partakers, and uncropt falls to the ground" (4.730–31). Despite Adam's praise of the pleasant labor, his stress falls on its overwhelming nature and on the need for the two of them to tackle the job together, Eve at his side.

Milton thus does not simply contrast labor and play. Rather, he shows how labor tests the primal couple. The potential danger is already clear in Eve's dream. If Adam stresses the magnitude of their labor, the result is anxiety for Eve. Eve's comment to Adam that she usually dreams "of thee, / Works of day pass't, or morrows next designe" (5.32–33) is telling. Concern and uncertainty over getting the gardening done resonate through Eve's satanically inspired dream. The angel (Satan) initially uses terms of pleasure—"Why sleepst thou *Eve?* now is the pleasant time" (4.38)—calling to Eve as to a lover. Significantly, however, what the angel seems to be calling Eve to (like Adam himself) is further gardening. The dream temptation to eat the fruit is couched in terms of unfinished gardening, a task that inevitably outgrows the laborer: "And O fair Plant, said he, with fruit sur-charg'd, / Deigns none to ease thy load and taste thy sweet, / Nor God, nor Man" (5.58–60). The earlier discussion about the over-abundance of the garden, which uncropped falls to the ground, is echoed in the angel's praise of the fruit "more sweet thus cropt" (5.68).

While Adam helps to resolve Eve's anxieties about having had the dream, he does not address her underlying anxiety about getting the gardening done. Indeed, Adam's conclusion—"And let us to our fresh imployments rise / Among the Groves, the Fountains, and the Flours" (5.125–26)—is an implicit reminder that they are late for work.

While the educative function and emblematic nature of gardening in *Paradise Lost* has been much stressed, less attention has been paid to this anxiety provoked by the overwhelming nature of the task.[17] Indeed, while labor in Eden marks the regard of God on all man's ways, separating Adam and Eve from the beasts who play around them, it seems to be an all but impossible task. The narrator, as well as Adam, comments upon the profusion and wildness of the garden. In sharp contrast to the cultivated beds of Caroline and Restoration pleasure gardens, this garden is "Wilde above rule or Art" (5.297). Descriptions of the garden are marked by innocent yet potentially threatening terms: "wanton," "luxuriant." Even more distressing, Adam notes that the very act of pruning makes the garden grow more, as "Nature multiplies / Her fertil growth, and by disburd'ning grows / More fruitful" (5.318–20).

This anxiety about labor throughout *Paradise Lost* makes more understandable Eve's much-debated comments in the separation scene. Although they have sometimes been taken to indicate (positively or negatively) unique aspects of her character, Eve's concerns about the abundance of work in fact closely echo what Adam and the narrator have said earlier:

> *Adam*, well may we labour still to dress
> This Garden, still to tend Plant, Herb and Flour.
> Our pleasant task enjoyn'd, but till more hands
> Aid us, the work under our labour grows,
> Luxurious by restraint; what we by day
> Lop overgrown, or prune, or prop, or bind,
> One night or two with wanton growth derides
> Tending to wilde.   (8.205–12)

Eve's speech is a tissue of echoes of what she has been told or heard earlier. "Labour" and "pleasant task" echo Adam's "pleasant labor"

(4.625), while "dress," "tend," and "prune" repeat Adam's "To prune these growing Plants, & tend these Flours" (4.438). "Lop Overgrown" and "wanton growth" recall Adam's "lop thir wanton growth" (4.629), while "Tending to wilde" evokes the narrator's observation that the garden is "Wilde above rule or Art" (5.297). Finally, "till more hands / Aid us" echoes Adam's "require / More hands than ours" (4.628–29) and the narrator's "for much thir work outgrew / The hands dispatch of two Gardning so wide" (8.202–03).

Yet while focusing on the same problem—too much work—Eve's follow-up suggestion, "Let us divide our labours" (8.214), boldly reverses Adam's earlier conclusion. If Adam draws upon the magnitude of unfinished work to urge Eve to go to bed, get up, and work beside him, it suddenly occurs to Eve that they might get more work done apart:

> For while so near each other thus all day
> Our task we choose, what wonder if so near
> Looks intervene and smiles, or object new
> Casual discourse draw on, which intermits
> Our dayes work brought to little, though begun
> Early, and th' hour of Supper comes unearn'd.   (8.220–25)

As Eve now recounts it, marital pleasures—conversation, looks, endearments—interrupt their labor and slow down the task they must accomplish. While Adam has consistently used the enormity of the task to keep Eve at his side, Eve notices that the opposite conclusion could be drawn: without her husband around the (metaphorical) house, she might get a lot more work done.

Adam, then, is forced to take a wholly different tack. While he praises Eve for studying "houshold good" (8.233), he asserts for the first time that their delight in each other, including kisses and amorous looks, is inextricably linked to their garden labor: "For not to irksom toile, but to delight / He made us, and delight to Reason joyn'd" (8.242–43). While Eve worries that looks, smiles, and casual discourse interfere with the gardening, Adam argues that such "sweet intercourse / Of looks and smiles" (8.238–39) mark them off from the animals, just as does their labor. Adam's ensuing comments are designed to reassure Eve:

> These paths and Bowers doubt not but our joynt hands
> Will keep from Wilderness with ease, as wide
> As we need walk, till younger hands ere long
> Assist us.   (8.244–47)

But Adam's words contradict what he has said earlier, what the narrator has said, and what Eve can see for herself: that there is too much gardening for the two of them to manage. Increasingly anxious that Eve will leave him, Adam drops the argument about working together to get the gardening done, and, reminding Eve of their joint foe, now simply asserts: "The Wife, where danger or dishonour lurks, / Safest and seemliest by her Husband staies, / Who guards her, or with her the worst endures" (8.267–69). No wonder, then, that Eve objects, recalling for the reader the angel's earlier warning to Adam that he must maintain his proper role over Eve, "who sees when thou are seen least wise" (7.1215).

In the separation scene, other pleasures—and their attendant anxieties—threaten to overwhelm Adam and Eve's pleasure in their joint labor, symbol of their voluntary obedience to God and "the regard of Heav'n on all [their] waies" (4.620). Adam's earlier account of his creation to Raphael shows how much Eve supersedes all the other pleasures in Eden for him, prompting a warning from the angel against "carnal pleasure" (7.1230). In recounting how he was brought in a dreamlike state to "the Garden of bliss, thy seat prepar'd" (7.936), Adam notes how much the walks, bowers, trees, and other natural delights of the garden surpass the greater Eden: "A Circuit wide, enclos'd, with goodliest Trees / Planted, with Walks, and Bowers, that what I saw / Of Earth before scarse pleasant seemd" (7.941–43). Yet Adam's pleasure in Eden, itself named for pleasure, is significantly hampered by his loneliness; the Almighty observes that Adam "wilt taste / No pleasure, though in pleasure, solitarie" (7.1038–39).

As he found all other natural pleasures to pale in comparison with the garden, Adam then finds Eve to surpass the fair garden:

> Under his forming hands a Creature grew,
> Manlike, but different sex, so lovly faire,
> That what seemd fair in all the World, seemd now
> Mean, or in her summd up.   (7.1107–10)

Adam's resolution to forgo all other pleasures without Eve indicates his potential overdependence on the wife whom he is supposed to guide: "She disappeerd, and left me dark, I wak'd / To find her, or for ever to deplore / Her loss, and other pleasures all abjure" (7.1115–17).

If Adam takes no pleasure while alone in a garden of pleasure, Eve has earlier shown the opposite tendency: an inclination to take pleasure in herself. The newly created Eve is pleased by her own image in the pool:

> I started back,
> It started back, but pleasd I soon returnd,
> Pleas'd it returnd as soon with answering looks
> Of sympathie and love.   (4.462–65)

Led away by a divine voice, Eve turns away from herself and to Adam, but her initial hesitation and the coercive language that she uses—"thy gentle hand / Seisd mine" (4.488–89)—show the possibility of her inclining back. In the separation scene, Eve for the first time insists on working alone, challenging Adam's view that they are more secure together and again playing on the meaning of Eden as pleasure: "Fraile is our happiness, if this be so, / And *Eden* were no *Eden* thus expos'd" (8.340–41).

When Eve goes off by herself, then, she is a beautiful woman walking alone and vulnerable to the advances of the lustful predator lying in wait. Walking in the pleasure garden without her male companion, she is suddenly open to sexual danger. Indeed, Satan is actively searching for Adam and Eve among the groves, fountains, and flowers:

> In Bowre and Field he sought, where any tuft
> Of Grove or Garden-Plot more pleasant lay,
> Thir tendance or Plantation for delight;
> By Fountain or by shadie Rivulet
> He sought them both.   (8.417–21)

In a striking parallel to the contemporary pleasure gardens in which Pepys observes how the gallants covertly watch and then light upon and "force the women," Satan—opportunely finding Eve alone—persuades her through a kind of sexual seduction, a temptation to "play" that will be seconded by Adam himself.

A kind of roving, would-be gallant, Satan destroys true pleasure in Eden through false and sexualized imitations. While he momentarily feels "Pleasure" (8.455) in beholding Eve working among her flowers, Satan comes into the garden not out of "hope here to taste / Of pleasures, but all pleasure to destroy" (8.476–77). The phallic serpentine form Satan assumes is itself a source of sexual pleasure and play: "pleasing was his shape / And lovely" (8.503–04), as he lures the "Eye of *Eve* to mark his play" (8.528).[18] The serpent argues for the fruit specifically in terms of pleasure "to pluck and eat my fill / I spar'd not, for such pleasure till that hour / At Feed or Fountain never had I found" (8.595–97).

False "pleasure" and "play" recur throughout the Fall. Eve responds to eating the fruit with a kind of giddy pleasure: "Satiate at length, / And hight'nd as with Wine, jocund and boon, / Thus to her self she pleasingly began" (8.792–94). Adam too uses language of pleasure: "Much pleasure we have lost, while we abstain'd / From this delightful Fruit" (8.1022–23), notoriously wishing for not one but ten forbidden trees. But while Eve's postlapsarian pleasure pertains to tending the forbidden tree, Adam has something very different in mind:

> But come, so well refresh't, now let us play,
> As meet is, after such delicious Fare;
> For never did thy Beautie since the day
> I saw thee first and wedded thee, adorn'd
> With all perfections, so enflame my sense
> With ardor to enjoy thee, fairer now
> Then ever, bountie of this vertuous Tree.   (8.1027–33)

As Adam and Eve settle down on the nearest shady bank, the scene is resonant of the seduction scenes observed (and sometimes enacted) by Pepys in the pleasure gardens. The moment of the fall is dangerous, idle play, a separation from labor and desire to seek pleasure in itself. Among its many resonances, the rebuke to Milton's own contemporaries seems clear.

Yet if the garden spaces in the poem, in 1667, serve on one level as a counterpoint to and rebuke of the leisure spaces of Restoration pleasure gardens, why doesn't labor prevent Adam and Eve's fall? Why, in fact, does labor seem to make things worse, since it is the argument about housework that separates the primal couple, makes them anxious, and leaves them more vulnerable to Satan's wiles? What goes wrong with the pleasant labor of Milton's Eden?

Those scholars who focus on the educative, developmental aspect of labor in the garden do not discuss the link with the Fall. But I would argue that, although Adam and Eve undoubtedly learn and progress in their first reasoning moments after their creation and in their dialogues with each other and with the angel, gardening itself does not evince such a developmental, progressive model, such a "plot."[19] Rather, their task, although "unlaborious," is repetitive, recurring, and, given the profuse and wanton growth of the Garden, decidedly nonprogressive. As such, gardening is more of a test than a task.

Adam and Eve's gardening, then, is analogous to a series of other seemingly impossible tasks assigned by God himself in *Paradise Lost*. The obedient angels in heaven expect to win against Satan and the rebel angels, but they do not. God padlocks hell with triple gates and a giant lock, then gives the key to Sin, who readily lets Satan out. The sharp-sighted Uriel cannot see the hypocrisy in Satan and in fact gives him directions to paradise. Gabriel and other angels guard the gate of paradise, but Satan simply jumps over the wall. The angelic guards, even when warned about Satan, fail to intercept him until after his dream temptation of Eve; they are nowhere in sight during the actual temptation and eventually return shame-faced to heaven, having seemingly failed. Perhaps the most spectacular instance of a divinely mandated task that cannot succeed is that given to Raphael, who is sent down to warn Adam and Eve, despite divine foreknowledge that they will fall. William Empson, provocatively, goes so far as to argue that it is Raphael's visit that gives them the idea.[20]

Yet, as scholars have maintained with these other instances, the point is not to complete a certain task, but to remain obedient and faithful. Thus, the angels in the war in heaven are commended, as are the returning guards from Eden. Raphael's mission is to make man accountable and without excuse, not actually to prevent the fall. Adam himself has it right when he tells Eve that "God left free the Will . . . / But bid her well beware" (8.351, 353). Adam and Eve must simply keep to their task, the same task, day after day in the garden, lopping, pruning, propping, and binding plants, branches, fruits, and flowers that within a night or two grow back. Similarly, in their inner gardens, they must continually prune back their recurrent tendencies to excessive or misguided pleasures: Adam's uxoriousness or excessive pleasure in Eve and Eve's vanity or misguided pleasure in herself.

After the Fall, these precise tendencies initially recur. The despairing Eve's suggestion that they refrain from sex, or even commit suicide, is in some ways a *reductio ad absurdum* of her earlier desire to work alone, well away from Adam's advances. While commending Eve's "contempt of life and pleasure" (9.1013), Adam suggests that abstinence or suicide goes too far, evincing "Not thy contempt, but anguish and regret / For loss of life and pleasure overlov'd" (9.1018–19). But Adam too mistakes appropriate pleasures. Once again lured by the pleasures of women and song, when he sees the "richly gay" women (10.578) and the "Tents . . . so pleasant" (10.603) in Michael's vision, Adam is advised:

> Judg not what is best
> By pleasure, though to Nature seeming meet,
> Created, as thou art, to nobler end
> Holie and pure, conformitie divine.   (10.599–602)

Judged with a curse on labor and rebuked for false or misguided pleasures, the fallen Adam and Eve might well seem to lose pleasure altogether.

Yet although Adam and Eve leave the literal space of the pleasure garden, *Paradise Lost* by no means gives up on either pleasure or play. If Adam and Eve must internalize the garden, following "conformitie divine," that divine image itself is attuned both to pleasure and play. When Adam and Eve move from false pleasure and play to woe, Milton reveals that they too are the object, rather than simply the subject of the gardens. The Son himself offers to the Father the fruits of repentance in Adam and Eve:

> Fruits of more pleasing savour from thy seed
> Sow'n with contrition in his heart, then those
> Which his own hand manuring all the Trees
> Of Paradise could have produc't, ere fall'n
> From innocence.   (10.26–30)

As God himself takes pleasure in Adam and Eve's repentance, the poem refocuses from human pleasure to divine. Earlier we are told that God grants freedom to Adam and Eve for his own pleasure, since if they obeyed only of necessity, "What pleasure I from such obedience paid?" (3.107). From his own displeasure with Eve, Adam intuits God's displeasure; and in their joint act of repentance, he hopes that God will "relent and turn / From his displeasure" (9.1093–94). That pleasure, in turn, is a model—and a comfort—for the sorrowing Adam and Eve.

Milton's 1667 *Paradise Lost* is thus situated not only in relation to a literary tradition of gardens but in a highly charged social and cultural atmosphere in which a pleasure-seeking society, headed by the king himself, sought out the spaces of gardens and parks for leisure and play. Milton's chastely laboring Adam and Eve provide a counterpoint to the goings-on in the arbors, groves, and alleys of Vauxhall and Mulberry Gardens, St. James's Park and Barn Elms. Their repentance after the Fall also contrasts to such pleasure-seeking. In Adam and Eve's unremitting attention to the garden without and within, Milton indicates his rejection of easy vice, and easy virtue. In literary form, Milton boldly reclaims the garden spaces of urban London and indicates their proper use. It is a lesson for 1667: and for the pleasure-seeking generations to follow.

"[N]ew Laws thou see'st impos'd"
Milton's Dissenting Angels and the Clarendon Code, 1661–65

Bryan Adams Hampton

Thomas Venner, a sometime cooper in London and the occasional preacher for a small congregation on Coleman Street, stood on the gallows under the bleak winter sun in January 1661. Before his sentence was carried out on the very street where the "false Master *Venner* had first promoted, encouraged and at last unanimously agreed upon the late Rebellion and Insurrection," Venner fervently denied that his actions were criminal. His last interlocutor upon the gibbet was "a brother Preacher of his in former time, but of late times better instructed," who acted as Venner's confessor. "*Now Mr.* Venner *you are going to your last home therefore confess your sinnes, and acknowledge this great fault and wickedness, for which you are now to dye,*" he admonished. Indignantly, Venner replied, "There must be conviction before there can be confession, which I cannot find in my own conscience." Venner's appeal to conscience was answered by an act of state. After "having hang'd the space of a quarter of an hour, he was cut down and quartered according to his Sentence."[1]

In the previous weeks, Venner had led a small contingent of Fifth Monarchists in an armed uprising, during which approximately 40 people were killed. They were hopeful that their actions would initiate the millennial kingdom with Jesus ruling through what Bernard

Capp calls "a new aristocracy of the godly." As Richard L. Greaves observes, however, the Vennerite rebellion initiated not the Parousia or the millennial kingdom of the saints ruling under King Jesus. Instead, the immediate outcome of the insurrection was swelling paranoia, increased surveillance, and the persecution of troublesome sects like the Quakers and Baptists who, like Venner, notoriously acted according to conscience. The uprising, though small, "confirmed the suspicions of conservatives," Greaves explains, "who viewed sectarian congregations as nurseries of sedition."[2] As the decaying bodies of regicides were dragged by sledge through London streets and newly hanged at Tyburn, located west of the City, Charles II issued a proclamation that prohibited the Quaker, Baptist, and Fifth Monarchist dissenters from holding private meetings. Enforcing the proclamation, however, met with limited success. Nonconformists overcrowded the prisons, sectarian conventicles continued to meet, and various other murky plots and conspiracies—chimerical or not—were uncovered in the months that followed. It became obvious to fiery royalist conservatives like Gilbert Sheldon, the Archbishop of Canterbury (raised from the bishopric of London in 1663), and even moderates like Edward Hyde, Earl of Clarendon, that tighter restrictions were required. New laws needed to be imposed.

This essay locates the angelic insurrection in *Paradise Lost* within this crackling atmosphere of persistent paranoia, political conspiracy, and importunate dissent. From 1661 to 1665 Sheldon and Clarendon spearheaded the Cavalier Parliament's passing of several laws, misnamed but collectively referred to as the Clarendon Code, that were directed against Nonconformists in order to minimize their potential threat and smother their "nurseries of sedition." The politics of the Clarendon Code ineluctably shaped Milton's depiction of the dissenting angels in the 1667 edition of *Paradise Lost*. Lucifer's objections at the raising of the Son in book 5 echo many of the "cases of conscience" voiced by Nonconformists in the face of the "new Laws . . . impos'd" (*PL* 5.676) by royal proclamation and parliamentary procedure.[3] The first section of this essay examines the politics of nonconformity and dissent in the early 1660s, and the Church of England's programmatic legislation against it through the Clarendon Code. In the second section, I discuss Milton's ambiguous response to these issues in the 1667 *Paradise Lost*.

The Politics of Dissent and the Clarendon Code

David Loewenstein observes that even though Milton eschewed direct appeals to particular radical sects, thereby maintaining a critical political and authorial distance, it is clear that throughout his career Milton openly supported the idea of dissent.[4] Heresiographers writing during the civil war and Interregnum years, such as Thomas Edwards and Ephraim Pagitt, however, represented radical dissent as a national and ecclesial disease while lamenting the spread of the sects in their thousand-page catalogs of heresy—both very popular works that saw multiple editions. Edwards remarks that if sectarianism is not stamped out, "a spark not quenched may burn down a whole house, and a little leaven leaveneth the whole lump: So small Errors at first . . . are grown now to many thousands." Mixing his metaphors, he admonishes that a nation and church that do not exercise proper censure or slothfully neglect the defense of doctrine are like a "Garden and Vineyard without a hedge and fences," a "City without walls and Bulwarks," or an "Army without Discipline," images with particular resonance when the large-scale enclosure of land was on the rise, and armies were gripped in bloody civil war.[5]

Edwards, whom Milton debases as "shallow" in his 1646 poem (published in 1673) "On the New Forcers of Conscience under the Long Parliament," desperately wanted to contain or eradicate heresy in England by erecting civil, ecclesial, and theological bulwarks and hedges against the encroaching sects that proclaimed them. In contrast to Edwards, in 1649 Milton affirms, "I never knew that time in *England*, when men of truest Religion were not counted Sectaries" (*Eikonoklastes*, YP 3:348). The weight of Milton's statement of support for dissenters must be gauged by the events of 1649, a tumultuous year that saw not only the execution of the king, but the appearance of Winstanley's bold declaration of a *New Law of Righteousnes Budding Forth* and the subsequent Digger experiment at St. George's Hill, the final publication of the Leveller manifesto *An Agreement of the People*, the stirrings of the Quaker movement under the preaching of George Fox, and the "revision" of the Blasphemy Ordinance of the previous year into the Blasphemy Act of 1650 against the Ranters.[6] Revisiting his conviction in *Of True Religion* (1673), his last pamphlet before his death, Milton offers continued support for the sects by declaring that "no true Protestant can persecute, or not tolerate his fellow Protestant, though dissenting from him in som opinions" (YP 8:421). To do so, he argues, violates an individual's liberty to search and try the Scriptures according to one's faith and reason, exercised apart from appealing to Church tradition or extrascriptural authority—the hermeneutical guideposts emphasized by the Roman Catholic Church. Any authority derived apart from the Scriptures is a source of genuine heresy for Milton, not the various doctrinal heterodoxies of the Anabaptists, Arians, Socinians, or Arminians. Milton does not deny that various sects may well be "in a true Church as well as in a false," but the latter occurs mostly when individuals uncritically follow their leaders in "implicit faith" rather than searching the Word of God for themselves (YP 8:422). Error is to be expected, he continues, but

> so long as all these profess to set the Word of God only before them as the Rule of faith and obedience; and use all diligence and sincerity of heart, by reading, by learning, by study, by prayer for Illumination of the holy Spirit, to understand the Rule and obey it, they have done what man can do: God will assuredly pardon them, as he did the friends of *Job*, good and pious men, though much mistaken, as there it appears, in some Points of Doctrin. (8:423–24)

Despite Milton's tenacious efforts to champion dissenting opinion, however, many conservatives in and around London continued to view dissent and rebellion as interchangeable, summoning to the minds of Restoration gentry not only the Vennerite uprising, but also the violent Anabaptist takeover of the north German city of Münster in 1534. Following a divine "revelation" given to Jan Matthys about the imminent arrival of the millennial kingdom, Jan Bockelson (John of Leiden) massacred Münster's magistrates, forced its citizens to choose between rebaptism or death, introduced polygamy, and instituted a form of communism. For royalists, religious "enthusiasm," whose Greek root *enthousiasmós* just as properly connotes demonic possession as much as it does "zeal" or divine inspiration, was nothing short of madness that inevitably led to chaos. Even on the eve of James II's 1688 Declaration of Indulgence, George Savile, the Protestant marquis of Halifax, warned in his *Letter to a Dissenter,*

"It is not so long since, as to be forgotten, that the *Maxime* was, *It is impossible for a Dissenter, not to be a* REBEL." Halifax remarks that the "Alliance" that many nonconformists make between "*Liber[t]y and Infallibility*"—as, for instance, in cases of conscience aligned with the dictates of the Spirit—"is bringing together the Two most contrary things that are in the world."[7] In the eyes of Halifax, those "contrary things" could only lead to chaos.

In order to demonstrate both the monstrosity of the proliferation of the "enthusiast" sects and the urgency of their containment, anti-sectarian literature often resorted to graphic and overblown images and metaphors of insect life in their pamphlet campaigns: swarms of bees, wasps, locusts, and maggots infest the nation.[8] These images remind us of Milton's description of the fallen angels—the original "dissenters" from heaven—that "Thick swarm'd" into Pandemonium, "Brush't with the hiss of rustling wings. As Bees / In spring time" that "Poure forth thir populous youth about the Hive / in clusters" (1.767–71). These distorted and nefarious representations of Nonconformists persist in Restoration England, and many royalists and moderate Presbyterians viewed the various sects with unease and alarm.[9] Interestingly, however, we also see the opposite impulse to diminish the menacing presence of the sectarians. Paul Seaward observes that the actual numbers of dissenters in Restoration England were comparatively small—a fact that Archbishop Sheldon wanted to publish widely when he ordered Bishop Henry Compton of London to issue a census in 1676, one that in Sheldon's eyes would be far more comprehensive than those previously implemented in 1665 and 1669. The archbishop hoped that the census would both reveal the elevated level of support for conformity and minimize the threat of Nonconformity within the Church of England.

But as Seaward relates, the results of the census are not conclusive or easily interpreted since they do not accurately account for cases of "partial" conformity, Catholic recusancy, or simply indifference.[10] Moreover, John Miller explains that in these decades the religious demarcations are more complex than comprehensive labels such as "Church of England" or "dissenter" suggest. In the former we must include the "overlapping visions of church-order" found among parish Anglicans, latitudinarians, some moderate Presbyterians, and church puritans. Meanwhile, the category of "dissent" is even more multivalent and includes a kaleidoscope of groups such as the Quakers, Baptists, Presbyterians, Independents, Muggletonians, Fifth Monarchists, and other millenarian groups, as well as a rising number of atheists. For many of these separatist groups there was "never any prospect of their being incorporated into the national church, because their conception of a church was exclusive rather than inclusive," and as Miller points out, the leaders and pamphleteers of these sects often engaged in bitter invective among themselves.[11] Nevertheless, Seaward insists that the results of the Compton census are perhaps useful as broad indicators of dissent being wide but not particularly deep: approximately 100,000 Nonconformists subsisted in a national population of 2.25 million, with the highest concentration living, ironically, in Sheldon's own Canterbury (10.5 percent) as well as London (7.2 percent), while the lowest concentration occurred in Bangor (0.8 percent).

This figure is decidedly low, and Paul Seaward and Barry Reay estimate that even in 1660 the Quakers alone claimed perhaps as many as 60,000 adherents, a number that is probably mirrored by the Catholics, while the Baptists accounted for at least 25,000.[12] These are numbers that likely would have increased by the time the Compton census was taken in the next decade. On the eve of Charles II's return and in the first years of the restored Stuart monarchy, many anticipated the militant potential of the dissidents, despite attempts by some Quaker and Baptist leaders to fashion their movements as civil and peaceful. Incidents such as the Quaker James Nayler's scandalous march into Bristol in 1656 in imitation of Christ's triumphal entry into Jerusalem, the Fifth Monarchist Vennerite rebellion of 1661, and the failed Baptist Derwentdale plot of 1663 to seize a cache of weapons, murder bishops and gentry, and burn the Book of Common Prayer did little to assuage popular and royalist fears of the sects.[13] In fact, Reay has persuasively argued that persistent fears of the number of Quakers and Baptists in 1659 did much to contribute to the restoration of a monarch who would prevent complete religious anarchy.[14] Furthermore, there is evidence to suggest that some gentry even sustained private militias to defend themselves against the sects. One gentleman of Norfolk, for instance, stockpiled arms in order to "secure himselfe agaynst Quakers & Annibaptists" whom he feared would "ryse to Cutt His throat, & if they did soe he was resolved to cutt theire throats First if he could."[15]

It is within this charged atmosphere that Clarendon and Sheldon intervene, but they do so with radically different tactics. The former was certainly no friend to seditious ministers or their congregants, nor was he sympathetic to enthusiasts like the Quakers, but Clarendon appears consistently to have made a distinction between "nonconformity" and separatist "dissent"—a crucial difference maintained by Presbyterian apologists like Richard Baxter—that Sheldon adamantly opposed.[16] Clarendon had coauthored with the exiled Charles the Declaration of Breda (April 4, 1660), which famously promised to extend "a liberty to tender consciences" to all citizens despite their "differences of opinion in matter[s] of religion" so long as these differences "do not disturb the peace of the kingdom."[17] Moreover, in the fall of 1660 Clarendon advocated compromise and comprehension before the convention's adjournment, and subsequently invited moderate divines and Presbyterian leaders to his home at Worcester House to discuss terms.[18] But Sheldon's own positions regarding nonconformity and dissent before and after the Restoration bear out Halifax's equating dissent with rebellion. "'Tis only a resolute execution of law that must cure this disease," Sheldon asserts, for "it's necessary that they who will not be governed as men by reason and persuasions should be governed as beasts by power and force."[19] As far as the archbishop was concerned, nonconformity was to be eliminated by root and branch through punitive legislation. In May 1661 Charles repealed his January proclamation that forbade the private meetings of Quakers and Baptists by freeing those Quakers who had been arrested in the aftermath of Venner's rebellion. But while then Lord Chancellor Clarendon and Charles made attempts to bring the tenor of Breda's promise of toleration to fruition through the king's first Declaration of Indulgence in December 1662, Sheldon and the Cavalier Parliament began shoring up the gap against any and all nonconformity. The Cavalier Parliament, dominated by Episcopalians, refused to ratify the declaration the following spring because they feared it would both open fissures in ecclesial and national unity and deepen the threat of Catholicism. Ironically, these are results that many Presbyterians, who desired a national church and could not stomach the spread of popery, wished to prevent as well. As N. H. Keeble comments, the failed declaration signaled to Charles that this Parliament, like that of the 1640s, "was prepared to disoblige its King if he threatened to encroach on its rights," and also communicated that "nonconformists were unwilling to become royal lackeys in order to secure their own relief."[20]

Clarendon's program of comprehension for moderates in the Church of England was a failure. But Clarendon shared Sheldon's life-long distaste for and distrust of the radical enthusiast sects, among these the "fanatic" Quakers in particular, whom the earl regarded as "a sort of people upon whom tenderness and lenity do not at all prevail."[21] The Vennerite rebellion and the Baptist Derwentdale Plot had demonstrated to Clarendon, Sheldon, and many in Parliament the pressing need for a legislative safety valve to prevent "differences of opinion in matters of religion" from effectively "disturb[ing] the peace of the kingdom." Hyde thus acquiesced in Parliament's passing the penal laws that collectively made up the Clarendon Code: the Corporation Act (1661), the Conventicle Act (1664), and the Five-Mile Act (1665).[22]

John Miller observes that many in the Cavalier Parliament feared the "substantial autonomy" that several of the towns possessed.[23] In order to secure them against rebellion, the Corporation Act required all magistrates, mayors, and government officials to swear oaths of allegiance that both prevented their taking up arms against the king and denounced any obligations to the Solemn League and Covenant; moreover, all present and future magistrates were required, as a kind of political litmus test, to take the Eucharist in accordance with the rites of the Book of Common Prayer. Those who failed to comply with any of these before the deadline on March 25, 1663, were to be immediately "removed and displaced" of their duties. While the Corporation Act was directed against nonconformist magistrates who may have been unsympathetic to the new order, the Conventicle Act sought to provide "further and more speedy remedies against the growing and dangerous practices of seditious sectaries and other disloyal persons, who, under pretence of tender consciences, have or may at their meetings contrive insurrections (as late experience has shown [in the Baptist Derwentdale Plot])." Constables with a warrant from the justice of the peace were granted the authority to enter any house under suspicion of worshipful gatherings of five or more that had been conducted without reference to the established liturgy or practices of the Church of England. A first offense carried a fine of £5, a second offense £10, and a third offense either £100 or banishment for seven years. The Quakers, against whose meetings this act was primarily directed, devised tactics to avoid prosecution by holding meetings outside or at night, by posting lookouts, and by meeting in groups of four in neighboring or adjoining houses while the minister preached from a window. The Second Conventicle Act (1670), consequently, was more explicit in its language of prohibition.[24] Meanwhile, the Five Mile Act legislated against ministers who "preach in unlawful assemblies, conventicles, or meetings, under colour or pretense of exercise of religion" and who "distil the poisonous principles of schism and rebellion into the hearts of his majesty's subjects, to the great danger of the Church and kingdom." The act stipulated a five-mile boundary around boroughs, towns, and cities that these clergymen were forbidden to cross unless they swore an oath of allegiance not to bear arms against the king and consented to the Book of Common Prayer; violators were subject to a £40 fine.

These acts of the Clarendon Code, along with the 1662 Act of Uniformity, which concluded that peace in the kingdom can be achieved only by "universall agreement in the Publique Worshipp of Almighty God," constituted the most aggressive campaign by the Church of England to stamp out nonconformity.[25] But many in the Cavalier Parliament remained frustrated because of the failure of local gentry to follow through with prosecution.[26] Blair Worden suggests that the aim of the Clarendon Code was not simply to "convert" dissenters to conformity within the Church of England, although this would be an ideal scenario. Rather, its more precise aim was to demonstrate the "*inconvertibility* of those at whom it was aimed."[27] Implicitly, the code thus sought not only to expose more clearly the theological and ideological fissures, but also to render the dissenters as hardened rebels who stubbornly persisted in their heresy. By their accounting, the "Golden Scepter" from which law proceeds and which Lucifer himself spurns in his dissent from heaven is turned now into "an Iron Rod to bruise and breake / Th[eir] disobedience" (*PL* 5.883–85). More than anything, however, the Clarendon Code fashioned and undergirded identity for both the Church of England and for the dissenters themselves.

Dissenting Angels and the 1667 Paradise Lost

Milton's "left hand" is stultifyingly silent regarding the Clarendon Code, but this is not the case with the *Paradise Lost* of 1667. The "new Lawes" imposed upon all of heaven at the raising of the Son in book 5 demonstrate the "inconvertibility" of those dissenting consciences, even as they harden dissenting identity: as both justified revolution against an oppressive conformity, and as pernicious rebellion in need of heavenly redress.

While Halifax admonished and bemoaned the tendency among Nonconformists to adhere to the dictates of an unerring conscience, we find that liberty and infallibility are precisely the "two contrary things" that Lucifer seems to bring together when he garners support before the war in heaven. We thus might profitably consider Lucifer and his cohort of angels as dissenters who, like many of Milton's radical contemporaries, object to the "monopoly" of worship prescribed in heaven. The crucial moment that demarcates Lucifer's resolve "to dislodge, and leave / Unworship't, unobey'd the Throne supream, / Contemptuous" (5.666–68) occurs after the exaltation of the Son as vicegerent of heaven. The Father decrees that all shall "abide" under the Son, "United as one individual Soule," wherein all shall remain "For ever happie"; yet "him who disobeys / Mee disobeyes, breaks union, and that day / [is] Cast out from God and blessed vision" (609–13). Following this declaration, what we might describe as the godhead's royal "Supremacy Act," and ecclesial "Act of Uniformity," all of the celestial inhabitants retreat to their "Pavilions numberless" where they are "Fannd with coole Winds" and participate in divine rest (650, 652). While "All but th' unsleeping eyes of God" close in the "duskie houre / Friendliest to sleep and silence" (645, 664–65), however, the preeminent angel restlessly churns with "envie" and "Deep malice" (659, 663).[28] This refusal to sleep is Lucifer's first claim to autonomy. It implicitly denies his own creation, for his being will no longer be sustained by God's Being, and ascribes to himself God's liberty to gaze upon the abundance of Creation without interruption. As he turns to Beelzebub, who is seemingly resisting divine rest as well, Lucifer notably inquires, "how then can now / Thy sleep dissent?" (675–76).

In his dissent from sleep, we may construe Lucifer here as the first anti-Sabbatarian. Absenteeism on the Sabbath was common in early modern England, and both Elizabeth and James passed legislation to curb its practice. Under the Elizabethan Act of Uniformity and the Jacobean Act against Popish Recusants, fines (referred to as "Sunday shillings") were levied against those who failed to show up for services in their parish church.[29] In the poem Satan lures others away from their Sabbath rest under the guise of preparing "Fit entertainment to receive our King / The great *Messiah*, and his new commands" (687–88). As is well known, James and Charles promoted their *Book of Sports* in 1618 and 1633, respectively, thereby legitimizing Sabbath-day celebration, but for many Puritans the Sabbath was to be devoted strictly to religious instruction and devotion. N. H. Keeble writes that the Stuarts politicized leisure by encouraging sports and entertainments as "statements of loyal opposition to Puritan dissent." With the return of the Maypoles in 1660, one of the "lawful recreations" approved in the *Book of Sports*, Keeble notes that "[p]artying signified a return to pre-war conditions" and royal prerogative.[30] Milton perhaps loosely alludes to these maypole celebrations when the restless Satan commands his followers to move the "great Hierarchical Standard" (698) to his palace in the north, "to his Royal seat / High on a Hill, far blazing," where he mockingly sits "Affecting all equality with God" (753–54, 760) in a royal reversal. Because Satan draws away the angels in a show of celebration, we are forced to consider the jovial atmosphere of the assembly gathered around the great standard to plan the "great reception of thir King" (766). Satan's initial address to the "Thrones, Dominations, Princedoms, Vertues, [and] Powers" (769) is an attempt to get above the mirthful din of those seduced away from their participation in Sabbath rest.

For Puritans like William Perkins, however, the freedom to return to one's labor or to engage in "honest pleasures and recreations" even after worship "doth quite abolish one of the commandments of the

Decalogue"; "to make the Lord's Day a set day of sport and pastime" is a "notable abuse of many."[31] The Milton who wrote *Of Reformation* (1641) agrees with Perkins's assertion. The Sabbath ought to be set apart "so that we might have one day at least of seven . . . to examin and encrease our knowledge of God, to meditate, and commune of our Faith, our Hope, our eternall City in Heaven, and to quick'n withal, the study, and exercise of Charity" (YP 1:589). At the end of Raphael's narration of Creation in book 7, he explains that the faithful angels commune to meditate on their hope in the puissance of God's great Name. "Great are thy works, *Jehovah*, infinite / Thy power" (7.602–03), they sing, as they recall Lucifer's failure to "diminish, and from thee withdraw / The number of thy worshippers" (612–13). As the Son rests "With his great Father" (588), and as the angels sing the praises of God's Name, Raphael tersely concludes, "Thus was Sabbath kept" (634). But any sense of the angels' ceremony on the Sabbath is checked in Milton's earlier prose, for in *Colasterion* (1645) he avers that "It is not the formal duty of worship, or the sitting still, that keeps the holy rest of the Sabbath; but whosoever doth most according to charity, whether hee work or work not; hee breaks the holy rest of Sabbath least" (YP 2:750). For Milton, work or play on the Sabbath is not the issue; at stake are the person's actions and attitudes toward his or her neighbor—one's formal disposition to God is secondary—and acts of charity are crucial to the performance of one's faith (YP 6:489). The Quaker James Nayler criticized a rigid Sabbatarianism because it fostered a single "day to abstain from the world," but allowed multiple "days to conform to the world."[32] Recalling Jesus' words in Mark 2:27 that the Sabbath was made for man instead of the reverse, Nayler's point is that the saints ought to devote every day to living in the Spirit for their own edification as well as for the benefit of their fellow creatures. Milton, with his life-long, stubborn devotion to everyday virtue, would agree. Moreover, in *De Doctrina Christiana* we find that Milton effectively turns the observation of the Sabbath into a case of conscience. The Sabbath was instituted for Israel as part of the law. Under the gospel, however, Milton argues that Sabbath rest refers to "a spiritual and eternal one" and that "the observation of it belongs not to this life, but to the next. . . . It must, in short, be spontaneous, not enforced, otherwise we shall be brought out of one Egypt and into another"

(YP 6:710–11). Milton's concern here is that devotion, even to commands in the Decalogue, cannot be legislated by civil powers. He thus concludes by stating, "our consciences must not be ensnared by the allegation of a divine command, borrowed from the decalogue" (YP 6:714).

Cases of conscience, the assertion that one's reason guided by faith must be used to evaluate and respond to issues of civil or ecclesial obedience, were on the rise in the 1660s.[33] Gary S. De Krey observes that for many Restoration sectarians, especially Quakers and Baptists who refused to acknowledge the legitimacy of the crown's ecclesial authority, "arguments for conscience became a wedge that loosened or uncoupled the nexus between prince and priest, and between magistrate and minister, that had been fundamental to English Protestantism since the 1530s."[34] Lucifer attacks this crucial connection between God and his worshipping angels. Dissenting in conscience from Sabbath sleep, Satan gathers his peers at the "Mountain of the Congregation" in "the limits of the North" (5.763, 752). Milton's description of this satanic congregation in the north is significant, for Quaker congregations began their rapid spread from the north of England—a geographical detail exploited by Quakers and their opponents alike. In George Fox's apocalyptic and bellicose pamphlet, *Newes Coming up out of the North, Sounding towards the South*, Fox zealously proclaims a trumpet blast of warning from the north as he prophesies the coming "day of slaughter" against all "who have made war against the Lamb and against the Saints." As he declares in another pamphlet, "A day of howling is coming" to the south of England, for the "glittering sword is drawn for the day of slaughter." To William Prynne, however, these auspicious Quaker beginnings resonate with Jeremiah 1:14, for the weeping prophet declares that from the north a great "EVILL SHALL BREAK FORTH UPON ALL THE INHABITANTS OF THE LAND."[35] From Lucifer's "Quarters of the North" (686) the archangel suggests that the declarations of the Father concerning his Word, far from being apodictic or beyond scrutiny, are subject to restless hermeneutical inquiry by free and reasonable consciences (787–99).

For Lucifer, the "New Laws from him who reigns, new minds may raise" to generate "new Counsels, to debate" (677–78)—activities done in "private," seemingly independent of the sanctioned purview of the

Father. Lucifer cannot worship the Father or accept the Son's newly exalted position because he locates these activities within the sphere of exercising his free and reasonable conscience *apart* from the authority, character, and "legitimizing" gaze of God. Provocatively, Blair Worden argues that while Nonconformists in the early part of the seventeenth century were often told by authorities and the established church that their consciences could err, the latter half of the seventeenth century began to witness a shift from a notion of conscience as "less a property leased to me by God, on his terms" and "more a property of my own."[36] Many of the radicals were holding strongly to the ideas of liberty of conscience and toleration, but many conservatives, such as Archbishop Sheldon, asserted that such arguments were "a cry for a radical individualism, an anarchical substitute for ecclesiastical order."[37] While the Father certainly sees his declaration to be eternal, unchangeable, and beyond dispute simply because he is God, Lucifer's appeal to individual conscience is a radical move toward secularization. This gesture is made clear as he poses a question to the "Natives and Sons of Heav'n" who are "*possest* before / By none": "But what if better counsels might erect / Our minds and teach us to cast off this Yoke?" (787–88, emphasis added; 782–83). God does not, nor has he ever, owned their consciences, which are all "Equally free" (789). Their breaking with Sabbath rest denies their ever having been "possest," sustained, or defined by God's Being in the first place. Thus, while the Father exalts the Son as his "great Vice-gerent" (609) through whom he shall rule, Lucifer exalts the merits of his own conscience. The leading Restoration Presbyterian Nonconformist John Humfrey, friend and colleague to Richard Baxter, polemically states, "if the Magistrate command a thing against my Conscience, that Command (at least to me) is void, and without power. Gods Vicegerent within me, my Conscience, makes his external Voice to cease."[38] For Lucifer, God's "external" voice embodied in the Son ceases to exist, but his own liberty of individual conscience remains.

Thomas Edwards observes that "the first time we read of Sathans [*sic*] making use of this plea of Liberty, in his Instruments and his Ministers, is in 2 *Pet.* 2.19. where the Apostle shewes the false Teachers that brought in the damnable heresies, did tell them of liberty, *while they promise them liberty*."[39] For Edwards, as it is for Sheldon a decade and a half later, liberty of conscience is responsible for the spread of heresy. Satan begins his speech before the jovial congregation by appealing to his followers' sense of prerogative, equality, and freedom as the "Thrones, Dominations, Princedoms, Vertues, [and] Powers" (769) of heaven whose "Imperial Titles" assert their "being ordain'd to govern" (798–99). These honorific titles actually have a "leveling" effect among heaven's celestial hierarchies. In some capacity, his strategy is reminiscent of popular responses to Leveller tracts during the turbulent 1640s and early 1650s, some of the polemic of which seemed geared toward eliminating social hierarchies. Lucifer's leveling strategy here is complicated by his own royal appearance before the Sabbath breakers, but it also reminds us of the Quaker and Baptist insistence on the voluntary association and egalitarian status of their sect's members, all of whom share in heaven's royalty and authority as saints who will someday govern alongside the Son. Like the Quakers and Baptists whose claim to hermeneutical freedom is seen as an insidious threat to the "universall agreement in the Publique Worshipp of Almighty God," these angelic dissenters, soon to be Satan's own "Instruments and his Ministers," are quickly labeled "Rebels" by heaven—insurgents whose pride the "Regal Power" will "subdue" and "quell" (736–39).

At this point, it is clear that Milton deliberately casts Lucifer and his cohort as dissenters in conscience from the monopoly of worship prescribed in heaven, and that the "new Lawes" imposed by Milton's God forge their dissenting identity. The first contest between the heavenly powers, however, registers for us an important shift. Recall that the zealous angel Abdiel, who is among the original host breaking with Sabbath rest to plan for the Son's mirthful reception, calls attention to Lucifer's false conscience and specious reasoning. Lucifer's leveling tactic is "blasphemous, false and proud," for as a created being he cannot justly accuse God, and we detect in Abdiel's retort an echo from Job:

> Shalt thou give Law to God, shalt thou dispute
> With him the points of libertie, who made
> Thee what thou art, & formd the Pow'rs of Heav'n
> Such as he pleasd, and circumscrib'd thir being?   (5.819–22)

What is genuinely "unjust," argues Abdiel, is not that God has imposed new laws, which in God's goodness can only serve "to exalt / Our happie state under one Head more neer / United"; the injustice lies in the fact that even though Satan is endued with a "great & glorious" nature, he claims equality with the Son, "by whom / As by his Word the mighty Father made / All things, ev'n thee" (826–28, 832–34). Here, Abdiel's confutation seems to invoke what Milton calls "that prudent and well deliberated act" (YP 7:246)—the Blasphemy Act of 1650, which was passed against enthusiasts, particularly the Ranters and Quakers, who claim equality with the Son. According to the act, justices of the peace were to bring to trial anyone who advanced "him or her self, or any meer Creature, to be very God, or to be Infinite or Almighty, or in Honor, Excellency, Majesty and Power to be equal, and the same with the true God, or that the true God, or the Eternal Majesty dwells in the Creature and no where else."[40] Such claims, according to the Blasphemy Act and Abdiel, are made only by those most "alienate from God . . . / Forsak'n of all good" (5.874–75).

It is appropriate that this zealous angel, "faithful found, / Among the faithless" (893–94), is the first to engage Lucifer on the battlefield. "All are not of thy Train," he defiantly declares, for there are those "who Faith / Prefer, and Pietie to God" (6.143–44). As we saw earlier in *Of True Religion,* dissenting opinion for Milton is sanctioned, even if it is found to be erroneous, if faith, piety, and an obedient heart accompany one's scriptural hermeneutic. Lucifer's own interpretation of the Word, so to speak, fails this crucial litmus test, and we might argue that the sect of rebel angels is guilty of assenting to the interpretations of their teacher out of the very "implicit faith" that Milton scorns. Abdiel's solitary rebuke of Lucifer in book 5 identifies him as being in the position of a "true" and pious dissenter within a false, impious, and erroneous dissenting sect. "I alone / Seemd in thy World erroneous to dissent / From all," he recounts, but now "my Sect thou seest, now learn too late / How few sometimes may know, when thousands err" (6.145–48). Lucifer now labels Abdiel the "seditious Angel" whose "tongue / Inspir'd with contradiction durst oppose / A third part of the Gods, in Synod met / Thir Deities to assert" (152, 154–57). "Synod" is a politically charged word; Milton's use of it is no accident, for he employs it again to describe the demonic council (2.391). Synods were small, localized groups of Presbyterian ministers and representatives, and they represented a clear and present danger to episcopacy in the Church of England in the same way that Nonconformist "conventicles" did.[41] Crucially, Lucifer's verbal attack allows Abdiel to argue that it is now *heaven* that is truly dissenting against the sect of this "Idol of Majestie Divine" (6.101), completing for us this radical shift.[42]

But how are we to account for heaven's nonconformity? Perhaps like some of Milton's radical dissenters who object to the Church of England's totalizing vision, Lucifer and his angels dissent from their Sabbath rest because they perceive that these "new Lawes" are a limitation put into place by a God who offers himself as a totality. They justify rebellion because such a totality appears to offer no other alternative but "new Subjection" under these "Strict Laws impos'd, to celebrate his Throne / With warbl'd Hymns, and to his Godhead sing / Forc't Halleluiahs" (2.239, 241–43). On the contrary, Abdiel suggests that the new laws do not create subjection, but provide all of heaven with a clearer glimpse of God's infinity and his infinite goodness (5.826–27). These laws help heaven's sect define a God who is "Omnipotent, / Immutable, Immortal, Infinite," and who is obscured by his own glorious beams (3.372–82). The faithful angels thus dissent from the totality that Satan will shortly set up in hell, an infernal totality governed by aggression and intimidation to which all the fallen angels have no choice but to conform, in favor of singing the infinite Name of God. This is not to say that Milton's God in *Paradise Lost* is "pluralistic." Milton is many things to many scholars, but he is most certainly *not* a religious pluralist; in fact, one could make the argument that, outside the world of the poem, Milton is just as guilty of substituting one kind of totality for another. But what Milton seems to be suggesting through his faithful dissenting angel is that the numberless blessed angels worship in numberless ways, each accounting for a fraction of that Infinite Name that cannot be exhausted. Consequently, each adds to the heavenly host's collective blessed vision of the divine. Milton needs only to turn to the prophet Isaiah to see that the seraphim are singing "Holy, holy, holy is the LORD of hosts" out of charity "one . . . unto *another*" (6:3;

emphasis added)—not principally to God. If this is indeed the case, then we might see Milton's God extending a great deal of "toleration" and freedom toward heaven's worshippers and exegetes who are not simply the slothful and slavish conformists that Lucifer decries before engaging Abdiel in combat (6.164–70). For Milton, the zealously faithful angels are actually radical Nonconformists within their own sect.

What emerges in the 1667 *Paradise Lost*, then, is not a heaven and a hell that we can neatly and statically cast into the roles of "Church of England" and "dissenters," respectively. Rather, what readers witness is a dynamic poem that is exceptionally sensitive to subtle (and not so subtle) historical, political, and theological fissures and shifts in standards of conformity. Clearly, Milton openly embraces the idea of dissent. Therefore, his poetic efforts to render the nonconformist rebellion of Lucifer and his sect in line with the tribulations of various dissenting groups in the early 1660s can be interpreted sympathetically. Readers in 1667 of the angelic insurrection, however, are subsequently pulled into a kind of Miltonic "rope-a-dope" through his radical reversal of roles. Milton is critical of adherents to the Church of England and its totalitarian program of conformity. But he is also critical of those who follow an "implicit faith" in factions of dissent that resist such a totalizing program at all costs without the corresponding task of "Govern[ing] the inner man, the nobler part" (*PR* 2.477). As he famously states in *Areopagitica*, both are perhaps equally guilty of failing in the "incessant labor to cull out, and sort asunder" the "cunning resemblances" of good and evil (YP 2:514).

Poetic Justice
Plato's *Republic* in *Paradise Lost* (1667)

Phillip J. Donnelly

Next to Homer and the inspired Hebrew poets, no author exercised a more powerful influence on the congenial sublimity of Milton's genius than Plato.
> —Benjamin Jowett, "The Genius of Plato"

Irony has always been a contour within the metaphysical (what did Plato believe?). The will to power is only a story, perhaps, but so is every metaphysics; and even as a story, its plot has often a poignantly dialectical logic.
> —David B. Hart, *The Beauty of the Infinite*

Readers of *Paradise Lost* have long observed that the shift to a twelve-book structure in the 1674 edition suggests a more direct engagement of Virgil's *Aeneid*; critical discussions of the initial ten-book structure of Milton's epic have tended, however, to emphasize numerological theories, rather than consider specific intertextual engagements that such a structure might afford.[1] In considering "why Milton ever chose ten Books" in the first place, John Hale casts doubt on such numerological readings and seems to give ultimate primacy to accidents of the writing process: "each book came forth first at the length compelled by the throes of composition—by a blind man, remember, who could compose only in the early morning and only in winter months." On this basis, Hale contends, for example, that only after writing book 10 (of the 1667 edition) did Milton realize its disproportionate length and decide to divide it in half in the 1674 edition.[2] Such an explanation does not, however, consider why Milton ever imagined that book of the epic initially as a single unit and as the final book in a set of ten. By contrast, David Norbrook proposes that "the original ten-book structure of *Paradise Lost* formed a parallel with [Lucan's] *Pharsalia.*"[3] Norbrook's argument cites various political and poetic similarities between the two epics, similarities that generally would be reinforced by having the same number of books. Such similarities do not, of course, entail that specific points of intersection between the two works are parallel in their arrangement. I contend that the ten-book edition of *Paradise Lost* does, however, offer a direct structurally symmetrical engagement of a different ancient text: Plato's *Republic*.

Reading the 1667 *Paradise Lost* in conjunction with Plato's *Republic* addresses numerous questions simply as a matter of course. Why narrate the Fall specifically in book 8 of the first edition?[4] How does the extended educational digression in books 5 through 7 relate to the ostensible topic of divine justice? Why does the apparently Virgilian vision of the future appear at the end rather than the middle of the epic, as in the case of the *Aeneid?* Although Milton begins with an apparently Dantean descent into hell, why does the narrative seem to peak metaphysically, as it were, in book 6, rather than at the end?[5] Similarly, why does the main narrative treatment of hell occupy exactly the first two books, no more nor less? All such questions are, of course, susceptible to multiple complementary answers, but I contend that the sustained engagement of Plato's *Republic* reveals an important part of the answer to each of them. In offering such an interpretation of Milton's epic, we need not presume that the *Republic* is any less aporetic than *Paradise Lost*. Nor should we imagine that simply identifying an intertext constitutes, in itself, an elucidation of Milton's poem, as though Milton were not capable of ironic appropriation of a text that already suggested ironic readings. Reserving a fuller comparison of the ultimate rhetorical aims of these two texts for a larger study, the main purpose of the argument here is to prove the existence of such a sustained intertextual engagement and to offer some characterization of how that engagement unfolds. By demonstrating such architectonic symmetries, the argument here does not imply that *Paradise Lost* is reducible to such intertextual connections. Rather, the arguments of the *Republic* constitute a major recurrent thematic portion of the weave (*textus*) that Milton subsumes and transforms in his own epic. Taking as a point of departure some general consideration of Milton's relation to Platonic texts, we can then trace the symmetrical development of the arguments in these two texts. I shall give sustained attention to their first and final books, but the most striking parallel is the central "educational digression" that occupies books 5 through 7 of both texts. The 1667 *Paradise Lost* does not merely address Platonic themes; the ten-book structure emphasizes a direct engagement and transformation of the major arguments in Plato's *Republic*.

I

Although critics have often cited the influence of Plato's writing upon Milton's prose and poetry, the precise character of that influence has been difficult to stipulate with much precision.[6] The difficulties arise partially from the fact that "by the seventeenth century the influence of Plato had so permeated European thought that few books Milton knew or might have known were untouched by it."[7] The ubiquity of Plato's influence can make attempts to discern Milton's relation to specific Platonic texts especially problematic. The argument here thus involves an unavoidable hermeneutic tension that cannot be overcome and must simply be negotiated. On the one hand, Milton's reading of Platonic texts was obviously shaped by the particularities of the Renaissance reception of those texts amid various competing or overlapping interpretive traditions. For instance, not only are there crucial differences between the medieval reception of Plato's *Timaeus* in the context of Augustinian theological traditions shaped by key Platonist teachings[8] and the Renaissance reception of the *Phaedrus* by Marsilio Ficino, but the latter context differs again in crucial ways from Henry More's appropriation of Plotinus in developing a response to Cartesian philosophy. On the other hand, Milton was clearly capable of reading a Platonic dialogue "with the same energy and independence that he brought to his interpretations of Scripture."[9] As Thomas Luxon explains with reference to Milton's reading of the *Symposium*, "[Milton] does not conflate all the symposiasts' erotic theories and hymns of praise into one teaching called Platonic. He explicitly rejects Aristophanes' fables and Pausanius' detailed prescriptions about when it is proper and dignified to gratify a lover, and he embraces Socrates' (or Diotima's) teaching about the procreancy of the soul."[10] In other contexts, Milton would be just as likely to distinguish the teaching of Socrates from that of Plato and feel free to disagree with both where necessary. But the larger point here is that we need to allow for both the competing interpretive frameworks that were available to Milton and his capacities as an independent reader.[11]

The most important point to understand about Milton's relation to Plato's texts is that Milton shared the ancient philosopher's view that all poetry was necessarily a kind of teaching, whether for good or ill; Milton also viewed Plato as a teacher of rhetoric. Notwithstanding the "ancient quarrel" between poetry and philosophy mentioned in the *Republic*, Plato was cited by early modern writers on both sides of the debate regarding the legitimacy of poetry. Milton was clearly among those who, like Philip Sidney, intended to "save both literature and Plato for Protestantism."[12] Milton makes explicit his view of Plato as a rhetorician in *Of Education* when he points out that, after studying grammar and logic, students should then be instructed in "a graceful and ornate Rhetorick taught out of the rule of *Plato, Aristotle, Phalereus, Cicero, Hermogenes, Longinus*" (YP 2:402–03). Such a view of Plato as a teacher of rhetoric appears in the very work that Milton mentions by Longinus, *Peri Hupsous* [On sublimity]. Longinus names, cites, and discusses in detail the writing of Plato as a model for rhetorical sublimity. The fact that Jowett would later, as in the epigraph above, associate Plato's influence upon Milton with the specific quality of "sublimity" is no mere coincidence. But Longinus does not engage Plato's texts in isolation: for Longinus, Plato is part of a rhetorical tradition that extends from Homer through Plato, Demosthenes, and Cicero to Longinus himself.[13] This point is crucial in order to avoid presuming that Milton viewed "rhetoric" and "philosophy" as being in some kind of fundamental opposition.[14] In multiple Platonic dialogues such a contrast does certainly appear,[15] especially if the claims of Socrates are read without attention to the

larger ironies of such texts; Milton's reading of Plato, however, seems
to be shaped by a tradition that had long distinguished the Socratic
critique of the Sophists from a rejection of rhetoric per se. *Paradise
Lost* does criticize specific kinds of rhetorical practice (see, for example, *PL* 2.108–228.), but Milton never opposes rhetoric per se and in
various places advocates a rhetorical practice that results from and
gives rise to a love for wisdom. As we shall see, Milton's ultimate
transformation of Platonist philosophical rhetoric results from his
Christian understanding of "wisdom."

As early as *An Apology against a Pamphlet* (1642), Milton had artic-
ulated his insistence upon a rhetoric informed by Platonist ethics.
Understanding epideictic poetry as a subgenre of epideictic rhetoric
(which is consistent with *Of Education*'s classification of imaginative literature), Milton declares: "He who would not be frustrate of
his hope to write well hereafter in laudable things, ought him selfe
to bee a true Poem, that is, a composition, and patterne of the best
and honorablest things; not presuming to sing high praises of heroick men, or famous Cities, unlesse he have in himself the experience
and the practice of all that which is praise-worthy" (YP 1:890). This
striking radicalization of an ancient rhetorical commonplace would
not be remarkable except for the fact that it comes in the midst of
a passage in which Milton reveals his familiarity with the Greek text
of Plato's *Republic* and some of its central claims. When Milton begins
addressing, in *Apology,* the charges against his chastity, he observes
regarding his accusers: "they shall not for me know how slightly they
are esteem'd, unless they have so much learning as to read what in
Greek *Apeirokalia* [vulgarity] is, which together with envie is the
common disease of those who censure books that are not for their
reading" (YP 1:888). Plato uses the term *apeirokalia* in the *Republic*
to indicate an ignorance of what is fitting and beautiful, which leads
a person to indulge in licentious sexual behavior.[16] In describing
how chivalric romances helped to instill in him an esteem for the
virtue of chastity, Milton explains that if one of those stories depicted
a knight who broke his vow of chastity, "I judg'd it the same fault
of the Poet, as that which is attributed to Homer; to have written
undecent things of the gods" (YP 1:891), which is to say that his
response was modeled on that of Socrates to Homer (see *Republic,*
377b–83c). The passage in Milton's *Apology* then culminates by

describing his own education and specifically how he was led "from the Laureat fraternity of Poets," to the "shady spaces of philosophy, but chiefly to the divine volumes of *Plato,* and his equall *Xenophon*" (YP 1:891). When Milton mentions "philosophy" in this context, he clearly does not mean what early moderns would call "dialectic," but the use of reason in moral judgment, the cultivation of which is integral to practicing the arts of poetry and rhetoric.[17]

Areopagitica offers one of Milton's most important prose engagements of Plato's writing and further reveals Milton's attention to Plato's rhetorical aims. At the most obvious level, with respect to Milton's argument against prepublication censorship, *Areopagitica* needs to address those who would legitimate censorship by citing the practices apparently recommended in the *Republic* (books 2, 3, and 10) as well as the *Laws* (book 7)—both of which Milton apparently read as "utopian."[18] Milton initially points out that the censorship described by Plato would limit human learning to "a Library of smaller bulk than his own dialogues": "But that Plato meant this [censorship] Law peculiarly to that Commonwealth which he had imagin'd, and to no other, is evident. Why was he not else Law-giver to himself, but a transgressor, and to be expell'd by his own Magistrates; both for the wanton epigrams and dialogues which he made, and his perpetuall reading of *Sophron Mimus,* and *Aristophanes*" (YP 2:522–23). Milton argues here specifically against those who would derive the wrong kind of political application from Plato's texts, but Milton does not disown the *allos topos* rhetorical practice per se. He thus opposes those who would "sequester" themselves "out of the world into *Atlantick* and *Eutopian* polities, which never can be drawn into use" (YP 2:526), not because the genre has no purpose but because its purpose is not to outline a political program. The root problem is that "*Plato*'s licencing of books," if understood as a political prescription for direct imitation by legislators, does not equip people to "ordain wisely," "in this world of evill, in the midst of which God hath plac't us":

> [Licencing] necessarily pulls along with it so many other kinds of licencing, as will make us all both ridiculous and weary, and yet frustrat; but those unwritt'n or at least unconstraining laws of vertuous education, religious and civill nurture, which *Plato* there mentions,

as the bonds and ligaments of the Commonwealth, the pillars and sus-
tainers of every writt'n Statute; these they be which will bear chief
sway in such matters as these, when all licencing will be easily eluded.
(YP 2:526–27)

In effect, Milton insists that Plato's larger point is to emphasize the
relation between poetry and the cultivation of virtue that results in
political stability and justice. Milton agrees with Plato that the primary means by which such "unconstraining laws of vertuous education" are inculcated is through poetry and music; but rather than
deduce, on that basis, a need for censorship, Milton deduces a calling for poetry that unites supreme truth, goodness, and beauty.[19] In
effect, for Milton, true civic virtue is cultivated among citizens not
by government censors but by great poets. Ultimately, Milton offers
in *Paradise Lost* a biblicist rhetoric that subsumes and transforms
the Platonic philosophic rhetoric.

II

The presentation of Satan in the first two books of *Paradise Lost*
is, I contend, a direct response to the "Thrasymachus problem" in
the first two books of the *Republic*. The two works share an explicit
concern with the topic of justice. Although often referred to as a
"theodicy," *Paradise Lost* does not, strictly speaking, aim to address
the customary topics of philosophical theodicy, whether ancient or
modern. For example, the poem presumes rather than argues for the
existence of God and his attributes of goodness and justice. The epic
takes such claims as points of departure for exploring the extent to
which biblical revelation helps to make divine goodness and justice
humanly intelligible. In the *Republic*, Socrates similarly presumes
that the gods exist and are wholly good (379c) and openly questions
the extent to which we can know what justice is. At the end of book
1, the Sophist Thrasymachus offers a challenge to Socrates that ultimately gives rise to the central argument of the dialogue. In response
to earlier attempts to define "justice," Thrasymachus aggressively
bursts into the discussion and asserts that "justice is nothing other
than the advantage of the stronger" (338c), or "the advantage of the
established rule," whatever the established regime may be (338e). In

effect, what people call "justice" is, according to Thrasymachus, a social construct that enables those in political power to perpetuate that power. In questioning Thrasymachus, Socrates attempts to argue that even a Sophist must presume the possibility of some knowledge regarding an objective good that gives content to the meaning of "advantage." At a deeper level, however, Socrates ultimately shows Thrasymachus that his very act of advancing such an argument embodies a contradiction. As the dialogue unfolds, Thrasymachus refines his position to the claim that what people commonly call "injustice" is actually "stronger, freer, and more masterly than justice" "if it is on a large enough scale" (344c). In the course of answering Thrasymachus, Socrates asks for explicit assurance from Thrasymachus that he really holds this position as his own (349a). Thrasymachus dismisses the question as irrelevant, which Socrates allows him to do easily; however, the ensuing exchange culminates with something that Socrates says he had "never seen before— Thrasymachus blushing" (350d). The act of blushing is obviously susceptible to a wide range of interpretations. At one level, Socrates succeeds in leading Thrasymachus to contradict unwillingly his own previous claims (350b–c). But the deeper difficulty becomes manifest only in book 2, where the argument of Thrasymachus is taken up by those who do not sincerely hold it, by Glaucon and Adeimantus.

What I have called the "Thrasymachus problem" is a problem of self-presentation. The position of Thrasymachus is, in effect, that of the Machiavel. The problem is that a Machiavel depends upon appearances, including the appearance that he is not a Machiavel. This explains why Socrates keeps asking Thrasymachus whether he really holds such a position as his own; for if Thrasymachus acted upon the belief that injustice is stronger and more beneficial, he would make a point of concealing such a belief so as to take advantage of appearing conventionally "just." Thus, in the course of arguing at length that what people call "justice" is really the "advantage of the stronger," Thrasymachus embodies a self-contradiction: a smart Machiavel would not publicize the fact that he is a Machiavel. This problem of self-presentation explains why the argument of Thrasymachus must be taken over in book 2 by Glaucon and his brother Adeimantus, who make the argument with the clarification that they do not hold such a view themselves. This shift between books 1 and 2 is necessary in order for the argument to continue. Only in book 2 does the central argument of the whole *Republic* become explicit. The challenge put to Socrates by Adeimantus is to show that "justice" is choiceworthy in itself, rather than for any of the extrinsic benefits that it might bring. As long as the benefits of justice are extrinsic to it, one needs only to appear just rather than to be just (362d–67e). Ultimately, Socrates will address that challenge by arguing that the just man in the midst of suffering unjustly is actually happier than the tyrant in the midst of all his apparent pleasures. The whole presentation of the *kallipolis* (or "good polis") that occupies the core of the *Republic* is ultimately to serve this twofold aim of defining justice and demonstrating that it is supremely choiceworthy in itself. The main, explicit purpose of the entire description of the *kallipolis* is thus to assist in understanding justice in the soul (368c–69b) and not necessarily to propose establishment of the *kallipolis* as a historical reality (471e–73a). But the first crucial point to notice regarding the argument's inception is that, although Thrasymachus continues as an incidental character in the rest of the dialogue, he never advances his position again in his own voice after book 1. In effect, the nature of his position is such that it must be presented by means of characters who do not hold it as their own.

In *Paradise Lost*, Milton deploys the character of Satan in order to probe this problem of self-presentation to its fullest extent. Initially, the ontological status of Satan as a fallen angel without hope makes him singularly appropriate to articulate the Thrasymachean position. Readers would not typically expect Satan to be virtuous; he can give authentic voice to the Thrasymachean position without any need to dissimulate regarding his relation to conventional notions of justice. The fact that both Thrasymachus and Satan have inspired ironic interpretations of the larger texts that they inhabit only suggests further the depth of similarity between the two figures.[20] As my use of the term "Machiavel" has already suggested, the views of Thrasymachus were most famously advanced in the Renaissance by the explicit advice given in *The Prince*, by Niccolò Machiavelli.[21] Although Milton is widely acknowledged to have engaged Machiavelli's writing in various ways, Milton would also have recognized the arguments of *The Prince* as transparently reiterating the view held by Thrasymachus and giving rise to the very same problem of self-presentation.[22] When Barbara Riebling thus contends that in *Paradise Lost*, "Milton deliberately evokes Machiavelli's prince in his portrayal of Satan," she is surely correct.[23] By understanding the Machiavel, however, as a recapitulation of the Thrasymachean Sophist we can appreciate more clearly why Milton begins his epic with and emphasizes such a characterization especially in the first two books.[24] After book 2 of the *Republic*, there are in the entire text only four passages in which Thrasymachus is mentioned by name.[25] A potential correspondence between Thrasymachus and Satan appears in each case, but the most suggestive instance appears in book 8, where Socrates reminds his interlocutors that they have now returned to the central question: whether or not they will be "persuaded by Thrasymachus to practice injustice" (545a).

Milton's depiction of Satan and his companions in book 2 of *Paradise Lost* allows a further interrogation of the *Republic*'s point regarding the need for the Machiavel to dissimulate, even as Milton's epic flatly contradicts the restrictions that Socrates would impose on poetic representations of the gods in book 2 of the dialogue. The first task that Socrates undertakes in describing the *kallipolis* is to stipulate, in the latter part of book 2 and the beginning of book 3, the kinds of stories that should be used in order to encourage civic virtues in the guardians of the city. The end of book 2 emphasizes the content of stories about the gods, while book 3 addresses the particular form that such stories should take.[26] Regarding the first topic, Socrates insists: "We won't admit stories into our city—whether allegorical [*huponoiais*] or not—about Hera being chained by her son, nor about Hephaestus being hurled from heaven by his father when he tried to help his mother, who was being beaten, nor about the battle of the gods in Homer" (*Republic* 378d). Throughout *Paradise Lost*, Milton, explicitly adapts the battle of the gods for his own purposes (especially books 1, 2, and 6), but two further points are crucial here: first, Socrates rejects such stories because they imply that the gods cause evil, act in morally corrupt ways, are subject to change, and are capable of dissembling (*Republic* 379a–82a); second, Milton's uncharacteristic use of explicitly allegorical narrative near the end of book 2 of *Paradise Lost* offers a direct contrast to the advice of Socrates at this corresponding point in the dialogue.

The shift in *Paradise Lost* from describing fallen angels (book 2) to describing the scene in heaven (book 3) corresponds to the shift in the *Republic* between emphasizing first the content and then the form of poetry about the gods in books 2 and 3. In depicting the fallen angels as dissimulating orators in book 2 of *Paradise Lost*, Milton implies that they do not finally escape the need to appear conventionally just, at least among themselves, suggesting that the Thrasymachean problem still persists.[27] At a deeper level, even Satan cannot ultimately maintain his position beyond book 2 without famously pretending that the evil he embraces is in some sense "good" (*PL* 4.110). But even before the end of book 2, readers encounter the first indications that Satan has managed to avoid the Thrasymachean problem only by relocating that very self-contradiction within his own psyche. Satan's encounter with the allegorical characters of Sin and Death depicts the self-alienation and self-ignorance that guides him. He does not at first even recognize Sin and Death as his own progeny. He must be instructed in his "lore" by his "daughter," Sin:

>   In sight
> Of all the Seraphim with thee combin'd
> In bold conspiracy against Heav'ns King,
> All on a sudden miserable pain
> Surpris'd thee, dim thine eyes, and dizzie swumm
> In darkness, while thy head flames thick and fast
> Threw forth, till on the left side op'ning wide,
> Likest to thee in shape and count'nance bright,
> Then shining heav'nly fair, a Goddess arm'd
> Out of thy head I sprung.
>   . . . .
>   But familiar grown,
> I pleas'd, and with attractive graces won
> The most averse, thee chiefly, who full oft
> Thy self in me thy perfect image viewing
> Becam'st enamour'd, and such joy thou took'st
> With me in secret, that my womb conceiv'd
> A growing burden.   (*PL* 2.749–58, 761–67)

Satan had apparently lost the knowledge that he has "known" sin. The ensuing "birth" of Death offers an extended dilation of James 1:13–17, but the narrative also offers more than an obvious allegorical claim that sin literally originates "from the mind of Satan." The fact that Sin's explanatory autobiographical narrative (*PL* 2.746–67) is modeled, in part, on the story of Athena's bursting from the head of Zeus is typical of Milton's response to Plato's critique of Homer. In effect, Milton implies that, while many of the Socratic objections regarding the content of poetry about the gods is valid if applied to the Christian God, such difficulties disappear if one interprets such gods as "false gods," which are for Milton reducible to demons or fallen angels. Moreover, the encounter with Sin and Death depicts Satan as an embodiment of what Socrates, at the end of book 2, calls "a *true* falsehood":

> Don't you know that a *true* falsehood, if one may call it that, is hated by all gods and humans?
>
> What do you mean?
>
> I mean that no one is willing to tell falsehoods to the most important part of himself about the most important things. . . . To be false in one's soul about the things that are, to be ignorant and to have and hold falsehood there, is what everyone would least of all accept, for everyone hates a falsehood in that place most of all. (*Republic*, 382a–b)

Satan seems to overcome the customary problem of representing the Thrasymachean position initially only because he has forced upon himself "a true falsehood" that results in the shattering of his own psyche, the fragments of which end up allegorically guarding the gates of hell.

In book 3 of the *Republic*, Socrates begins his critique of the modes of poetry and especially dramatic "imitation" (392c–98b). That argument is not finally complete until book 10, but already Socrates emphasizes that the only kind of drama permitted in the *kallipolis* would be that which "would imitate the speech of a decent person," rather than speak in the direct voice of a vicious character (398b). *Paradise Lost* clearly offers both kinds of speech, but Milton's supreme instance of the speech of a virtuous character is arguably that of the Son in book 3. As I have elsewhere observed, the most striking characteristic of the Father-Son dialogue in book 3 is the fact that it happens at all, given the apparent presumption involved in such poetic representation; but Milton's depiction of the Father and Son as characters in a dialogue is based on a conflation of biblical models.[28] The key point here is that Milton's biblicist adaptation of the Homeric poetic mode (that is, "mixed" dialogue and narrative) corresponds directly to Plato's initial critique of that mode for representing the gods in book 3 of the *Republic*.

III

The particular shape of the overall argument in both of these texts constitutes the most compelling evidence that Milton intended his biblical epic as a direct engagement of the *Republic*. In briefly outlining the overall argument as it unfolds in each text, we can trace the structural symmetries that run through all ten books. We can then consider in more detail just a few of the several points of engagement that might otherwise seem incidental. Intrinsic to the treatments of justice in both the *Republic* and *Paradise Lost* is a purported attempt to envision complete human virtue. Both accounts aim not merely to describe complete virtue but also to explain how vice could ever arise amid such imagined perfection. As part of their argument, both of these texts give readers, specifically in book 4, their initial glimpse of the moral perfection envisioned: the *kallipolis* in Plato's text and Eden in Milton's. In book 4 of the *Republic* Socrates first declares the *kallipolis* "established" and begins to describe the virtues within it (427d–35b). In book 4 of *Paradise Lost*, readers get their first full description of Adam and Eve in Eden, in their state of complete virtue, albeit through the eyes of Satan initially (4.194–535). The latter circumstance of Satan's perspective implies Milton's emphasis upon the limited capacities of fallen humans, including himself, to imagine such moral perfection. By contrast, although Socrates elsewhere allows for human limitations like mortality and insists upon the connection between moral and intellectual virtues, in book 4 of the *Republic* he does not evidence Milton's skepticism regarding the contingent but universal human moral inability to understand complete virtue.[29] But the more important point here is that both texts first offer their imagined depiction of complete virtue in book 4.

From the latter part of book 5 through book 7, both texts focus on the education of the wisdom lovers who rule the good city, or Eden, which is intended to protect the virtue first described in book 4. Both of these educational digressions "peak," as it were, in book 6, with explicitly analogical accounts of "the good" that informs all justice. Book 7 of both Plato's and Milton's texts offer differently enigmatic discussions of astronomy as part of the educational digression. Although they address various educational topics in contrasting ways, both works imply that an understanding of divine justice requires an account of the relation between the temporal cosmos and its eternal cause. Only in book 8 of both texts is there an explicit return to the main action postponed by the digression in books 5 through 7. In book 8 of the *Republic* Socrates attempts to describe how the *kallipolis* could ever begin to go into decline, despite the "philosophic" education of its rulers. Book 8 of *Paradise Lost* describes how, despite their preparatory education through Raphael, Adam and Eve fall into sin. Book 9 of both texts then delineates the consequences of that fall from virtue. Book 10 of both texts offers an inset narrative specifically aimed to instruct readers who must adapt to the circumstance of living outside the *kallipolis* or Eden. A schematic outline of the progression in topics appears in table 1.

Once we begin to discern this overall symmetry in the progression of topics, numerous other points of engagement appear that might otherwise seem incidental. The most striking similarity between the two works is the locations of the educational digressions in books 5 through 7. In book 5 of the *Republic,* Socrates explicitly sets aside his account of virtue in the polis in order to address three potential "waves of objections" (472a) to the *kallipolis* that he envisions. Three aspects of the good city would differ radically from Athens, but the last element is the one to which Socrates anticipates the greatest opposition: (1) educational equality between the men and women (451c–57c); (2) the holding of all things in common, including wives and children (457c–61e); (3) philosophers becoming rulers or rulers becoming philosophers (472a–540c). Two points are crucial for our purposes here: first, Socrates needs to address these arguments before he can complete his account of virtue and vice in the polis; second, the answer to the third and final wave of objections extends from

Table 1. Outline of topics in the *Republic* and *Paradise Lost* (1667)

Republic	Book	*Paradise Lost* 1667
Thrasymachean account of justice	1	Satan as authentic voice of Thrasymachean view
Content of poetry about the gods	2	Poetry about demons to explain false gods
Modes of poetry about the gods	3	Poetry depicting God as a character
Establishment of kallipolis and account of virtues complete	4	Reader's first view of newly completed Eden
Digression: protect *kallipolis* by educating rulers	5	Digression: protect Eden by by educating Adam and Eve
Digression peaks in sun analogy	6	Digression peaks in revelation of Son
Conclusion of philosopher-king education	7	Conclusion of prelapsarian education
Explanation of how *kallipolis* could decline	8	Narration of how Eden was lost
Stages of decline in virtue of polis and psyche	9	Consequences of the Fall: psyche, polis, cosmos
Critique of "imitative poetry" and myth of Er	10	Didactic narration of fallen human history

the latter part of book 5 through book 7 and includes an account of how such philosopher-kings might be educated.[30]

The last "wave" is most important, but I should note briefly how *Paradise Lost* also reconfigures the first two topics. The entire digression in the *Republic* arises in book 5 in response to a passing comment that Socrates made earlier in book 4 to the effect that "the having of wives and the procreation of children must be governed as far as possible by the old proverb: Friends possess everything in common" (423e–24a). Milton does not address this issue in book 5 because communal marriage is preemptively ruled out in book 4 of his epic in a passage that corresponds closely to the point at which the topic first appears in the *Republic:* "Haile wedded Love, mysterious Law, true source / Of human ofspring, sole proprietie, / In Paradise of all things common else" (*PL* 4. 750–52). The topic of equality in educational opportunity for men and women in either the *Republic* or *Paradise Lost* warrants a detailed independent treatment that must be postponed here. I will, however, at least observe that until the midpoint of book 7 Adam and Eve are both instructed by Raphael and they are indeed both naked, as Socrates recommends (while attaching an explicitly figurative meaning to the proposal) (*Republic* 457a–b).

In contrast to the three waves of objections that Socrates must address, the narration of divine justice in *Paradise Lost* must deal with one major objection, but the answer to that objection corresponds directly to the discussion of the "third wave" in the *Republic*. The Genesis account of the Fall depicts not merely a freely chosen disobedience on the part of Adam and Eve, but disobedience under the influence of deception and temptation. The poem needs to show that the allowance of such extenuating circumstances does not compromise divine justice. The epic narrator makes explicit the need to address this issue in the poem by calling out for a "warning voice" from heaven (4.1). In dilating the biblical narrative, Milton addresses this challenge in two ways. Conceptually, the poem emphasizes that, although the facts of deception and temptation do not mitigate the event of the Fall itself and its immediate consequences, such extenuating circumstances do provide a basis for restoration that would not otherwise be available (*PL* 3.86–134).

The other way in which Milton addresses the challenge to divine justice is by providing, in the angel Raphael, the warning voice that had been requested. Despite those critics who find the Father's reasons for sending Raphael indecorously tendentious, the narrator explicitly observes that in doing so, God "fulfilld / All Justice" (5.246–47). Thus, at the level of narrative structure, Milton devotes the latter part of book 5 and all of books 6 and 7 to Raphael's visit. The angelic educational instruction against temptation is intended to prepare Adam and Eve against temptation by providing knowledge of their enemy and their own place in the cosmos. Thus, in the same way that the latter part of book 5 through books 6 and 7 of the *Republic* discusses the education of the philosopher-kings in order to address the objections against philosophers ruling, *Paradise Lost* depicts the education of Adam and Eve through the corresponding books in order to address the objection that the divine allowance of temptation in Eden contradicts justice.

Book 6 of the *Republic* reaches its apex of metaphysical speculation in an extended analogy between the sun and "the good."[31] Socrates insists that the good is actually ineffable but that we can get some sense of what it is like by comparing it to the sun: "What the good itself is in the intelligible realm, in relation to understanding and intelligible things, the sun is in the visible realm in relation to sight and visible things" (508b–c). The whole analogy begins, however, when Socrates disowns the ability to speak about the good directly: "But I am willing to tell you about what is apparently an offspring of the good and most like it. . . . So here then is this child and offspring of the good. But be careful that I don't somehow deceive you unintentionally by giving you an illegitimate account of the child" (506e–07a). Milton is, in a sense, being utterly conventional in adapting the sun analogy, with its language of father and child, to Christian theology:[32] "Effulgence of my Glorie, Son belov'd, / Son in whose face invisible is beheld / Visibly, what by Deitie I am," says the Father (*PL* 6.680–82).

By emphasizing this imagery in book 6, Milton's description of the Son's appearance to the angels in the "Chariot of Paternal Deitie" (6.750) corresponds directly to the Socratic sun analogy. In effect, in *Paradise Lost* the Son is manifest as the form of the good who makes all other forms intelligible to human understanding.[33] This further explains why the epic deploys the imagery of light in such close proximity to the Son's description of his own actions as a revelation of the good that informs both justice and charity:

> and on his Son with Rayes direct
> Shon full, he all his Father full exprest
> Ineffably into his face receiv'd,
> And thus the filial Godhead answering spake.
> O Father, O Supream of heav'nly Thrones,
> First, Highest, Holiest, Best, thou alwayes seekst
> To glorifie thy Son, I always thee,
> As is most *just.* . . .
> 　　　　. . . . .
> Scepter and Power, thy giving, I assume,
> And gladlier shall resign, when in the end
> Thou shalt be All in All, and I in thee
> For ever, and in mee all whom thou *lov'st:*
> But whom thou hat'st, I hate, and can put on
> Thy terrors.　　　　　　　(6.719–26, 730–35; my emphasis)

The epic presents the expulsion of Satan and his followers as a matter of justice that follows from the same good that informs the enjoyment of divine love.[34] The crucial difference between the respective accounts of the good offered by Milton and Plato is that Milton's use of narrative requires that he render in sequence a reality that Socrates insists is atemporal.

IV

Because the 1667 *Paradise Lost* narrates the Fall in book 8, this section of the epic offers one of the most crucial parallels with the *Republic* that appears only in the first edition. Only after completing the educational digression in the *Republic* does Socrates propose a return to the earlier account that he had postponed at the beginning of book 5: the account of the various kinds of constitutions and corresponding souls that are dominated by vice. In book 8, Socrates proposes, "let's recall the point at which we began the digression that brought us here, so that we can continue on the same path" (543c). His first challenge, however, is to explain how the *kallipolis* could ever go into decline, given its presumed perfection: "How, then, Glaucon, will our city be changed? How will civil war arise, either between the auxiliaries and the rulers or within either group? Or do you want us to be like Homer and pray to the muses to tell us "how civil war first broke out? [*sic*] And shall we say that they speak to us in tragic tones, as if they were in earnest, playing and jesting with us as if we were children?" (545d). When *Paradise Lost* begins to tell the story of the Fall in book 8, the narrator similarly marks a return to the earlier topic after a digression and similarly invokes the tragic genre:

> No more of talk where God or Angel Guest
> With Man, as with his Friend, familiar us'd
> To sit indulgent, and with him partake
> Rural repast, permitting him the while
> Venial discourse unblam'd: I now must change
> Those Notes to Tragic; foul distrust, and breach
> Disloyal on the part of Man, revolt
> And disobedience.   (*PL* 8.1–8)

The narrator seems to offer in earnest what Socrates, given his own repudiation of the tragic genre, can do only in mockery, yet the clear parallel remains.

The root issue to which I draw attention here is the radically different causes that the two texts cite as precipitating each respective fall from an imagined state of complete virtue. In one of the most obscure and numerologically dense passages in the *Republic,* Socrates suggests that the demise of the *kallipolis* is inevitable (546a). The rulers of the *kallipolis,* despite their knowledge of eternal forms, will not be immune to error in their eugenics practices because such practices depend upon combining "calculation together with sense perception" (546a–b). The moral and intellectual flaws in the ensuing generation of rulers will begin the decline of the polis into various stages in the progression of vice (546a–47a). In effect, Plato's equation of eternal and unchanging being with the good leads him to locate the origin of the moral decline of the polis in blameless error arising from the need to unite intelligibility ("calculation") and temporal mutability ("sense perception").[35] By contrast, one of Milton's major aims in *Paradise Lost* is to emphasize the moral freedom of Adam and Eve before the Fall. The narrative emphasizes at length that the human will is the crux of moral consequence. The epic leads readers through a series of distinctions showing that to be deceived is not to be fallen, to be mistaken about the facts of a given situation is not to be fallen, and to be tempted is not to be fallen.[36] Thus, despite all of these conditions being present in Eve's situation in book 8, *Paradise Lost* implies that her decision whether to obey the divine command is free. Here we come to the core of Milton's critique of Plato's treatment of justice in the *Republic.* The moral corruption of the *kallipolis* is inevitable, according to Socrates, because of his assumption that there is an insurmountable ontological difference between unchangeable eternity and changeable temporality.

The engagement of themes in the final book of both texts also suggests that Milton intends to offer an alternative to the *Republic*'s account of "being." The ostensible argument against "imitative poetry"[37] in book 10 of the *Republic* begins with the ontological claim that poetry, through analogy with painting, is at a "third" remove from the truth it purports to imitate. Rather than imitate an eternal form, whether of a given object or a virtue, a poem merely imitates the appearance of an embodiment that is itself a temporal imitation of an eternal form (595b–601a).[38] Writing after Sidney's *Apologie for Poetrie*, not to mention Plato's manifestly inconsistent presentation of the argument, Milton had no need to address directly such doubtful and ironically analogical claims.[39] But the initial ontological critique of poetry is really in service to a further claim that Socrates makes regarding the morally corrupting effects of poetry like Homer's. Although Homer was an epic poet, Socrates depicts him as the leader (in terms of form and content) of all tragic poets, who were the most powerful "imitative poets." Most crucial is Homer's reputation as a teacher of virtue—which Socrates undertakes to attack. On the basis of previous divisions between the rational, spirited, and appetitive parts of the soul, Socrates argues that tragedy encourages people to be ruled by irrational desires, rather than their rational desire for truth. Socrates is especially concerned with how tragedy trains people to respond poorly to suffering:

> The law says, doesn't it, that it is best to keep as quiet as possible in misfortunes and not get excited about them? First, it isn't clear whether such things will turn out to be good or bad in the end; second, it doesn't make the future any better to take them hard; third, human affairs aren't worth taking very seriously; and finally, grief prevents the very thing we most need in such circumstances from coming into play as quickly as possible.
> What are you referring to?
> Deliberation. . . .
> Accordingly, we say that it is the best part of us that is willing to follow this rational calculation. (*Republic*, 604b–c)

By contrast, a soul that is subject to the lower appetites for glory or bodily pleasure will "lead us to dwell on misfortunes" (604d). Ultimately, according to Plato, the "enjoyment of other people's sufferings" that is inherent to tragedy "is necessarily transferred to our own," such that "the pitying part, if it is nourished and strengthened on the suffering of others, won't be easily held in check when we ourselves suffer" (606b). As if offering a direct response to such a charge, the angel Michael explains to Adam that the specific moral purpose served by the revelation of human history that Adam is about to

receive, a story that depicts much suffering, is to fortify the ability
to endure hardship:

> Ere thou from hence depart, know I am sent
> To shew thee what shall come in future dayes
> To thee and to thy Ofspring; good with bad
> Expect to hear, supernal Grace contending
> With sinfulness of Men; thereby to learn
> True patience, and to temper joy with fear
> And pious sorrow, equally enur'd
> By moderation either state to beare,
> Prosperous or adverse: so shalt thou lead
> Safest thy life, and best prepar'd endure
> Thy mortal passage when it comes.   (*PL* 10.356–66)

In the *Republic*, the attempt to prepare humans for the "mortal passage" is also the explicit aim in presenting the "myth of Er" that then follows the critique of imitative poetry. In this way, Milton sets his own summary of biblical history in didactic competition with the myth of Er.

The final book of the 1667 *Paradise Lost* thus suggests intertextual connections that the twelve-book edition tends to obscure. For example, many readers of Virgil's *Aeneid* who have also read the 1674 *Paradise Lost* are impressed by the similarities between the prophetic vision of the future in book 6 of the *Aeneid* and Michael's prophecy to Adam in the last two books of Milton's epic. William Porter further points out that the passage in the *Aeneid* draws upon "the story of Er in book 10 of Plato's *Republic*" as well as Homer and Cicero (98). Because Porter, quite reasonably, works from the twelve-book edition of *Paradise Lost*, he does not consider that Milton may have been engaging the myth of Er directly rather than through the *Aeneid*. Milton does indeed clearly appropriate the prophetic vision of history from the *Aeneid*, book 6, but I contend that he locates that vision in the tenth book of the 1667 *Paradise Lost* in order to address the problems that Milton saw in the myth of Er. The inset narrative in Plato's dialogue offers a report from a messenger regarding the "world beyond" (614b). The myth aims to induce devotion to wisdom above wealth, power, or glory by narrating an atemporal state in which immortal souls choose their respective destinies. In contrast, the revelation that Michael presents to Adam in *Paradise Lost* is intended to induce faith, hope, and charity through an account of temporal events in view of an eschatological horizon.[40] Both stories aim to instruct in virtue those who must cope with life outside the *kallipolis* or Eden, but Milton seems to offer his inset narrative as, in effect, a better vindication of the Socratic claim that justice is its own reward.

Paradise Lost also transforms the explicit ontology presented in the *Republic* regarding two crucial claims: the view that being is atemporal; the tendency to describe the moral decline from perfect virtue as originating in a failed attempt to unite eternal truth and temporal mutability. The argument of the *Republic* does not imply that the body is intrinsically evil but that the possibility of injustice arises from the condition of temporal embodiment. Nor must we presume that the surface teaching of the *Republic* offers Plato's complete account of the body or temporality. Nevertheless, Milton's epic transforms the *Republic*'s explicit distinction between "seeming" and "being." Whereas for Socrates, in the *Republic* at least, the difference between appearance and reality is absolute and permanent, such that changeable appearances cannot participate in being, for Milton that very difference is temporal. In *Paradise Lost*, there is a continuity between the truth of what is (being) and what seems, such that even a reality that is hidden at present will appear over time. The classic case would be Milton's treatment of the effects of the Fall, whether angelic or human; the truth may be hidden for a time but will later become manifest. Milton does not deny that there are, at times, discrepancies between "seeming" and "being," as in the case of Abdiel's reaction to Satan at the beginning of book 6 (*PL* 6.114–16); however, such discrepancies result from a temporal "fold" in the appearance that is being, not from an incommensurable difference between being and time.[41]

In emphasizing the parallels and similarities between the overall argument development in the *Republic* and the 1667 *Paradise Lost*, the analysis offered here has, in effect, established the need for further investigation of several points that I have mentioned only briefly. In view of this argument, we might reasonably ask, "If Milton was so invested in the initial ten-book structure, why did he change the number of books to 12 in 1674?" Most striking is the way that the twelve-book structure neatly obscures this engagement of Plato's text. The critical tone in Milton's prefatory headnotes to *Paradise Lost* and *Samson Agonistes* should be kept in mind here. At one level, Milton was clearly willing to accommodate the growing neoclassical popularity of Virgil in the late seventeenth century England, even if such accommodation to Virgilian tastes could be intentionally ironic.[42] Milton also likely judged that the majority of such a reading public—those who expected prefatory plot summaries and rhyming couplets—were the same ones who welcomed the Restoration and cheered the execution of Milton's friends. I contend that Milton's accommodation to public taste involved a willingness to let his own structural purposes become obscured from such readers. He would not deform his verse by subjecting it to the "modern bondage" of rhyming, but Milton was apparently willing to give those readers the appearance of what they thought they wanted: something more like the *Aeneid*. In effect, Milton was willing to let Restoration neoclassicism enable a kind of self-deception among the religiously conforming, rhyme-loving public regarding the larger purposes implied by the logical shape of his epic.

The 1667 edition of *Paradise Lost* remained, I contend, Milton's preferred version. Only when we keep in view the ten-book structure does the consistent engagement of Plato's *Republic* become readily apparent. *Paradise Lost* is not, of course, a philosophical dialogue; that would be Milton's point. His epic sharpens the dialectical encounters within it by foregrounding the competing narrative frameworks that Plato's dialogues typically leave implicit. But Milton does not simply privilege rhetoric or narrative over dialectic: the Logos revealed at the apex of his epic encompasses and enables human participation in both. For Milton, only a specifically biblical epic, informed by the biblical story of Creation, Fall, incarnation, redemption, and eschaton, enables the epic form to overcome the Socratic indictment of poetry, resulting in poetic justice.

The Mysterious Darkness of Unknowing
Paradise Lost and the God Beyond Names

MICHAEL BRYSON

In 1667, John Milton dropped a bomb on the literary and intellectual world of England. Unfortunately, that bomb proved initially to be a dud, an object of curiosity rather than an immediate literary sensation. Received with more of a collective raised eyebrow than with the buzz and stir for which Milton must have hoped, the ten-book edition of *Paradise Lost* proved to be a difficult sale, and goes nearly completely unread today.[1] Published without any of the editorial apparatus modern readers take for granted, the first edition of *Paradise Lost* was also published without the "arguments" or miniature plot summaries that have become so familiar to readers of later editions (including the now dominant twelve-book version of 1674). In effect, the first printing of *Paradise Lost* was loosed upon a world that was not yet ready for it, in a form that it could not—and did not—fully digest.[2] Though the 1667 *Paradise Lost* does all the same work that the 1674 version does, perhaps the audience it sought, though "fit," was far too "few" for the work to have sufficient impact or to provide its author with a legacy that the world would not willingly let die.

So why read, much less write about, the 1667 *Paradise Lost* today? Much can be written about the difference in form between the 1667, ten-book edition, and the more famous 1674, twelve-book edition. Choosing the ten-book format, rather than the twelve-book format

183

is, as Barbara Lewalski argues, "an overt political statement . . . [as] Milton eschewed Virgil's twelve-book epic format with its Roman imperialist and royalist associations for the ten-book model of the republican Lucan."[3] Even more politically suggestive, however, is the timing of the poem's publication, coming after the plague of 1665 and the devastating fires of September 1666, and after the conclusion reached by many that the disasters were the judgment of God upon a debauched and dissolute nation.[4] Robert Elborough provides an excellent example of this way of thinking in his 1666 sermon, entitled "London's Calamity by Fire":

> What is it that God saith to others by *Londons conflagration?* Oh have a care of *Londons abomination*. If you partake of *London*, as to its *sinning*, you shall partake of *London* as to its *suffering*. . . . alas, who will not acknowledge that God hath dealt severely with *London?* . . . God comes with the *Plague* and that don't work; God comes with the *Sword*; & that don't work; at last he comes with a *Fiery Judgment*, that so he may not come with this, *London adieu*, and *England Farewel*, thy house is left desolate unto thee, and thou are left desolate without an house.[5]

Thomas Vincent, a Nonconformist minister who is one of our most vivid sources of descriptive detail about London during the 1665 plague, argues in *Gods Terrible Voice in the City* (first printed in 1666) that both the plague and the fire were sent as judgments from God: "The Plague is a terrible Judgment by which God speaks unto men," and "God spake terribly by fire when London was in flames."[6] Like Elborough, Vincent is not at all shy about assigning blame for the disasters; in fact, he offers a list of 25 sins prevalent in London that caused God's anger. Among the highlights are the eleventh sin, "*fullness of Bread, or intemperance in eating*"; the fifteenth sin, "*Drunkennesse*," and the twenty-first sin, "*Prodigality and profuse spending*."[7] But more than these sins, for Vincent it seems to have been the various provisions of the Clarendon Code (specifically, the Act of Uniformity of 1662, and the Five-Mile Act of 1665) that angered God to the point that he sent plague and fire as punishments:

> Here I might speak of the Judgment executed, August 24th 1662, when so many Ministers were put out of their places, and the judgments

executed, March 24, 1665, when so many Ministers were banished five miles from Corporations. . . . Gospel-Ordinances, and Gospel-Ministers were the safeguard of London, the glory and defence. But when the Ordinances were slighted, and the Ministers were mocked . . . God is provoked.[8]

Barbara Lewalski quotes a letter of the same period (dated September 1666) that questions the prevailing mindset by seizing on the fact that various groups in England offer widely disparate—and self-serving—explanations for the back-to-back disasters:

"All see the same desolation, yet, by looking on it with different opinions and interest, they make different constructions as if the object were so. Some thinking it a natural and bare accident, while others imagine it a judgment of God. . . . The Quakers say, it is for their persecution. The Fanaticks say, it is for the banishing and silencing their ministers. Others say, it is for the murder of the king and the rebellion of the city. The Clergy lay the blame on schism and licentiousness, while the Sectaries lay it on imposition and their pride."[9]

Each of these explanations, with the exception of the "natural and bare accident" theory, involves a different notion of the active judgment of God. In turn, each of the "judgment of God" theories involves a construction of the deity that is different from every other theory. For example, the Quaker theory constructs a God who devastates London as punishment for the persecution of Quakers, while "Fanaticks" (such as Vincent) construct a God who is angry over the treatment of non-Anglican ministers, and unnamed royalist "Others" construct a God who lays waste to the city as delayed retribution for the execution of Charles I. Each complaining group creates a God in its own image, a God that is especially sympathetic to the group's grievances. Against this background, the constructions of God in *Paradise Lost* demand attention, especially because the poem was first published in a setting where urban disasters were commonly read as the judgment of God, and in which the constructions of God varied as widely as did the "sins" being "judged."

Why read the 1667 edition, then? The answer, for me, is a simple one: because of its context, 1667 calls for a different and perhaps more intensely focused kind of reading than does 1674. What a

consideration of the 1667 edition allows us to do, even demands that
we do, is to read this work as a reflection of the prevalent contemporary tendency to imagine God as one's own partisan (a view of God
that Milton had once shared), and to read without reference to
Milton's later poetic works.[10] What such a reading brings to the fore-
front is that the epic—*in its earliest published form*—rejects partisan notions of God, including (but not limited to) those commonly
expressed in the wake of London's disastrous mid-1660s. Despite its
frequent use of human imagery to facilitate poetic descriptions of the
Father and Son characters presented as alternate models of deity,
Paradise Lost often expresses nervousness, doubt, and hesitancy
about such imagery. Positive (in the sense of *posited*) images of deity
are cross-examined, countered, and finally negated. *Paradise Lost* presents both positive images of deity and negations of those images,
negations ultimately informed by an apophatic or negative theology.
When reading the 1674 edition, placed in the context of *Paradise
Regained* and *Samson Agonistes*, the strain of negative or apophatic
theology in *Paradise Lost* can be more easily brought into focus as
each of those works presents an image of a deity that radically differs from the other and from those presented in the epic. But a close
reading of several passages will show that it is readily discernible
in the 1667 edition, even without the context that the later poems
provide.

The God Beyond Names: Negative Theology

At its most fundamental level, negative theology suggests—much
like its modern relative, deconstruction—that there is a fundamental gap between our language and those subjects and objects our language attempts to describe.[11] For the negative theologian, the ultimate
subject / object of language is "God." But what *is* God? Can this
"God" be described at all, much less in ontological terms, terms of
being, or *is*-ness? For the negative theologian, the answer to this last
question is "yes, but no," while the answer to the first question is
"I do not (or cannot) know."

Negative theology is actually something of a misnomer. The
Greek term *apophatic* is more to the point. Meaning "without voice"
or "unsayable," apophatic theology is an attempt to highlight the

limits of human reason, imagination, and discourse in any consideration or meditation upon the divine. Apophatic theology is a way of speaking—without speaking—about that which cannot accurately be spoken. It is a dismantling of images, a denial of concepts, and a negation of the qualities that are posited to the divine in *cataphatic* ("with voice" or "sayable") or positive theology. However, negative theology is a complement to, not the enemy of, positive theology, serving to remind us of our limits and to prevent us from concretizing our images and metaphors, thus serving the believer as an aid in the attempt to avoid idolatry. The relation between positive and negative theologies is one of the central dynamics of Western theology— a tension between the God with qualities and the God without qualities. This tension, most famously presented in the works of Pseudo-Dionysius, can be described as a continuous process of affirmation and negation, a "yes, but no" approach to trying to understand that which, ultimately, is beyond human understanding. The "yes, but no" pattern posits and then negates qualities (goodness, being, righteousness, and the like) that might be used to understand the divine.

Pseudo-Dionysius, in his works the *Divine Names* and the *Mystical Theology*,[12] establishes the essential pattern of affirmation and negation. Starting with "the most important name, 'Good'" (*DN* 68), Dionysius argues closely for an understanding of the divine that emerges from "the processions of God" (*DN* 68). Each of these "processions" (Good, Being, Wisdom, Truth, and so on) is best understood in causal terms, that is, in terms of God as the cause of Goodness, Being, Wisdom, and Truth as they manifest in creatures and the created world. It is an inductive approach to the divine, reasoning from the manifestation to the cause thereof, from the observable instance to the unobserved (and unobservable) principle or cause. These "processions of God," then, are the observable effects of the divine as translated into human terms; much like Milton's "wayes of God to men," these processions are the conceivable and categorizable "aspects" and "actions" by which human beings are able to represent God to themselves in the world.

The language of "processions" here is from Proclus, the fifth century Neoplatonist whose *Elements of Theology* is frequently echoed by Dionysius (and is thus one of the major proofs for the pseudonymous nature of the Dionysian texts).[13] For Proclus, procession (πρόοδοσ—going forth), is the method through which all things are brought into existence, and the basis for how the ineffable may be apprehended, if not actually known. Qualities may be affirmed about the divine—in a strictly limited way—through observing the characteristics of creatures and the created realm. This indirect, or affirmative, method allows for a partial apprehension of the divine, based on extrapolation: "differences within a participant order are determined by the distinctive properties of the principles participated . . .; to each cause is attached, and from each proceeds, that effect which is akin to it."[14] The idea is that each creature (what Proclus calls an existent [ὄντα—that which exists]) participates in (from μετέχο; share in, partake of) the level of existence above it, sharing in the qualities of that higher level, and this chain continues all the way up until it is broken at the point of the One (τοὄν; the highest divine, especially as conceived in the third century A.D. by Plotinus), or what Proclus calls "the unparticipated."[15] This unavailability is precisely why, according to Dionysius, the affirmative method can only ever take the worshipper a limited distance: "we have a habit of seizing upon what is actually beyond us, clinging to the familiar categories of our sense perceptions, and then we measure the divine by our human standards and, of course, are led astray by the apparent meaning we give to the divine and unspeakable reason" (*DN* 106). The words we use about God only point to that which cannot be truly spoken, cannot be captured, summed up, or defined in human terms. The "words we use about God. . . . must not be given the human sense" (*DN* 106).

The words we use about God, in fact, must be withdrawn almost as soon as they are uttered. No name, no quality, and no combination—even infinite combinations—of names and qualities can do any more, ultimately, than point to our own inability to describe and understand the divine:

> we use the names Trinity and Unity for that which is in fact beyond every name, calling it the transcendent being above every being. But no unity or trinity, no number or oneness, no fruitfulness, indeed, nothing that is or is known can proclaim that hiddenness beyond every mind and reason of the transcendent Godhead which transcends every being. (*DN* 129)

And so negation, or apophatic theology is required—not merely as a correction to, but in a fuller sense as a complement to, the affirmations of more traditional cataphatic or positive theology. As Oliver Davies and Denys Turner point out,

> The interdependence of the Mystical Theology and the Divine Names shows the dialectical pulsation between affirmations and negations that characterises the enterprise of Christian negative theology as whole. Here negation is not free-standing, but secures the theological character of the affirmative speech patterns in address to God or speech about God. . . . a movement of negation, as "forgetting", is held in tension with a movement of affirmation . . . and each informs the other.[16]

Nicholas of Cusa, the fifteenth century German theologian, emphasized this interdependence by arguing that negative theology serves as the only safeguard against idolatry: "the theology of negation is so necessary to the theology of affirmation that without it God would be worshipped not as the infinite God but as creature; and such worship is idolatry, for it gives to an image that which belongs only to truth itself."[17]

The complementary nature of the relationship between cataphatic and apophatic—positive and negative—theologies is one of procession and return, a descent from, and ascent to, the divine. As Michael Lieb notes, "Pseudo-Dionysius maintains that [cataphatic theology] embodies a descent from first things to last, that is, from the most abstruse conceptions of deity to their concretization in symbolic form," while its necessary complement, apophatic theology, "involves a return or *epistrophē* upward from last to first things. In this return we discover an obliteration of knowing, understanding, naming, speech, and language as the seer travels into the realm of unknowing, divine ignorance, the nameless, the speechless, and the silent."[18]

When positive and negative theologies are held in a complementary tension, they can be seen as an ongoing attempt to make our theological reach exceed our linguistic grasp. We form images and concepts of the divine in part because that is how we make sense of our experience of the physical world. But these images and concepts are merely symbols, which must remain provisional, fluid, and flexible in order to serve effectively the purpose of bringing humans into relation with the divine. Once these symbols begin to be concretized, once the image or concept begins to be mistaken for that to which it merely points, negation is necessary in order to clear the way again. For Jean-Luc Marion, this difference between the rigid and fluid, the opaque and the transparent, is the signal distinction between "the idol" and "the icon." The idol "expresses a concept of what it then names 'God,'" which process renders the divine (or the *invisable*—Marion's term for that which cannot be aimed at or taken into view) "disqualified and abandoned." The icon, on the other hand, seeks "to allow that the visible not cease to refer to an other than itself."[19] In other words, the idol serves to focus attention to and on itself, while the icon seeks to focus attention beyond itself. The idol is concrete and opaque. The icon is transparent to transcendence. The icons of positive theology remain effective only so long and only so far as they remain transparent to transcendence. Once this transparency begins to cloud, and the icon begins to be regarded as pointing to itself rather than "to an other than itself," the icon has become an idol. Idolatry, or what Marion calls "the idolatrous gaze," arises out of "a sort of essential fatigue," a fatigue that grows out of the strain of worshipping that which cannot truly be contained in human images or concepts. "The gaze settles only inasmuch as it rests—from the weight of upholding the sight of an aim without term, rest, or end." The further "the gaze" pursues this "aim without term, rest, or end," the greater grows the temptation to harden icons into idols, to concretize symbols, to "rest" within "the scope of [what] particular human eyes [or understandings] can support."[20]

Positive theology starts out as an aid to focus beyond the visible, the constrainable, and the definable, but inevitably—as the limits of human sight, understanding, and imagination are reached—it becomes a trap, a prison whose walls are the very images that once served as aids, but now have become impediments. Negation is what can remove these impediments, and can remind us that our images and our concepts are not identical to that to which they merely point. Negation reminds us of our limits. In Dionysius's words, "the more we take flight upward, the more our words are confined to the ideas we are capable of forming" (*MT* 139); thus, it is imperative to remember that the divine is "beyond intellect" and that as we approach it "we shall find ourselves not simply running short of words but actually speechless and unknowing" (*MT* 139). From this point of view, what we say about "God" says little or nothing about the divine itself, but it says a great deal about us, our world, our concepts and categories. The divine as it actually *is*, is "beyond every assertion and denial. We make assertions and denials of what is next to it, but never of it" (*MT* 141).

Dionysian ideas were, of course, available to Milton and to his contemporaries (an English translation of the *Mystical Theology* was published in 1653);[21] though due, at least in part, to the controversy surrounding the authorship and dating of the texts, they were viewed with suspicion by such reformers as Luther (post–1516) and Calvin. The Swiss reformer characterizes Dionysius, "whoever he was," as having "skillfully discussed many matters in his *Celestial Hierarchy*," but judges the discussions to be "for the most part nothing but talk."[22] Luther, in his early work, *Dictata super Psalterium* (Lessons on the Psalms, generally dated between 1513 and 1515), sounds remarkably at one with Pseudo-Dionysius. Dennis Bielfeldt writes of "Luther's praise of Dionysius and the *via negativa*," further showing that "Luther points out that God dwells in 'inaccessible light' such that 'no mind is able to penetrate to him.'" Finally, Luther follows Dionysius up the ladder of negations: "Luther claims that it is Dionysius who taught the way of 'anagogical darkness' which 'ascends through negation. For thus is God hidden and incomprehensible.'"[23] Later, however, as David Steinmetz argues (in a summary of earlier work by Erich Vogelsang),

> Luther rejected Dionysian mysticism absolutely after 1516, in spite of the fact that he makes occasional positive references to it. Dionysian mysticism is too speculative for Luther, too impatient with a God who is found in the humiliated and crucified Jesus. Rather the Dionysian mystic wishes to scamper up a graded ladder of ascent to a God who reigns in glory. But the only ladder to God, Luther believes, is the ladder provided by the humanity of Jesus of Nazareth.[24]

Luther's rejection of Dionysian mysticism is borne out by his characterization of Dionysius as *plus platonizans quam christianizans* (more of a Platonist than a Christian):

> Indeed, to speak more boldly, it greatly displeases me to assign such importance to this Dionysius, whoever he may have been, for he shows hardly any signs of solid learning. . . . in his *Theology*, which is rightly called *Mystical*, of which certain very ignorant theologians make so much, he is downright dangerous, for he is more of a Platonist than a Christian.[25]

Even for Luther, however, who sees a "humiliated and crucified Jesus" as a necessary soteriological element, Steinmetz argues that "Faith penetrates the cloud beyond thinking and speaking where God dwells."[26]

Thus, the basic insight of Pseudo-Dionysius—that images and concepts of God, the realm of "thinking and speaking," must finally be regarded as lesser than that which lies beyond (or within) "the truly mysterious darkness of unknowing" (*DN* 137)—is shared even by the later, more skeptical Luther. The Milton who declares, in *De Doctrina Christiana*, that "God, as he really is, is far beyond man's imagination, let alone his understanding" (YP 6:133), or in the original, "nam Deus, prout in se est humanam cogitationem, nedum sensus longe superat,"[27] would have had no trouble agreeing with that basic Dionysian idea.[28] But Milton goes far beyond Luther here, as is evidenced by his refusal ever to imagine, fully and poetically, the very "humiliated and crucified Jesus" that Luther finds indispensable. Salvation never explicitly requires such a Jesus in Milton's poetry, and a "graded ladder of ascent"—as Steinmetz describes it—is frequently (if often obscurely) outlined for Adam and Eve in *Paradise Lost*. For example, Barbara Lewalski maintains that Milton has Raphael encourage Adam "to love Eve's higher qualities as a means to make a Neoplatonic ascent to heavenly love" in *Paradise Lost*.[29] Though, according to Steinmetz, "Luther does not mean to commend speculative theology"[30]—even on those occasions when he seems to speak favorably of Dionysian ideas—for Milton, it is precisely such a speculative theology that appears in *Paradise Lost*, a theology that regards the divine, as it actually is, as "beyond every assertion and denial."

Milton is hardly alone in such speculative theology, nor is the judgment of Luther and Calvin on Dionysius necessarily that of Milton's contemporaries. Examples abound: from John Everard's posthumously published translation of Dionysius in 1653; to Francis Rous, whose mysticism in *Mystical Marriage* (1631) and *Heavenly Academie* (1638) is indebted to such figures as Thomas à Kempis, Bernard of Clairvaux, and Dionysius; to the Cambridge Platonist Henry More, who was deeply versed in Plotinus, Proclus, and Dionysius (as well as Tauler's mystical *Theologia Germanica*)—in Milton's lifetime, Neoplatonic and apophatic ideas return to the fore with a vengeance. In his epic, Milton actively engages with these ideas, using (as Anna Baldwin argues) "the 'emanationist' view [of nature] associated with Plotinus, [that] vivifies his understanding of nature and of man" in *Paradise Lost*.[31] Baldwin goes on to suggest that Milton may have found these ideas through a reading of Plotinus (either in Greek, or in the Latin translation by Ficino), but he may also have come to them indirectly. Neoplatonic ideas

> were Christianized early on by Byzantine thinkers like Gregory of Nyssa, Dionysius the Areopagite and Maximus, who had been assimilated into the West largely through John Scotus Eriugena in the ninth century. His systematized account of Nature, the *Periphyseon*, opens with an "emanationist" explanation of how all Creation flows out from God, and is destined to ascend back to him. . . . Milton's account of nature sometimes follows Eriugena so closely as to suggest direct influence.[32]

Eriugena, the ninth century Irish monk whose major undertakings included Latin translations of the works of Dionysius, is almost entirely responsible for keeping Neoplatonic and apophatic ideas alive in the Latin West through the early Middle Ages (though the Eastern church always kept the Dionysian corpus as part of its Greek philosophical and theological heritage). But whether Milton adapted his theories of creation and the nature of God from those found in Eriugena, Dionysius, and Plotinus, or simply made them up out of whole cloth, the parallels between his thinking and theirs are profound. As presented in *Paradise Lost*, Milton's is an apophatic theology that gestures toward the transcendent deity by making "assertions and denials of what is next to it, but never of it" (*MT* 141), assertions and denials that are only hinted at in *De Doctrina Christiana*.

De Doctrina Christiana, Paradise Lost, *and Milton's Divine Representations*

The relation of *De Doctrina Christiana* to *Paradise Lost* is a vexed one, and though I believe those who have vigorously pursued the argument that Milton was not, in fact, the author of the theological treatise have not proven their case,[33] the question about the extent to which the treatise can be used as a guide to the poem remains open. To what extent can the positions outlined in the treatise be ascribed to the poem?

A thought-provoking suggestion about the treatise is made by Neil Graves, who argues that Milton's theory of accommodation differs radically from the "traditional theological . . . attempt to explain the difference between the nature of God and the textual images or mental conceptions of him." This theory, which "functions by expressing the incomprehensibility of God in terms which 'accommodate' God to human understanding . . . presupposes that language cannot adequately describe God, while yet authorizing the attempt to depict him, conscious that the resulting image is not a true representation of the deity."[34] Graves suggests that, rather than following this traditional theory—which maintains that "God is accommodated in language through metaphor"—Milton in *De Doctrina Christiana* "envisages a synecdochic theory of scriptural accommodation" that "claims that the image embodies the truth—but not the whole truth" of God. Thus, argues Graves, when Milton writes, "God has revealed only so much of himself as our minds can bear" (YP 6:133), what he means is that "God has actually revealed himself, although incompletely, and not that he has revealed merely a symbol for himself." In discussing Milton's analysis of the "back parts" of God in Exodus, chapter 33, Graves seizes on Milton's idea that "we do not consider that what are called *the back parts* of God in Exodus xxxiii, are, strictly speaking, God, yet we do not deny that they are eternal" (YP 6.312). Graves argues that this illustrates Milton's departure from an accommodationist model: "*The back parts* themselves are not an accommodated image which bears no direct congruence to the personage of God, but instead are a partially perceived aspect of God's being itself and as an existent substance are thus accorded the predicate 'eternal.'"[35]

Here, the Neoplatonic underpinnings of negative theology can help bring Graves's argument into clearer focus: when Milton argues that "the back parts" are not God, but are eternal, he is not attempting to have it both ways—they either are or are not God. For Milton, they are not. But as Graves expresses it, they are "a partially perceived aspect" of God and, as such, are eternal. Plotinus (the "Father," if you will, of Neoplatonism), describes the divine in a way that helps to make sense of Milton's description of the "back parts" as eternal. The One (Plotinus's ultimate divine—beyond all categories and description) "can produce nothing less than the very greatest that is later than itself." This product of the One is "the Divine Mind," or *Nous* (the intelligent, active divine). In turn, *Nous* gives rise to "soul" or *Psyche* (the divine that can be perceived operating in humankind and the world), which "is an image and must look to its own original."[36] *Nous* is eternal, but it is not the One. *Psyche* is neither eternal, nor the One. But both have their source in the One, and continually look both below (*Nous* to *Psyche*, *Psyche* to the world of the senses) and back to the One. What Milton does, in explaining "the back parts" of God as eternal, is to borrow a recognizably Neoplatonic, or Plotinian, trope—explaining what might otherwise seem a metaphor ("back parts") as an emanation ("not, strictly speaking, God, yet . . . eternal"), or as Graves characterizes it, "a partially perceived aspect" of God. The back parts (or the *kavod*—rendered by the KJV as "glory") of Exodus 33:22 are not God in the sense of *containing, rather than being contained by,* the totality of the divine (or the One, in Plotinian terms)—after all, as Yahweh insists to Moses at 33:20, "Thou canst not see my face: for there shall no man see me, and live"—but they are, as Pseudo-Dionysius puts it, "what is next to it" (*MT* 141). In other words, in a synecdochic theory (rather than the orthodox accommodationist view), the images of God presented in Scripture would have their source, not in a divine condescension to a limited human understanding, but in a divine reality (emanation) that a limited human understanding can only partially perceive, seeing though a glass darkly, as it were. But either way, the limits of human speech and thought are the same: we make "assertions and denials of what is next to it, but never of it" (*MT* 141). Ultimately, all we can speak about is the image (the symbol or the part), not what is referred to by the image (the symbolized or the whole).

Barbara Lewalski has suggested a reading of Milton's images of the divine that is quite similar to that of Graves, though she goes on to apply the theory of images in *De Doctrina Christiana* to *Paradise Lost*. Lewalski argues that Milton

> entirely repudiates all attempts to explain what seems unworthy of God by anthropopathy (the figurative ascription of human feelings to God), making the radical claim that every aspect of God's portrayal of himself in the Bible—including his expression of humanlike emotions and his manifestation in something like human form—should form part of our conception of him.[37]

Milton, who avers, "We ought not to imagine that God would have said anything or caused anything to be written about himself unless he intended that it should be a part of our conception of him" (YP 6:134), is, according to Lewalski, using this idea to "find biblical warrant for portraying God as an epic character who expresses a range of emotions . . ., who makes himself visible and audible to his creatures by various means, and who engages in dialogue with his Son and with Adam."[38]

Regardless of their origin, and despite being what Milton characterizes in *De Doctrina Christiana* as God's own self-revelation ("God has revealed only so much of himself as our minds can bear" [YP 6:133]), these images (or revelations) are too often misunderstood by their human perceivers. In the passages Lewalski highlights, Milton repeatedly references the idea of human imagination and belief: "We ought not *to imagine*"; "*let us believe* that he did repent"; "*let us believe* that it is not beneath God to feel . . ., to be refreshed . . ., and to fear" (YP 6:134–35; emphasis added). These are not arguments about what God *is*, but about how God should be *imagined* or *understood* by human beings. Whether Milton's theory of representation is metaphorical or synecdochic, the danger is the same. Just as the danger with metaphor (the basis for orthodox accommodation theory) is that the metaphor will be concretized, that the symbolic nature of the relation of unlikes that comprises the metaphor will be lost or literalized, so the danger with synecdoche is that the part, which merely *represents* the whole, will be mistaken *for* or *as* the whole. Taking a part of the divine, and identifying it as the whole of the divine, is just as much idolatry as is taking an accommodated image of the divine and losing track of the distinction between the image and what that image represents.

But the question of the relation of *De Doctrina Christiana* to *Paradise Lost* remains. Peter Herman argues that "it seems that Milton abandoned working on this text at the Restoration to concentrate on writing verse," and that "the movement from *De Doctrina Christiana* to *Paradise Lost* also entailed a movement from confidence to doubt."[39] Herman puts this "movement from confidence to doubt" in the context of a failed revolution, and a realization on Milton's part that his confidence—rooted in his image of God—had been misplaced. Milton's assertions had turned out to be disastrously wrong: "Milton built his theology and self-confidence on the reassuring certitude of God's approbation of the Revolution." In other words, "God is on the republican's side," rather than that of the royalist. If Milton is, as Herman argues, "engaged in a wholesale questioning of just about everything he had argued for in his prose works," and if "*he does not come to a conclusion*," perhaps that is because there is no positive conclusion to be reached.[40] In that case, what Milton struggles with in *Paradise Lost* is a project of negation, challenging or even dismantling the certainties on which he had once relied—certainties about what God is, about what God wants, about whom God supports—in favor of uncertainty, undecidability, and unknowing. The "movement from confidence to doubt" that Herman argues for can be seen as Milton's radical reevaluation of his beliefs about God. The synecdochic theory of divine imagery that Graves finds in *De Doctrina Christiana*, and that Lewalski applies to *Paradise Lost*, requires a measure of conviction that I think Milton had come to question in the years immediately following the Restoration. In essence, Milton's move from *De Doctrina Christiana* to *Paradise Lost* is a move away from the idolatry inherent in being *certain* about what cannot be reduced to certainty, and being *knowing* about what cannot be known in human terms.

Milton's is an argument against idolatry, no matter what the ultimate source of the "idol" may be. I believe that what Milton is doing in *Paradise Lost* is highlighting the distinction between the image and that which is imagined, between the metaphor and that which is represented. In so doing, Milton is making assertions and denials about what is next to the divine (the concepts and images through which humans understand and worship a "God" they can only dimly, if at all, perceive, a divinity that is far beyond their thinking and imagining), but never of the divine itself. The images of the divine that are put forward, critiqued, confidently asserted, or nervously and doubtfully expressed—these are what is next to "it," but they are not "it." *Paradise Lost,* though it has (too) often been read as if it expressed a vigorously positive theology, is a constantly shifting poetic ground, one where negation, not affirmation, is both the prime moving energy for, and the interpretive principle that makes sense of the conflicts between confidence and doubt that so often threaten to rend Milton's great epic. The conflicts are not resolved, nor can they be. They are, I believe, meant to be experienced as painful, and as irresolvable. Milton does not present what God *is*—indeed he cannot do so—in *Paradise Lost*. But what he can, and does, do is show his characters' various attempts along the same lines, highlighting the contradictions along the way. To each and every image that is raised, to each and every definition that is offered, the poem's response is *not this*.

May I Express Thee Unblamed: Negative Theology in Paradise Lost

Paradise Lost contains numerous passages where uncertain or contradictory ideas of God are expressed. The instances I will focus on here—the expressed ambition to "justifie the wayes of God to men" of book 1; the invocation to light in book 3, followed by the perspective on God of the poem's narrator; the devils' perspectives on God from books 1 and 2; Raphael's curious remark about God's mixing "destruction with creation" in his conversation with Adam; and Adam and Eve's prayer that they receive only good from God—all illustrate the doubts and incongruities that abound in *Paradise Lost* when the topic turns to the nature of the divine. Each of these constructions of the deity is an artifact that says more about the one constructing it than it does about the deity itself. And each of these constructions is contradicted or negated almost as soon as it is made.

In the context of apophatic theology (which insists that God is above being, and therefore no being at all, a nothing, or no-thing), how can one make sense of the attempt to "justifie the wayes of God to men" (1.26)? After all, it would seem to be only common sense that one "justifies," not a nothing, but a something (or a someone) that actually exists. While I have discussed elsewhere the theological implications of "justifie," the part of the famous phrase to focus on here is "the wayes of God."[41] Milton's famous ambition relies on a crucial distinction that is strongly reminiscent of that made by such Byzantine church figures as Gregory Palamas (1296–1359), whose Hesychast (stillness or quiet, from Greek *hesychia*) theology was affirmed by the Eastern church at the councils of 1341, 1347, and 1351 in Constantinople.[42] These councils established a real distinction between the unknowable essence of God and the energies or observable acts of God (what Milton calls "the wayes of God").[43] It is these acts (or ways) that enable humans to have a relationship with a God that is beyond their understanding. Palamas's understanding of the divine owed much to Pseudo-Dionysius and, more generally, to apophatic theology.[44] Likewise, Milton's attempt to justify, not God, but the *ways* of God makes a distinction between the unknowable essence and the observable acts of God, a distinction that makes a positive / cataphatic argument for the possibility of human relatedness to the observable acts of God (including personal revelations of the kind found in Scripture), but also makes a negative / apophatic argument for the impossibility of knowing the God beyond names. The difference between an attempt to justify the ways of God, and an attempt to justify God could not possibly be greater—the first project, though it sounds impossibly hubristic, is quite the opposite—acknowledging the gap between human understanding and the unknowable divine essence. The second project would be hubristic in the extreme, implying that its undertaker (Milton) knew both the knowable and unknowable aspects of the divine. The difference is so great that Milton's care in spelling out which project he was undertaking must be noted, and accounted for, in reading the poem that pursues the project of justification.

The parallels between Milton's projects in *Paradise Lost* and the apophatic and Neoplatonic tradition are further demonstrated in a consideration of Milton's use of an *ex Deo* (out of God) theory of Creation. Christopher Hill contends that Milton "did not believe that God created the universe *ex nihilo*," which would have "seemed to Milton both logically meaningless and an impossible translation of the relevant Hebrew, Greek and Latin texts of the Bible. He believed in creation *ex deo*."[45] J. H. Adamson refers to this as Milton's "poetically conceived" theory:

> It was the theory advanced by Plotinus of creation *ex Deo*, a theory dominated by the metaphor of the sun and its radiance. As the sun poured out an eternal stream of light, so the Uncreated Essence overflowed with life which penetrated down into all levels of being. Having reached the lowest level, it turned again and, yearning for its source, traveled back through the levels of being until it once more reached the Divine.[46]

For Pseudo-Dionysius, creation is accomplished by emanation, a process through which the divine is "enticed away from his transcendent dwelling place and comes to abide within all things" (*DN* 82). This divine that abides within all things is what the Eastern Hesychast tradition refers to as the energies of God (essentially, the divine as manifested in creation). For Milton, in *De Doctrina Christiana*, and again later in *Paradise Lost*, God creates not *ex nihilo* (out of nothing) but out of preexisting material that was part of God's own substance.[47] Though neither of these ideas is a precise analogy to the unwilled process of emanation as explained by Plotinus in the *Enneads* (5.1.6), or the course of procession and reversion outlined by Proclus in *The Elements of Theology* (sections 25–39),[48] they are analogous to the extent that each idea insists that the creation shares intimately in the nature of the Creator.[49] But how can that shared nature be realized if the divine is only knowable "through a glass darkly," through the acts, energies, or "wayes of God to men"? This can not, certainly, be accomplished merely through the established rites and rituals of the external church (West *or* East)—though as long as the symbolic nature of these rites and rituals is not forgotten, as long as the metaphor is not concretized, and the symbol mistaken for that to which it merely points, such churches can serve a valuable function. No, something more is needed. It is this something more that is imagined by Dionysius as a wordless, silent state beyond concepts and images. It is this something more that Gregory Palamas imagined as the *hesychia*, the quiet, the stillness necessary to achieve spiritual union with God through a vision of divine light. It is this something more that Milton imagines in terms remarkably similar to the inner light of his contemporaries, the Quakers, an idea to which he gave poetic expression as "A Paradise within thee, happier farr" (10.1478) than the Eden of Adam and Eve.

With the distinction between God and the ways of God, however, comes the tension between positive and negative approaches to the divine. The tensions between positive and negative theologies, between the ideas that the divine can, and cannot, be known or imagined are especially evident in the invocation to light of book 3:[50]

> Hail holy light, ofspring of Heav'n first-born,
> Or of th' Eternal Coeternal beam
> May I express thee unblam'd? since God is light,
> And never but in unapproached light
> Dwelt from Eternitie, dwelt then in thee,
> Bright effluence of bright essence increate.
> Or hear'st thou rather pure Ethereal stream,
> Whose Fountain who shall tell? before the Sun,
> Before the Heavens thou wert, and at the voice
> Of God, as with a Mantle didst invest
> The rising world of waters dark and deep,
> Won from the void and formless infinite.   (3.1–12)[51]

This invocation expresses both positive (in the sense of *posited*) images of the divine, and a corresponding unease about the appropriateness, the limits, even the accuracy of those images. Starting with "holy light," an abstract image that manages to make the divine available to the human visual imagination without anthropomorphic imagery, the invocation moves immediately to something more concrete, more human: "ofspring of Heav'n first-born." But then the narrator immediately retreats back into the abstract, and still more abstract: what, after all, is an "Eternal Coeternal beam"? The images so far on offer exist in a liminal space between the almost purely conceptual and abstract ("Eternal Coeternal beam"), the ethereal yet measurable ("holy light"—a phrase that holds together both the immeasurable—"holiness"—and the measurable—"light"), and the anthropomorphic ("ofspring" and "first-born"). What follows, however, is the key to the entire invocation: "May I express thee unblam'd?" The question is asked in all seriousness—may I, without blame, without fault, without making a fundamental error, use *any* of the aforementioned images as ways of truly expressing (not just describing, but capturing, through words and images, the reality, the substance of that which is described—think of "express" as ex-press: to press out or squeeze out) the divine? May I, without reducing the object of my description, express the divine with words? Does even the very process of such expression reduce the irreducible, take as an object that which is not any kind of object, treat as a noun requiring a predicate that upon which no thing can be predicated? The dilemma is palpable, confusing, and urgent. If the divine cannot be described, cannot be expressed, how ever can this poem achieve its stated ambition to "justifie the wayes of God to men" (1.26)?

The very next phrase seems to indicate a return of confidence, a return, at least, of confidence in language's facility for describing God: "God is light." But the language quickly becomes unsteady, indicating uncertainty about the relationship of God and light that had seemed certain and easily defined in the initial three-word phrase. If "God is light" and "never but in unapproached light / Dwelt from Eternitie" and "dwelt then in thee," then a tenuous equation seems to hold between God, the dwelling place of God, and the "thee" being addressed in the invocation.[52] Who, or what, is being addressed here? Is it the Son, who will play so crucial a role in the rest of book 3? Is it the Father, with whom the Son will argue for mercy to be shown to as-yet-unfallen humankind? Is it what a Trinitarian Christian might refer to as the Holy Spirit ("hail holy light")? Is it the poetic muse? Is it Wisdom or *Ḥokmah*, the feminine figure who existed with God before Creation, and was by his side, "daily his delight, rejoicing always before him" (Prov. 8:30) as the works of creation unfolded?

Milton is addressing all of these things. But more importantly, he is addressing none of these things. In a few brief lines, Milton's poetry both proffers and withdraws positive (or posited) images and ideas through which the divine might be understood in—or reduced to—human terms and concepts. "God is light" and dwells in "unapproached light" from "Eternitie," *and* "dwelt then in thee / Bright effluence of bright essence increate." Here is a profusion of concepts and images (naturalistic, philosophical, Trinitarian) offered as ways of understanding the divine. But then—immediately—doubt creeps in, with the use of a single word: "or".[53] "Or hear'st thou rather pure Ethereal stream, / Whose Fountain who shall tell?" Or is it none of these things, neither light, nor offspring, neither the "Eternal Coeternal beam" nor *of* the "Eternal Coeternal beam"? Perhaps it is (or is of) this "Ethereal stream" with a source (or without a source?) that cannot be told, or even known.

Perhaps. And perhaps not. The undecidability, the unknowability, is the point. Conventional explanations that would have readers understanding this passage as a repetition of the standard epic call to the muse, or an Arian description of the subordinate nature of the Son's relation to the Father, or an "orthodox" treatment of the Son / Father relationship that merely nods toward either Antitrinitarianism or "subordinationism" all remain firmly within the positive tradition.[54] These explanations insist that Milton is trying to force his poetry to say—in one way, or in several contradictory ways—that God *is* this, or God *is* that. However, the structure of the invocation, the alternating moments of confidence and doubt, and the profusion of definitions that are no sooner offered than negated argue for a different way of understanding Milton's project here, and throughout *Paradise Lost.* Just as for Pseudo-Dionysius, so for Milton, "the more we take flight upward, the more our words are confined to the ideas we are capable of forming" (*MT* 139). Milton's narrator is expressing, not God, but the state that Dionysius describes as "the truly mysterious darkness of unknowing" (*DN* 137). The narrator does not know—*cannot know*—to whom or to what he is referring in this invocation.[55] Henry Vaughan, in his poem "The Night," achieves much the same effect as does Milton in describing the indescribable: "There is in God (some say) / A deep, but dazzling darkness" (49–50)—a darkness that represents, poetically, the inability of humans to see and think beyond the limits of their senses and intellects. But where

Vaughan seems to take this state of affairs as a given (ending the poem by wishing for "that night! Where I in him / Might live invisible and dim" [53–54]),[56] Milton throughout *Paradise Lost* pushes, with almost Samsonic force, against the limits of his descriptive capabilities, having his various characters try one, and then another, and still another image or concept that might be used to nail down the nature of the divine, to shine a light on that deep but dazzling darkness. But each description, each light, tells the reader more about the describer, about the shiner of the light, than it does about the ostensible object being described and illuminated. In essence, each character in *Paradise Lost* creates his or her own "God," as can be seen through a comparison of the narrator, Satan and his "infernal crew," Adam and Eve, and Raphael.

The narrator gives us "the Almighty Father" who "High Thron'd above all highth, bent down his eye, / His own works and their works at once to view" (3.56, 58–59). This God is, like Lear, every inch a king—a deliverer of imperious pronouncements who will thunder forth with the emotion of the moment and then just as quickly retreat into mildness and affectionate regard. His speech on the Fall of mankind (3.80–134) is a masterpiece of emotional volatility, rising from the flat desert plains of the consideration of "our adversarie, whom no bounds / Prescrib'd, no barrs of Hell / . . . can hold" (81–82, 84) to the volcanic peaks of his rage against humanity, "whose fault? / Whose but his own? ingrate, he had of mee / All he could have" (96–98), to the self-justifying descent into equivocation, "if I foreknew, / Foreknowledge had no influence on their fault, / Which had no less prov'd certain unforeknown" (117–19), before finally coming to rest in the valley of mercy, "Mercy first and last shall brightest shine" (134). A deity this volatile is far from the impassible "Unmoved Mover" of Aristotle, or the character that Stanley Fish describes as one whose "presentation is determinedly non-affective."[57] The narrator constructs a God very much along the lines of the biblical Yahweh—"Great are thy works, *Jehovah*, infinite / Thy power" (7.602–03)—and Yahweh is about as passible and affective as deities get.[58]

The God constructed by Satan and his compatriots is quite different, colder, more calculating, and infinitely more in control than the narrator's God.[59] Satan's God is a tyrant, "hee / Who now is Sovran" (1.245–46), who had long "Sat on his Throne, upheld by old repute, / Content or custome" (1.639–40) while slyly not showing all in order to tempt Satan into the very misstep he has just made: "but still his strength conceal'd, / Which tempted our attempt, and wrought our fall" (1.641–42). In the debate scenes of book 2, the demons construct a portrait of a God whose wrath is premeditated, a deliberate strategy rather than a spontaneous outpouring of negative emotion (in contrast to the God the narrator describes). For Moloch, God is a "Torturer" (2.64), but one who inflicts pain coldly, through technology and invention, what Moloch describes as *"Tartarean* Sulphur, and strange fire, / His own invented Torments" (2.69–70). Belial, on the other hand, pictures God as an all-seeing eye (my apologies to J. R. R. Tolkein and Peter Jackson): "what can force or guile / With him, or who deceive his mind, whose eye / Views all things at one view?" (2.188–90). Belial also sees God as a judge who might, just *might*, be placated into giving the demons, if not time off, at least tortures off for good behavior: "Our Supream Foe in time may much remit / His anger, and perhaps thus farr remov'd / Not mind us not offending" (2.210–12). Mammon sees God as both a tyrant and a master of shifting appearances—Mammon's God is at once the object of bile in the phrase "how wearisom / Eternity so spent in worship paid / To whom we hate" (2.247–49), and a dweller in darkness, deep but dazzling in its own way:

> How oft amidst
> Thick clouds and dark doth Heav'ns all-ruling Sire
> Choose to reside, his Glory unobscur'd,
> And with the Majesty of darkess round
> Covers his Throne; from whence deep thunders roar
> Must'ring thir rage, and Heav'n resembles Hell?   (2.263–68)

For the demons, God is a tyrant who can only be dealt with head-on, a torturer who can only be fought with his own inventions, a judge who *might* be reasoned with or placated, and an implacable tyrant who can neither be reasoned with nor overcome, but whose facility with appearances might profitably be imitated. Beelzebub and Satan put the finishing touches on this incoherent picture by positing a God who cannot be placated, reasoned with, or attacked head-on, but who *can* (despite Belial's picture of God as an all-seeing eye) be fought indirectly, by attacking the outermost and least-defended portion of creation: Earth and its inhabitants, Adam and Eve.

Adam and Eve's constructions of God, as well as that implied in Raphael's story of Creation, revolve around anxiety, specifically a fear that God is just as capable of and inclined to providing evil as he is disposed to providing good. Where the narrator's God is emotionally volatile, the God constructed by Adam, Eve, and Raphael is quite nearly schizophrenic. Fear—in the sense of terror, not respect—is the primary response to such a deity. Eve, who in book 5 dreams of the tree of life, and of her own future action of eating from it, elicits just such fear in herself and in Adam, who begins to worry over Eve, the source of the dream, the nature of evil, and the ability of God to entertain, and possibly act upon, evil:

> The trouble of thy thoughts this night in sleep
> Affects me equally; nor can I like
> This uncouth dream, of evil sprung I fear;
> Yet evil whence? in thee can harbour none,
> Created pure.
>   . . . .
> Evil into the mind of God or Man
> May come and go, so unapprov'd, and leave
> No spot of blame behind: Which gives me hope
> That what in sleep thou didst abhorr to dream,
> Waking thou never wilt consent to do.   (5.96–100, 117–21)

Evil thoughts may, and do, come, says Adam, but as long as we do not act upon such thoughts, such evil leaves no taint, does no damage. So far, so good. But Adam's explanation is made to seem like so much whistling past the graveyard when he and Eve specifically pray that they be given only good by God, praying, in essence, that God lets whatever evil comes into his mind pass unapproved, and unacted upon:

> Hail universal Lord, be bounteous still
> To give us onely good; and if the night
> Have gathered aught of evil or conceald,
> Disperse it, as now light dispels the dark.   (5.205–08)

Why is such a prayer necessary? An invocation requesting "onely good" from God—one that regards such good as a bounty or boon from the deity at that—is a tacit admission that the speaker of the invocation regards God as a potential source of good *and* evil. Much like the God spoken of in Job 2:10, a deity from whose hands "we receive good" and "receive evil" (or like the deity spoken of at Lamentations 3:38, where the question is asked: "Out of the mouth of the most High proceedeth not evil and good?"), the figure to whom Adam prays here, though *currently* a benefactor, is clearly also regarded as a potential threat.

This image of God is reinforced by Raphael's curious characterization of the Father as being quite capable of mixing destruction with creation, and doing so as the result of a temper tantrum. Raphael cannot give Adam a firsthand account of Adam's creation (thus opening the door for Adam to do so himself), because he had been sent on a mission:

> For I that Day was absent, as befell,
> Bound on a voyage uncouth and obscure,
> Farr on excursion toward the Gates of Hell;
> Squar'd in full Legion (such command we had)
> To see that none thence issu'd forth a spie,
> Or enemie, while God was in his work,
> Least hee incenst at such eruption bold,
> Destruction with Creation might have mixt.   (7.866–73)

Unlike Adam, who seems to hope against hope that the God he fears will not act upon the evil that comes into his mind, Raphael takes for granted, not only that God *can* but that God *will* act upon such evil, and all because he cannot control his anger. But it gets better (or worse, depending on your point of view)—Raphael's God is not just irrational, not just temperamental, not just inclined to destructive behavior: no, Raphael's God is also a royal hypocrite (literally). The offered rationale for mixing destruction with creation is the "eruption bold" of a "spie" or "enemie" from hell, who might catch a glimpse of the creative process in action, and thus spoil it by causing God to lose his temper and break the very thing(s) he had been making. (Here, Raphael's God appears as an auteur in high dudgeon—a volatile and high-maintenance *artiste* who would not be out of place in any high-culture capital today.) To avert this destructive scene, Raphael testifies that he was sent with a full legion to prevent a jailbreak, thus warding off both the intrusion and the tantrum. But such an "eruption bold" could only have happened, as Raphael explains, because God *allowed* it to happen:

> Not that they durst without his leave attempt,
> But us he sends upon his high behests
> For state, as Sovran King, and to enure
> Our prompt obedience.   (7.874–77)

In other words, Raphael was sent on a mission in order to prevent an "eruption bold" that he would have been unable to prevent—because it would have been undertaken with the permission of the very God who sent Raphael in the first place—and the mission was assigned, not with any realistic prospects of success in mind, but simply to further ingrain obedience (to even the most irrational of commands) in the already obsequious angel.[60] Since the entire bizarre mission was undertaken, according to Raphael, to deflect the possibility that God "Destruction with Creation might have mixt" (7.873), it seems then that Raphael and his crew were especially "Glad [to have] return'd up to the coasts of Light" after having found "fast shut / The dismal Gates" (7.883, 877–78), and glad primarily from a sense of relief that God's violence (rather than Satan's) had been forestalled.

Each of the preceding examples shows characters (the narrator, Satan and his angels, Adam and Eve, and Raphael) whose thinking is firmly ensconced within a positive theological framework—for these characters, God *is* what they perceive him to be and what they define him as being. But each definition is different, often quite radically so, from every other definition—and the individual definitions are often themselves contradictory or tentative. Satan, for example, defines God as a tyrant in books 1 and 2, but seems to waver in the famous soliloquy of book 4, only to return to his earlier definition. Adam and Eve are certain that God is good, except when they fear that God is not good (or is, at least, *potentially* not good or the potential source of that which is not good). Raphael cheerfully assumes that the human pair's fears are correct—God *is* the source of destruction.

But Raphael also defines God as the source of a perfect creation—despite what he seems to think is the very real possibility that the very same God might, at any moment, have mixed destruction into his creation:

> O *Adam*, one Almightie is, from whom
> All things proceed, and up to him return,
> If not deprav'd from good, created all
> Such to perfection, one first matter all.   (5.469–72)

So which is it? Is God good? Yes. Is God potentially evil? Yes. Is God almighty? Yes. Is God light? Yes. Is God a king? Yes. Is God a tyrant? Yes.

But no.

The contradictions, the descriptions that offer first one image of God and then another—very different—image, are included, even highlighted in *Paradise Lost* in order to make a simple, but supremely important point: these "Gods" are not God. The narrator's abstract light image is not God. The narrator's glorious king is not God. Satan's dark, opprobrious tyrant is not God. Adam and Eve's provider of good, who is still "bounteous" enough not to bring evil, is not God. Raphael's preemptory and obedience-inuring commander is not God. Each and every one of these constructions says more about the speaker than about what is ostensibly being spoken of or described. What each of Milton's characters worships, fears, loves, resents, or merely speaks of, is an idol, in Marion's terms, rather than an icon. The narrator's king is not transparent to transcendence, pointing beyond himself, but is opaque, pointing rather insistently right at himself. Satan's tyrant is not transparent to transcendence either, and in fact is so opaque an idol that it is just as insistent in pointing at Satan and the Father (or the God-image Satan has created) as is it is in not pointing beyond itself to an ineffable, unknowable God. A tyrant, after all, is neither ineffable nor unknowable.

Why does Milton, the famous iconoclast, present such a profusion of divine imagery in *Paradise Lost?* Like so many other religious thinkers who have come to the point that they are ready—even impelled in some way—to move beyond images, Milton is attempting, in the terms of Meister Eckhart's famous prayer to be able "for

God's sake [. . . to] take leave of god,"[61] to leave off worshipping that which he understands (his own images and concepts of God) and begin worshipping that which he does not, and can never, fully understand—the God beyond names. In *Paradise Lost,* Milton creates and rejects images of God—showing the divine as a warrior king, as a tyrant, as a creator and destroyer, a deliverer of sometimes irrational-seeming commands, an imperious figure whose sole delight is in obsequious shows of obedience and submission, and even as a tentatively conceived abstraction (light)—in order to emphasize that such images are merely images, generated by and for human beings. In making such a point, Milton refuses to take comfort by applying what Neil Graves suggests is the synecdochic theory of divine representation in *De Doctrina Christiana* to *Paradise Lost,* and in so refusing, Milton moves away, as Peter Herman suggests, from the "reassuring certitude of God's approbation" as part of an overall "movement from confidence to doubt."[62]

In so moving, Milton is swimming directly upstream. At a time when God is loudly asserted to be the avenger of sins, a bringer of plague and fire, and either an Anglican or Nonconformist partisan, the 1667 edition of *Paradise Lost* is at least as bold as any of Milton's earlier prose works—whether against the episcopacy or the monarchy—because this time the "double tyrannie, of Custom from without and blind affections within" (YP 3:190) that Milton takes on is nothing less than the "tyrannie" inherent in imagining God as one's own partisan.

Here, perhaps, a comparison to our own day may be in order, given that God is again being invoked to explain disasters that have brought death and destruction after them. Fawzan Al-Fawzan, a professor at Al-Imam University in Saudi Arabia, claimed—in a television interview about the devastating tsunami of December 2004 in Indonesia—that "these great tragedies and collective punishments that are wiping out villages, towns, cities and even entire countries, are Allah's punishments of the people of these countries."[63] In 2001, the American televangelist Jerry Falwell, in an interview on fellow televangelist Pat Robertson's show, *700 Club,* declared that the September 11 attacks on the World Trade Center towers were a result of God's judgment on a sinful United States of America:

what we saw on Tuesday, as terrible as it is, could be miniscule if, in fact God continues to lift the curtain and allow the enemies of America to give us probably what we deserve. . . . God will not be mocked. . . . I really believe that the pagans, and the abortionists, and the feminists, and the gays and the lesbians who are actively trying to make that an alternative lifestyle, the ACLU, People For the American Way, all of them who have tried to secularize America. I point the finger in their face and say "you helped this happen."[64]

Make a few minor alterations to the names of the groups being accused, as well as the roll call of so-called sins, and this statement could very well have been made in response to the disasters of mid-1660s London, where sexual, epicurean, and various other broadly ideological "sins" were blamed for the tragedies of plague and fire. It is precisely this kind of thinking, this knowingness about the judgments (or nonjudgments) of God, that Milton is rejecting in *Paradise Lost*. In the England of the mid-1660s, there were more than enough Robert Elboroughs and Thomas Vincents declaring death and destruction to be the punishments inflicted by God on a wayward and sinful people. In publishing *Paradise Lost* in 1667, in this milieu of hysteria, presumption, and idolatry posing as piety, Milton is not seeking to join their numbers, but is, instead, throwing down his gauntlet in response to those who would presume to know the unknowable.[65] In undertaking to "justifie the wayes of God to men" (1.26), Milton presents so bewildering a variety of conceptions of who that "God" is, and what those "wayes" are, that it finally becomes impossible to decide between them. Looked at from one perspective, *Paradise Lost* becomes a celebration of the perfections of divine kingship.[66] From another perspective, *Paradise Lost* becomes a critique of images of kingship, both human and divine, a critique, in fact, of the habit of imagining the transcendent deity in the terms of a human political role.[67] Much ink can be spilled arguing which of these—or many others—opposing perspectives on Milton's "God" (the character he creates) is correct. But such arguments, I think, are all part of the overall structure of the attempt to see Milton's work in—or force his work into—the terms of a rarely questioned "positive" theology. In this essay I hope to have stepped outside the positive (cataphatic) tradition of reading Milton's "God," but I must make my point as clearly and forcefully as I can: we have missed the point.

We have gotten Milton wrong in a crucial way.

To the extent that any of us interpret Milton's great epic as if he were trying to define what God actually *is*, I believe we are fundamentally misreading the poem. By reading Milton as if he were using the occasion of an epic poem to defend that God against charges of wickedness, although demonstrating, rather than defusing the charges,[68] we miss something crucial. Likewise, in reading Milton as if he were using his poem to demonstrate the goodness of the same God,[69] or using the epic to demonstrate the sinfulness of the reader who does not immediately and consistently agree that the goodness of God has, indeed, been demonstrated[70] we have missed an essential feature of *Paradise Lost*. We have taken Milton's repeated examples of *not this, not this*, as if they were positive statements, as if they were *this, this*. Published at a time when all too many of Milton's contemporaries were positive they knew both that God *had* chosen to bring plague and fire down upon London, and *why* God had chosen to visit such disasters on the city's people, *Paradise Lost* tried valiantly then, as it continues to try now, to pull its readers up the graded ladder of ascent from such easy and idolatrous certitudes to the mysterious darkness of unknowing. The multiplicity of perspectives on "God" in *Paradise Lost*, which, like the garden therein, "with wanton growth derides / Tending to wilde" (8.211–12), serves not to define the deity, but instead to call attention to the limits—and dangers—of the attempt at definition itself.

"That which by creation first brought forth Light out of darkness!"
Paradise Lost, First Edition

John T. Shawcross

Authorial revisions are instructive in many ways. We may think of the alternate ending of Charles Dickens's *Great Expectations* or of the numerous alterations that William Butler Yeats made to many of his poems, notably "Sailing to Byzantium," or the significantly different text of the second version of William Faulkner's "The Bear." These authorial revisions give us an insight into the development of a writer's thought; his or her decisions to present a text that is more accurate, more connotational and referential or allusive, more exacting in language and image; they may point to changed aims or revised points of view or reconsidered strategies in presenting those aims or points of view. Authorial revisions may have significance for the author in demonstrating his sorting out what he wants to say and how he wants to say it, but also for the reader in clarification of what the author says and wants that reader to recognize and weigh. And we have a number of examples from John Milton's work of revision that may point to any or all of these purposes. The second edition of his epic *Paradise Lost* in 1674 points to these same concerns as well as a bowing down to commercial demands.

At a Solemn Music is worked out in the Trinity manuscript in three and a half versions, yet its last line is not doctrinally and logically

213

corrected until it appears in print in 1645. Four times Milton presents the multitude with palms in their hands before the throne of God (from Rev. 7:9): "till God e're long / to his celestiall consort us unite / To live & sing wth him in endlesse morne of light." Of course, God did not join in the singing, but it is not until the poem was printed that Milton altered the last line to: "To live with him, and sing in endles morn of light." Even after a poem had appeared in print, it might sustain change, as in lines 143–44 of *Ode on the Morning of Christs Nativity*, which in 1645 read:

> Yea Truth, and Justice then
> Will down return to men,
> Th'enameld *Arras* of the Rainbow wearing
> And Mercy set between.

In the second edition of the *Poems* in 1673 these lines became:

> Yea Truth, and Justice then
> Will down return to men,
> Orb'd in a Rain-bow; and like glories wearing
> Mercy will sit between.

The first version of 1629 celebrates the end of time when the Age of Gold will return to humankind, and through Christ, Peace, symbolized by the rainbow, will reign, as the confluence of the other three daughters of God—Truth, Mercy, and Justice—predicates. The term "Arras," unfortunately, can suggest a covering over of something (a wall) by a fabric with some kind of design on it, and having Truth and Justice "wear" such a fabric or garment does not present them as pure and forthright personifications. Further, "enameld" implies not only a colorful, semitransparent, and glossy surface, but an application of those colors onto some kind of hard metallic object, not a fabric, setting up a contradiction in the image. However, that the arc of the rainbow (Noah's "bow in the cloud") had affinities to fabric for Milton early on (in 1634) can be seen in *A Mask*: "but first I must put off / These my sky robes spun out of *Iris* woof / And take the weeds and likenes of a swain" (82–84).

Further still, the verb "set" requires that someone placed Mercy between the other two, a placement that emerges in the source of

the image, Psalm 85:10: "Mercy and truth are met together; righteousness and peace have kissed each other." But Milton's own ren-
dition of that text in 1648 is:

> Mercy and Truth *that long were miss'd*
> Now *joyfully* are met;
> *Sweet* Peace and Righteousness have kiss'd
> *And hand in hand are set.*   (41–44)

By 1673, however, he seems to have realized the problem with an
"enameled" "Arras" and with wearing anything that might tend to
obliterate unclouded concepts of Truth and Justice, and the problem
of having God explicitly act to unite these concepts or symboliza-
tions of himself. Now Truth and Justice are "orbed" (enclosed) in a
rainbow, and the glories that such exaltation projects are shared by
(worn by) Mercy, who "sits" between them.

When we heed Milton's revisions in new editions of the prose, we
find with at least two of them what amount to two different works,
not simply a second edition. *The Doctrine and Discipline of Divorce*
(1643) and *The Readie & Easie Way to Establish a Free Commonwealth* (1660) present texts in their second editions that constitute
very different books. The volume on divorce offers its argument in
forty-eight pages (with two pages of errata), but the second edition
of 1644 ("Now the second time revis'd and much augmented, In Two
BOOKS") creates a new book of eighty-two pages with an eight-page
preface. *The Readie & Easie Way* (a quarto) has eighteen pages, and
"The second edition revis'd and augmented" (a duodecimo) expands
to 106 pages of text. The argument of the first edition is more than
just further developed; in the words of Stanley Stewart, "He also
enriched the tract by reinterpreting the political situation in biblical terms. And he amplified his own voice by inviting associations
of it with prophetic models."[1]

Thus when we come to consider the *Paradise Lost* of 1667 alongside its second edition of 1674, we are confronted with an artifact
that is quite different, a text presented in a different setting with some
revisions that have likeness to that in the Nativity ode but most importantly with revision here and there as a result of that different setting. The book that is the 1667 *Paradise Lost* has only very seldom

been discussed (aside from bibliographic descriptions), but it deserves our importunate awareness of the "creation" that "first brought forth" Milton's interrogation of evil and his exemplification of how to bring "Light out of darkness."

"The poem we read is Milton's creation, a similitude of God's creation; because of its subject matter he functions as a surrogate of God for man to 'repair the ruins of our first parents by regaining to know God aright.'" "[A]nd like God, he has had to accommodate his message to the comprehension of his readers."[2] The 1667 *Paradise Lost* has ten books, with numbers seven and ten being very long. These have as their subject matter the Creation and some of the biblically reported aftermath of the Fall. Revision in 1674 disrupts the unity of these books: first, by separating the general Creation of God through the Son (in new book 7) and the discourse upon the universe of humankind's world, the creation of Adam, and the creation of Eve (in new book 8); second, by separating what happened up to the Flood (in new book 11) from the new world of Abraham and the covenant and those who followed it or defied it up to the advent of Christ (in new book 12). The division of original book 10 has probably been part of the reason that critics have seen the two books 11 and 12 as an "untransmuted lump of futurity" and have wondered about the rapid jumps in time covered. The biblical history that is the foundation of most of the content of books 11 and 12 is a panorama of selective personages who are types of the antitype, Christ, or negative representatives of the antitype. It is not a telling of biblical history per se but a deliberate series of examples of what Milton's readers could become according to how they live their lives. The emphasis in the epic is upon the figure of the Son and what he denotes (or rather *should* denote) as the source for and the exemplar for humankind to bring the light out of the darkness within themselves and within the existent world around them. (Perhaps we should also think of "When I consider how my light is spent, / E're half my days in this dark world and wide.") The emphasis in books 11 and 12 should not be upon a recitation of history, which, at best, is here incomplete and skewed. *Paradise Lost* (1667) presents a significant meaning for the reader that *Paradise Lost* (1674) obscures.

Even more so, I think, the division has helped to remove recognition of the substruct of the temptation motif that will be more directly and unavoidably offered in *Paradise Regain'd* in 1671 (acknowledging Ellwood's prompting of Milton to say something about "Paradise found" in 1665 as a frequent unfortunate and inadequate reading of the poem). The temptation motif, drawn from Matthew 4 and Luke 4 and elaborated upon by various clerical authors in the years before Milton wrote, recounts a temptation of the flesh (where temperance is its counter); a temptation of the world that emerges in the form of lures of *voluptaria*, *activa*, and *contemplativa* (where prudence and justice are the virtuous opposites), and a temptation of the devil (where fortitude and faith are evoked).[3] In *Paradise Lost* the first temptation appears in 11.527–31 and following:[4]

> There is, said *Michael*, if thou well observe
> The rule of not too much, by temperance taught
> In what thou eatst and drinkst, seeking from thence
> Due nourishment, not gluttonous delight,
> Till many years over thy head return.

The second temptation, part 1 (stressing bodily matters), underlies 11.569 and following, where "a different sort" of men "descended" "to the Plain," who "by thir guise / Just men . . . seemd," but who soon after "behold / A Beavie of fair Women" who "sung / Soft amorous Ditties, and in dance came on."

> The Men though grave, ey'd them, and let thir eyes
> Rove without rein, till in the amorous Net
> Fast caught, they lik'd, and each his liking chose;
> And now of love they treat till th' Eevning Star
> Loves Harbinger appeerd; then all in heat
> They light the Nuptial Torch, and bid invoke
> Hymen, then first to marriage Rites invok't.

Temptation two, part 2 (stressing ownership, war, glory), is reprised in 11.634 and following, where "Cities of Men with lofty Gates and Towrs" threaten war "and bould emprise," "Single or in Array of Battel rang'd," while others drive "A herd of Beeves, fair Oxen and fair Kine / From a fat Meddow ground; or fleecy Flock, / Ewes and thir bleating

Lambs over the Plaine, / Thir Bootie," but this "tacks a bloody Fray; . . . Where Cattel pastur'd late, now scatterd lies / With Carcasses and Arms th' ensanguind Field / Deserted" and while "Others to a Citie strong / Lay Siege, encampt; by Batterie, Scale, and Mine, / Assaulting." Such war of "these Giants, men of high renown" "shall be held the highest pitch / Of human Glorie, and for Glorie done / Of triumph, to be styl'd great Conquerours."

The third part of the second temptation (stressing ease and intellectual boasting) is rendered as "Those . . . Who having spilt much blood, and don much waste / Subduing Nations, . . . achiev'd thereby / Fame in the World, high titles, and rich prey" by their changing "thir course to pleasure, ease, and sloth, / Surfet, and lust, till wantonness and pride / Raise out of friendship hostil deeds in Peace" (11.783–92), and those "coold in zeale / Thenceforth shall practice how to live secure, / Worldlie or dissolute." A hint of the lure of *contemplativa* also appears in 11.605–08:

> studious they appere
> Of Arts that polish Life, Inventers rare,
> Unmindful of thir Maker, though his Spirit
> Taught them, but they his gifts acknowledg'd none.

But this "sober Race of Men" "yeild up all thir vertue . . . to the traines and to the smiles / Of these fair Atheists, and now swim in joy, / (Erelong to swim at larg) and laugh" (11.617, 619–22).

Because of the separation of book 10 into two books (11 and 12) we do not encounter the third temptation until new book 12, line 24 and following (that is, line 916 in the first edition), in the presence of Nimrod,

> Of proud ambitious heart, who not content
> With fair equalitie, fraternal state,
> Will arrogate Dominion undeserv'd
> Over his brethren, and quite dispossess
> Concord and law of Nature from the Earth.

The Tower then built (to be juxtaposed, we realize, with Pandemonium), in great contrast with the temple in Jerusalem where Jesus will be tempted with *superbia vitae*, receives God's derision, followed by "a jangling noise of words unknown," "a hideous gabble . . . Among the Builders," and in turn this is followed by "great laughter . . . in Heav'n," recalling Psalm 2 and the Lord's having the kings of the earth in derision. The second edition contributes to, nay, helps create, the lack of understanding of how paradise is to be found that the first edition led Ellwood to express.[5]

Space allows for just two examples from the texts of *Paradise Lost* 1667 and 1674 to suggest similar matters to those I have noted with *At a Solemn Music* and the Nativity ode. The first is the much dis-cussed lines from book 1, 504–05: "In *Gibeah*, when hospitable Dores / Yielded thir Matrons to prevent worse rape," changed in 1674 to "In *Gibeah*, when the hospitable door / Expos'd a Matron to avoid worse rape." The commentary has been particularly incensed because of the gender bias implicit in the lines—that forced homosexuality is worse than forced heterosexuality, although some readings have stressed the concept of hospitality and the duty of the old man toward his guest. What Milton is doing here is repeating the Bible (Judg. 19:22–29) to characterize the sons of Belial, and it is the old man who offers his daughter, a maiden, and the guest's concubine (the plural "Matrons" being used). The "worse rape" has been inter-preted as homosexual rape that is condemned by most religious groups and, apparently, by the old man in Judges, "but unto this man do not so vile a thing." It is the Bible that has the sons of Belial demand "the man . . . that we may know him." It is Milton who calls that potential rape "worse" (the word appears in both versions). But examination of the full story, which is seen as a rewriting of the events in Genesis 19, should also suggest that further (heterosexual) rape in general that would repeat the brutal dismemberment of the per-son raped as in the biblical account is what is considered "worse."

The changes in the text from the first edition to the second are what concern us here, and they indicate a movement toward a more biblical text. The first edition unexplainedly says "prevent," whereas the manuscript, which was the copy text for the edition, has "avoyde" altered to "avoid" and this is the infinitive given in 1674. While the two words seem almost interchangeable, a nuance enters when we observe that 1667 has "Dores" and "Matrons" and has dropped the definite article, apparently indicating more than just the old man's home in Judges where rapes of matrons in those houses might have occurred, thereby implying other subjections to such demands from Sons of Belial. The "prevention" is to stop more than this one rape to occur that night. To "avoid" a rape confines the forced rape of "a Matron" to only that rape. The biblical text gives no indication of any rape beyond the gang-rape of the matron, that is, the concubine. Seemingly more representative of Milton's thought, the lines are *not* really faithful to the biblical text; the 1674 revision is, though inexplicit about what happened. The biblical text itself is confused, for the men "would not hearken to him," yet "the man took his concubine, and brought her forth unto them; and they knew her, and abused her all the night until the morning."[6] The change from "Yielded" to "Expos'd" would seem to shift blame from the old man: his "hospitable door" only "exposed a matron" (the concubine). In 1667 we see a confusion that makes "that night" a more general situation than the Bible presented, and in 1674 we find a closer biblical text that points to an occurrence that exemplifies what might happen at any time "when Night / Darkens the streets" and "the Sons of Belial" "wander forth," "flown with insolence and wine." In 1674 it is only "a Matron," the concubine of the Bible story, who is assaulted, with Milton's not elucidating whether the men hearkened not to the old man and thus the man was raped, or whether he was not raped since "the man took his concubine, and brought her forth unto them." The 1674 text, appearing through the form written down by an amanuensis, does not elide "th' hospitable" as it should and replaces the Miltonic spelling of "Dores" with a standard form, which also appears in the manuscript. Milton's word "worse" does seem to refer to the demand of the Sons of Belial to "know" the guest "so wickedly" and "do . . . this folly," but the question may be one that should be directed toward the biblical account, not to Milton.

As a second example I suggest a crux in lines 241–42 of book 9 (book 10 in 1674): Sin and Death are awaiting word of Satan's assault on Adam and Eve. If there has been a mishap, she posits, "Ere this he had return'd, with fury driv'n / By his Avenger, since no place like this / Can fit his punishment, or their revenge." In 1674 the change is made to "Avengers," and, as Harris Fletcher notes, "To agree with the number of the pronoun **their** in the next line, the change seems to be deliberate." But surely Sin means, and can mean, only God as the Avenger. She cannot be including the Son, and to be referring to the faithful angels would require knowledge that Gabriel, Uzziel, Ithuriel, and Zephon were in Eden on guard. Is it perhaps "their" that is not correct? Has a change in 1674 alerted us to a textual error in 1667 that has been inaccurately corrected? Should it not have been "no place like this / Can fit his punishment, or his revenge"? Is there not indeed a "new epic" to read?[7]

There were six issues of the first edition with seven title pages, as discussed by Stephen Dobranski in this collection. The first issue was registered on August 20, 1667, and the third issue seems to have appeared in May 1668, but we do not know the months of the other four issues. There are various states of the text (sometimes two states, sometimes three states of the same page).[8] So many press corrections indicates either poor composing or poor copy text; there were errata printed in the second 1668 issue. The first issue of *Paradise Lost* did not have arguments attached, as we all know; they were added all together at the beginning of the poem in this issue of 1668 (the fourth issue of the poem) along with the preface called "The Verse" and "The Printer to the Reader." (The arguments are dispersed in the second edition, those for books 7 [new 7 and 8] and 10 [new 11 and 12] being divided.) Samuel Simmons's statement appears in two forms, one in four lines, not mentioning "The Verse," and the other in six lines, adding "and withall a reason of that which stumbled many others, why the Poem Rimes not." Did Simmons forget at first that "The Verse" was also included, or was it added after printing had begun on this issue? Milton's argument for blank verse appears to have been provoked and influenced by John Dryden's "Essay on Dramatick Poesie" (registered August 7, 1667, but not published until 1668). The sheets with the four-line statement also appear in the fifth issue in 1669, as does the six-line statement. The statement is omitted entirely in the second issue of 1669 and there are alterations in the arguments and "The Verse," with signatures A, a, Z, and Vv being reset.

I have previously argued for the significance of a ten-book epic, indicating the symbolic meanings of numbers (such as the "perfection" and completeness that ten implied) and the placement of certain subjects in symbolically significant books (such as the introduction of Adam and Eve in book 4 and of Creation in book 7).[9] The removal of the Fall from book 8, for example, creates confusion; eight in Christian number symbolism denotes a weak number and as the cube of two it illustrates the triumph of Satan, of Sin in Eve's succumbing, and of Death in Adam's willful choice. As an event in book 9 it conflicts with the symbolism of defect amid perfection, and as the cube of three, God's will, which the 1667 book 9 does exhibit, exposing the faults of Adam and Eve, upon whom judgment is given and with their repentance expressed in duplicated lines because of its significance. In this book, too, the bad success of Satan is countered in the images of hissing serpents and the apples of Sodom. Remark too the contrast of book 3 (with its prolepsis of the Fall) with the original book 8 (the Fall) and the golden section relationship of the two (8 representing .616 of the total lines of the two together, and book 3, .384), which is erased through revision. In all there are 15 added lines in 1674, incorrectly offsetting the important center of the poem at 6.762.

Further, a major significance of the center of the poem at 6.762 has been pointed out by Michael Lieb in an essay on the occult where he argues, "In the ten-book edition in particular, the elements of Neoplatonism customarily associated with *merkabah* speculation in the early modern period came to the fore." The placement of the Chariot of Paternal Deity in the middle of "the sixth book becomes the matrix for the convergence of past, present, and future events."[10] Whereas the center of the poem in 1667 was 6.762, the addition of 15 lines in 1674 made 6.742 the central line of the poem, obliterating Milton's structural scheme. The major cause of error was the mislinage of book 3 in 1667, which Milton, unawares and relying upon an amanuensis to prepare the revised text, accepted and thus added too many lines in the wrong place.[11]

Discussing the ten-book poem and structure of Milton's original epic, Louis Martz points out the significance of Richard Fanshawe's translation of Camões's *The Lusiad; or, Portugals Historicall Poem* (1655): "in 1667 Milton chose to present the second half in an asymmetrical division into four books. This deliberate violation of the obvious Vergilian expectation suggests that Milton, after all those many years of planning his epic, must have had some compelling design in mind when he offered us this poem in ten books."[12] After having reviewed various parallels between the heroic poems of Camões and Milton, Martz concludes: "The voice of the bard, full of trouble and hope and personal opinion, thus plays an essential part in the meaning and in the success of both these epics. For in each the poet stands forth as the representative of an ideal, spoken by a human being who has suffered the woes of mankind and who yet believes that man can overcome his woe."[13]

The alteration into a twelve-book Virgilian form appears to be a case of publication consideration to make the poem agree with reader expectation. Likewise, Milton's justification of blank verse against "lame Meeter" and his supplying arguments as help for the easily daunted join his reorganization of his symbolically significant text to accord with the expectation of "Custom."

Appendix

Changes in Format and Verbal Alterations between Paradise Lost *First Edition (1667) and Second Edition (1674)*

Arguments to the Books
   1667–68 (issues 1–3): no arguments
   1668–69 (issues 4–6): arguments gathered in preliminary position
   1674: arguments dispersed before each pertinent book

The Verse
   1667–68 (issues 1–3): not included
   1668–69 (issues 4–6): included in preliminary position
   1674: included in preliminary position

Individual Books
   1667–69 (all issues): Books 1–10
   1674: original books 7 and 10 each divided into two, books 7 and 8, and books 11 and 12. Original book 8 became book 9; original book 9 became book 10.

Thus:

1667–69	1674
Book 1	Book 1
Book 2	Book 2
Book 3	Book 3
Book 4	Book 4
Book 5	Book 5
Book 6	Book 6
Book 7	Book 7
	Book 8
Book 8	Book 9
Book 9	Book 10
Book 10	Book 11
	Book 12

Some changes in indentation throughout.

Verbal Changes (First Edition, 1667 / Second Edition, 1674)

Book 1

Argument: The / This
25: th'Eternal (corrected by erratum) / Eternal
504: hospitable Dores / th'hospitable door
505: Yielded thir Matrons to prevent / Expos'd a matron to avoid
530: fainted / fainting
703: founded / found out
758: and Band (corrected by erratum) / Band and

Book 2

Argument: should (1669 printing) / shall
282: where / were
483: thir / her
527: his / this
881: great (corrected by erratum) / grate

Book 3

Argument: the right hand (1669 printing) / his right hand
Argument: plac't there (1669 printing) / plac't here

594: Which / With
741: with (state 1, corrected by erratum) / in

Book 4

Argument: find him out (1668 and 1669 printings) / find him
451: on / of
627: walks / walk
705: shadier / shadie
928: The / Thy

Book 5

Argument: appearing (1669 printing) / appearance
627: [missing] / now
636: [missing] / On flours repos'd, and with fresh flourets crownd,
637: with refection / in communion
638–39: [missing] / Quaff immortalitie and joy, secure I Of surfet
   where full measure onely bounds
640: Are fill'd, / Excess,
659: [missing] (added by erratum) / in
830: our (State 1) / one

Book 7

25: tongues; (1669 printing) / dayes,
126: a (1669 printing) / as
224: his (1669 printing) / the
366: his / her
451: Fowle / Foul [should be Soul]

Book 8 (7, 641–1290, in first edition)

Argument: *Adam* then inquires (1668, 1669 printings) / *Adam*
   inquires
Argument: seek (1669 printing) / search
1–3: added in second edition
4: To whom thus *Adam* gratefully repli'd. / Then as new wak't thus
   gratefully repli'd.
269: as / and

Book 9 (8 in first edition)

92: fleights / sleights

186: Not / Nor
213: hear / bear
347: ought / aught
394: Likest / Likeliest
632: make / made
922: hast / hath
1019: we / me
1092: for / from
1093: from / for

Book 10 (book 9 in first edition)
  Argument: Angels (1669 printing) / Son
  Argument: meet / met (state 1)
  Argument: full assembly (1668, 1669 printings) / full of assembly
  Argument: taste (1668, 1669 printings) / take
  58: may / might
  241: Avenger / Avengers
  397: those / these
  408: prevail, / prevailes,
  550: fair / [omitted]
  827: then / [omitted]

Book 11 (Book 10, lines 1–897 in first edition)
  Argument: and declares (1669 printing) / but declares
  Argument: Cherubims (1669 printing) / Cherubim
  380: to amplest / to the amplest
  427: sin derive / derive
  485–87: added in second edition
  551–52: Of rendring up. *Michael* to him repli'd. / Of rendring up,
      and patiently attend | My dissolution. *Michael* repli'd,
  579: lost (corrected by erratum) / last
  651: tacks / makes
  879: that / who

Book 12 (book 10, lines 898–1541 in first edition)
  Argument: thence from the flood relates, and by degrees explains,
      who that Seed of the Woman shall be; / The Angel . . . in the
      Fall;

1–5: added in second edition
191: This / The
238: them thir desire, / what they besaught
534: Will / Well

N.B.: many changes in 1674 are errors. Changes in spellings, indentations, capitalization, and the like, are not indicated above.

NOTES

Notes to Lieb, "Back to the Future"

1. Parenthetical references to the first edition of *Paradise Lost* by book and line number are to *Paradise Lost: A Poem Written in Ten Books: An Authoritative Text of the 1667 First Edition* from Duquesne University Press. That edition is a transcription of a copy owned by the Newberry Library, collated with a copy owned by the British Library. I also have had recourse to *Milton's Poetical Works in Photographic Facsimile with Critical Apparatus*, 4 vols., ed. Harris Francis Fletcher (Urbana: University of Illinois Press, 1948), as well as to John Milton, *Paradise Lost 1667* (Menston, England: Scolar Press, 1968) and *Paradise Lost, as Originally Published by John Milton, Being a Facsimile Reproduction of the First Edition*, intro. by David Masson (London: Eliot Stock, 1877). Aside from the first edition of *Paradise Lost*, references to Milton's poetry in my text are to the *Complete Poetry of John Milton*, ed. John T. Shawcross, 2nd ed. rev. (Garden City, N.Y.: Doubleday, 1971). References to Milton's prose are to *The Complete Prose Works of John Milton*, 8 vols. in 10, gen. ed. Don M. Wolfe (New Haven: Yale University Press, 1953–82), hereafter designated YP and followed by volume and page number in the text. Corresponding references to the original Latin (and to the English translations) are to *The Works of John Milton*, 18 vols. in 21, ed. Frank Allen Patterson et al. (New York: Columbia University Press, 1931–38), hereafter designated CM. Milton makes the distinction between "brief" and "diffuse" epic in *The Reason of Church-Government* (YP 1:813).

2. Frank Capra, *The Name above the Title: An Autobiography* (New York: Macmillan, 1971), 216–17. Capra not only confuses "editions" with "issues" but also is wrong about both the circumstances surrounding the publication of the first edition and Milton's relationship with his publisher Samuel Simmons. I am grateful to my colleague Virginia Wexman for alerting me to this text.

3. A helpful source of information on matters relating to editions, issues, variants, and the like is Fredson Bowers, *Principles of Bibliographical Description* (Princeton: Princeton University Press, 1949). Broadly speaking, "*an* EDITION *is the whole number of copies of a book printed at any time or times from substantially the same setting of type-pages.*" An edition includes all issues and variant states within its typesetting. "*An* ISSUE

229

is the whole number of copies of a form of an edition put on sale at any time or times as a consciously planned printed unit and varying in relation to the form of an 'ideal copy' of this unit." In turn, *"STATE is synonymous with VARIANT, and can be applied to any part of a book exhibiting variation in type-setting"* (37–42).

4. In this regard, see Stephen B. Dobranski, "Simmons's Shell Game: The Six Title Pages of *Paradise Lost,"* in this volume. See also Dobranski, *Milton, Authorship, and the Book Trade* (Cambridge: Cambridge University Press, 1999). Also of importance are Peter Lindenbaum's two articles: "The Poet in the Marketplace: Milton and Samuel Simmons," in *Of Poetry and Politics: New Essays on Milton and His World,* ed. P. G. Stanwood (Binghamton, N.Y.: Medieval & Renaissance Texts & Studies, 1995), 249–62, and "Authors and Publishers in Late Seventeenth Century: New Evidence on Their Relations," *The Library* 17 (1995): 250–69. Although certainly helpful, Fletcher's commentary on the facsimile edition of the *Complete Poetry* must be used with care.

5. Given the customary association of Milton's name in connection with the controversial subject of divorce and the support of the regicides, might the use of initials indicate an attempt to mask identity? Such an explanation is at best surmise.

6. According to John Toland, "we had like to be eternally depriv'd of this Treasure [*Paradise Lost*] by the Ignorance and Malice of the Licenser [Thomas Tompkins]; who, among other frivolous Exceptions, would needs suppress the whole Poem for imaginary Treason" in the lines that allude to the light that "with fear of change / Perplexes Monarchs" (1.594–99). See Toland, *Life of John Milton* (1698), in *The Early Lives of Milton,* ed. Helen Darbishire (New York: Barnes and Noble, 1965), 180.

7. This is the running title of the manuscript thus reproduced. See *The Manuscript of Milton's Paradise Lost Book I,* ed. Helen Darbishire (Oxford: Clarendon Press, 1931). Now housed in the Pierpont Morgan Library, New York, the manuscript of book 1 is the only one extant. One might well question the significance of using lowercase *"lost,"* as opposed to uppercase *"Lost"* both in the first edition and in the manuscript.

8. Referring to the unstable nature of the first edition of *Paradise Lost* and its propensity to undergo change, Leah Marcus adopts the telling phrase "the unfixity of print." See her discussion in *Unediting the Renaissance: Shakespeare, Marlowe, Milton* (London: Routledge, 1996), 178.

9. Simmons's statement has two forms, both of which appear in copies of the fourth and fifth title page issues, respectively. The statement does not appear in the sixth title page issue. It is ironic that there should be an insistence in defending the reason "why the Poem Rimes not," when, in fact, *Paradise Lost* is a poem that does contain a good deal of rhyme.

10. This is the point that Dobranski makes so effectively in *Milton, Authorship, and the Book Trade,* 33–40.

11. Here, I make use of John T. Shawcross's invaluable *Milton: A Bibliography for the Years 1624–1700* (Binghamton, N.Y.: Medieval & Renaissance Texts & Studies, 1984), 86 (#318).

12. Marvell's poem significantly associates Milton with such prophets as the blind Tiresias, and concludes with slighting remarks aimed at "the *Town-Bayes*," that is, John Dryden, whose "opera" *The State of Innocence* (licensed in 1674), based on *Paradise Lost,* was never performed. Because the commendatory poems of S. B. and A. M. in the second edition of *Paradise Lost* are in effect responding to the first edition, they implicitly represent additional ties between the first and second editions. For a discussion of these poems, see the entries in *A Milton Encyclopedia,* 9 vols., gen. ed. William B. Hunter Jr. (Lewisburg, Pa.: Bucknell University Press, 1978–83), s.v. On Samuel Barrow, see my essay "S. B.'s '*In Paradisum Amissam*': Sublime Commentary," *Milton Quarterly* 19 (1985): 71–78.

13. Nonetheless, it is well known that the prose arguments that preface each book can also be misleading. See, in this volume, Joseph Wittreich, "'More and More Perceiving': Paraphernalia and Purpose in *Paradise Lost,* 1668, 1669."

14. With the appearance of the 1674 edition, one can find no external evidence to account for Milton's decision to publish his epic in twelve books rather than ten. Despite all claims to assess the rationale underlying the change, the attempt to document motive has been frustrated at every turn. Shawcross, *With Mortal Voice: The Creation of "Paradise Lost"* (Lexington: University Press of Kentucky, 1982), 63–66, has offered the most pragmatic argument, based on the idea that the second edition appeared in the twelve-book version to increase sales, which can hardly be described as robust. This is later reiterated in Shawcross, "Commercialism: Early Editors of Milton and Their Publishers," *Milton Quarterly* 33 (1999): 61–66. John K. Hale, "*Paradise Lost:* A Poem in Twelve Books, or Ten," *Philological Quarterly* 74 (1995): 131–49, reviews the arguments offered to explain Milton's reasons for effecting the change from ten to twelve books and comes up with explanations of his own. Beginning with an analysis of prevailing explanations (textual, numerological, arithmetical, and structural), he offers what he considers to be "external or biographical" evidence, but this too is finally conjectural. See also Hale, "The 1668 Argument to *Paradise Lost,*" *Milton Quarterly* 35 (2001): 87–97. In the present volume, Phillip J. Donnelly, "Poetic Justice: Plato's *Republic* in *Paradise Lost* (1667)," advances the notion that the structure of the first edition of *Paradise Lost* has important ties with Plato's *Republic.*

15. In the authoritative edition of *Paradise Lost* (1667) edited by Shawcross and Lieb, see the section titled "Discussion of the Edited Text."

16. Additional changes in format between the 1667 edition and the 1674 edition may be noted here. Whereas 1667 employs running heads in arabic numerals (such as "Book 4"), 1674 employs them in roman (such as "Book IV"). One finds pagination in 1674; none in 1667. Finally, 1667 has line numbers every ten lines; 1674 has no line numbers. Despite the presence of line numbers in 1667, the first edition contains errors in linage, especially in book 3. This fact becomes important to any claims of numerical balance of one edition as opposed to the next. Perhaps the presence of errors in the linage of 1667 accounts in part for the omission of linage altogether in 1674.

17. Shawcross, *Milton: A Bibliography for the Years 1624–1700*, provides detailed bibliographical accounts of these editions, as well as the various issues associated with them. See also R. G. Moyles, *The Text of "Paradise Lost": A Study in Editorial Procedure* (Toronto: University of Toronto Press, 1985). I have also examined the editions cited here. The second edition of 1674 was reissued in 1675, and the fifth edition of 1691 was reissued in 1692 with a different title page.

18. David Masson, *The Life of John Milton, narrated in connexion with the political, ecclesiastical, and literary history of his time*, 7 vols. (1877–96; reprinted, New York: Peter Smith, 1946), 6:785.

19. John T. Shawcross, *Milton: A Bibliography for the Years 1624–1700*, 96 (#345).

20. See, in this regard, Ants Oras, *Milton's Editors and Commentators from Patrick Hume to Henry John Todd, 1695–1801* (1931; rev. ed., New York: Haskell House, 1967).

21. Marcus Walsh, *Shakespeare, Milton, and Eighteenth-Century Literary Editing* (Cambridge: Cambridge University Press, 1997), 31, 53–57.

22. John T. Shawcross, introduction to *Milton: The Critical Heritage*, ed. John T. Shawcross (London: Routledge & Kegan Paul, 1970), 25. According to Shawcross, the 1688 edition of *Paradise Lost* is "the first edition of a poem to owe its existence to printing by subscription" (2).

23. For a full treatment of that *Nachleben*, see Nicholas von Maltzahn, *The Making of a National Poet: Milton and His Readers, 1650–1750*, forthcoming.

24. The reference, of course, is to the description of Satan in *Paradise Lost* (2.1–10).

25. William Butler Yeats, "A Coat," *The Yeats Reader*, rev. ed., ed. Richard Finneran (New York: Scribner, 2002), 53.

26. For treatments of the text of the first edition of *Paradise Lost*, see in particular John T. Shawcross, "Orthography and the Text of *Paradise Lost*," in *Language and Style in Milton: A Symposium in Honor of the Tercentenary of "Paradise Lost*," ed. Ronald David Emma and John T. Shawcross (New York: Frederick Ungar, 1967), 120–53; "The Texts of Milton's Works," in *The Riverside Milton*, ed. Roy Flannagan (Boston: Houghton Mifflin, 1998), xi–xxxii. See also Fletcher's *Facsimile* edition, 4:9–216.

27. Dobranski, "Simmons's Shell Game," this volume.

28. Compare Adrian Johns's enactment of a similar drama (grounded in *Areopagitica*) in *The Nature of the Book* (Chicago: University of Chicago Press, 1998), 58–62.

29. According to Hugh Wilson, "The Publication of *Paradise Lost*: Censorship and Resistance," in *Milton Studies*, vol. 37, ed. Albert C. Labriola (Pittsburgh: University of Pittsburgh Press, 1999), 33, given both the political and literary climate that prevailed at the time, Milton's title "had a sardonic flavor that must have seemed especially pointed in light of all the realms of gushing royalist propaganda." Compare Voltaire: "The title alone was revolting, and everything connected with religion was then out of fashion," in *The Life Records of John Milton*, 5 vols., ed. J. Milton French (New Brunswick, N.J.: Rutgers University Press, 1949–58), 4:429.

30. We recall perhaps that the same situation is true for the 1671 title page of *Paradise Regained*, which has "PARADISE REGAIN'D. A POEM. In IV *BOOKS*. To which is added *SAMSON AGONISTES*. The Author *JOHN MILTON*." The title page of the 1674 edition has *"Paradise Lost. A Poem In Twelve Books."*

31. See *The Reason of Church-Government* (YP 1:813) and *Of Education* (YP 2:405). In the first instance, Milton speaks of "that Epick form whereof the two poems of *Homer*, and those other two of *Virgil* and *Tasso* are a diffuse, and the book of *Job* a brief model." In the second instance, he speaks of "what the laws are of a true *Epic* poem."

32. As a synonym for "epic," Milton adopts the phrase "Heroic Song" (1667 edition, 8.25), which carries its own meanings quite distinct from those associated with the "epic." What is true of *Paradise Regained* is finally no less true of *Paradise Lost* as the designation of a work that presumes to portray deeds above heroic; compare *Paradise Regained*, 1.14–15. Even once we are certain that what we have before us is an epic (a genre, of course, that was itself the subject of heated debate in the early modern period), we must still acknowledge that the ten-book structure departs from both the Homeric and the Virgilian models, despite the fact that the epics of Homer and Virgil are certainly (and obviously) crucial sources of influence in other respects.

33. Ten-book (or ten-canto) narratives extend from Lucan's unfinished epic *Pharsalia* to Camoens's *Os Lusiadas*. See Barbara K. Lewalski's account of such structures in *The Life of John Milton: A Critical Biography* (Oxford: Blackwell, 2000), 447. For a discussion of Milton and Lucan, see David Norbrook, *Writing the English Republic: Poetry, Rhetoric and Politics* (Cambridge: Cambridge University Press, 1999), esp. 439–67. For a discussion of Milton and Camoens, see Louis L. Martz, *Poet of Exile: A Study of Milton's Poetry* (New Haven: Yale University Press, 1980), 155–68.

34. Lewalski conjectures that "the Proem to Milton's Book VII, which recalls Virgil's invocation to the second half of his poem near the beginning of his Book VII, contains Milton's line 'Half yet remains unsung' (21): this is strictly true for an epic in twelve books but not for a ten-book poem." Yet, as indicated in my own discussion, the precise numerical length of the 1667 edition is vitally important in locating the true "middle" of the poem.

35. Cyriack Skinner (the Anonymous Biographer), in *The Early Lives of Milton*, 33.

36. In *Paradise Lost, 1668–1968: Three Centuries of Commentary*, ed. Earl Miner et al. (Lewisburg, Pa.: Bucknell University Press, 2004), 32–33. Hobart is one of several early readers of the first edition of *Paradise Lost* on record. These include John Beale, a royalist and Anglican divine, whose correspondence with John Evelyn mentions the poem. For additional references, see William Poole, "Two Early Readers of Milton: John Beale and Abraham Hill," *Milton Quarterly* 38 (2004): 76–99; the essays of Nicholas von Maltzahn, "Laureate, Republican, Calvinist: An Early Response to Milton and *Paradise Lost*," in *Milton Studies*, vol. 29, ed. Albert C. Labriola (Pittsburgh: University of Pittsburgh Press, 1993), 181–98; "The First Reception of *Paradise Lost* (1667)," *Review of English Studies* 47 (1996):

479–99, among others; James M. Rosenheim, "An Early Appreciation of *Paradise Lost,*" *Modern Philology* 75 (1978): 280–82. See also John T. Shawcross, *Rethinking Milton Studies: Time Present and Time Past* (Newark: University of Delaware Press, 2005), 169–71.

37. Martz, *Poet of Exile,* 158.

38. Shawcross, *With Mortal Voice,* 42–55. See the accompanying diagram of the "Symmetries of *Paradise Lost*" (46).

39. See Shawcross, *Complete Poetry,* 383 n. 52; and *With Mortal Voice,* 43: "The exact middle of the first edition came with lines 761 and 762 of Book VI, 5275 lines lying before and after" (43). See also Shawcross, "Pictorialism and the Poetry of John Milton," *University of Hartford Studies in Literature* 13 (1982): 143–64.

40. See Shawcross's chapter, "Numerological Relationships" in *With Mortal Voice,* 56–67.

41. Ibid., 56.

42. See Gunnar Qvarnström, *The Enchanted Palace: Some Structural Aspects of "Paradise Lost"* (Stockholm: Almqvist & Wiksell, 1967), 55–89; Maren-Sofie Røstvig, "The Hidden Sense: Milton and the Neoplatonic Method of Numerical Composition," *The Hidden Sense, and Other Essays* (New York: Humanities Press, 1963), 24–36; Røstvig, "Structure as Prophecy: The Influence of Biblical Exegesis upon Theories of Literary Structure," in *Silent Poetry: Essays in Numerological Analysis,* ed. Alastair Fowler (London: Routledge & Kegan Paul, 1970), 32–72; and Røstvig, "Images of Perfection," in *Seventeenth-Century Imagery: Essays on Uses of Figurative Language from Donne to Farquhar,* ed. Earl Miner (Berkeley and Los Angeles: University of California Press, 1971), 1–23; the notes and introductory material in the John Carey and Alastair Fowler edition of *The Poems of John Milton* (London: Longman, 1998), esp. 440–43, 763–65; Alastair Fowler, *Triumphal Forms: Structural Patterns in Elizabethan Poetry* (Cambridge: Cambridge University Press, 1970), 116–17; and Claes Schaar, *The Full Voic'd Quire Below: Vertical Context Systems in "Paradise Lost,"* Lund Studies in English 60, ed. Claes Schaar and Jan Svartvik (Lund: CWK Gleerup, 1982), 31–33.

43. Michael Lieb, "Encoding the Occult: Milton and the Traditions of *Merkabah* Speculation in the Renaissance," in *Milton Studies,* vol. 37, ed. Albert C. Labriola (Pittsburgh: University of Pittsburgh Press, 1999), 42–88.

44. Line numbers are evident in the manuscript of book 1 of *Paradise Lost.* See Darbishire's edition of *The Manuscript of Milton's "Paradise Lost" Book I.*

45. On this point, see William B. Hunter, "The Center of *Paradise Lost,*" *English Literary Notes* 7 (1969): 32–34.

46. In this regard, see Albert R. Cirillo, "Noon-Midnight and the Temporal Structure of *Paradise Lost,*" *English Literary History* 29 (1962): 372–93. Compare John 19:13.

47. Underscoring that movement is the description of the table as a symbol of perfection embodied in the squaring of the circle, a theme of crucial importance to Milton's epic: "Rais'd of grassie terf / Thir Table was, and mossie seats had round, / And on her ample Square from side to side" (5.391–93).

48. See, among other studies, those of Thomas Stroup, *Religious Rite and Ceremony in Milton's Poetry* (Lexington: University Press of Kentucky, 1968), and Achsah Guibbory, *Ceremony and Community from Herbert to Milton: Literature, Religion, and Cultural Conflict in Seventeenth-Century England* (Cambridge: Cambridge University Press, 1998). See also Regina Schwartz's study of sacramentalism in Milton and others in *"When God Left the World"* (forthcoming).

49. See Roy Flannagan, "Milton's Gout," *Milton Quarterly* 15 (1981): 123–24.

Notes to Wittreich, *"'More and more perceiving'"*

The quotation in the title to this essay is from "The Argument: Of the Ninth Book" [a2v]. All quotations from *Paradise Lost*, unless otherwise indicated, are from the first edition of the poem, citations for which are hereafter given parenthetically within the text of my essay. The quotations, furthermore, correlate with two different issues of the poem, both in the New York Public Library Rare Book Room: (1) [double-ruled border] / **Paradise lost.** / **A** / **POEM** / **IN** / **TEN BOOKS.** / [bar] / The Author / *JOHN MILTON.* / [bar] / [ornament] / [bar] / *LONDON,* / Printed by *S. Simmons,* and to be sold by *S. Thomson* at / the *Bishops-Head* in *Duck-lane, H. Mortlack* at the / *White Hart* in *West-minster* Hall, *M. Walker* under / St. *Dunstans* Church in *Fleet-street,* and *R. Boulter* at / the *Turks-Head* in *Bishopsgate* street, 1668. / [this copy is identified by the New York Public Library as first edition, fourth title page]; and (2) [double-ruled border] / **Paradise lost.** / **A** / **POEM** / **IN** / **TEN BOOKS.** / [bar] / The Author / *JOHN MILTON.* / [bar] / *LONDON,* / Printed by *S. Simmons,* and to be sold by / *T. Helder* at the Angel in *Little Brittain.* / 1669. / [this copy is identified by the New York Public Library as first edition, seventh title page]. Compare John T. Shawcross, *Milton: A Bibliography for the Years 1624–1700* (Binghamton, N.Y.: Medieval and Renaissance Texts and Studies, 1984), 79, where the first of these copies is identified as "Issue 4" and the second of them as "Issue 5." For the epigraphs to this essay, see Jonathan Richardson Sr., "Life of the Author," *Explanatory Notes and Remarks on Milton's "Paradise Lost"* (1734, by Father and Son), in *The Early Lives of Milton,* ed. Helen Darbishire (1932; rpt. London: Constable, 1965), 315 (my italics). All other quotations of Milton's poetry are from *The Complete Poetry of John Milton,* rev. ed., ed. John T. Shawcross (New York: Anchor Books, 1971); and quotations of the prose (unless otherwise indicated) are from *Complete Prose Works of John Milton,* 8 vols., ed. Don M. Wolfe et al. (New Haven: Yale University Press, 1953–82), hereafter cited as YP.

1. See Shawcross, *Milton,* 78–80, 86–87; compare Richardson, "Life of the Author," esp. 293–310. John K. Hale, "Books and Book-Form in Milton," in *Milton as Multilingual: Select Essays, 1982–2004,* ed. Lisa Marr and Chris Ackerley (Dunedin, New Zealand: Otago Studies in English 8, 2005), remarks that "Milton altered, revised, expanded and cared for his poem through serial improvements up to his death" (135).

2. Richardson, "Life of the Author," 291, 293.

3. Ibid., 293

4. Samuel Taylor Coleridge, entry 15, in *The Romantics on Milton: Formal Essays and Critical Asides*, ed. Joseph Wittreich (Cleveland: Press of Case Western Reserve University, 1970), 159.

5. Richardson, "Life of the Author," 299.

6. Jerome McGann, "How to Read a Book," in *New Directions in Textual Studies*, ed. Dave Oliphant and Robin Bradford (Austin, Tex.: Harry Ransom Humanities Research Center, 1990), 34. Jennifer Andersen and Elizabeth Sauer, "Current Trends in the History of Reading," *Books and Readers in Early Modern England: Material Studies* (Philadelphia: University of Pennsylvania Press, 2002), conjecture that Milton views books "as 'systems' or parts of a socio-cultural matrix" (1); and see also Hale, "Book and Book-Form in Milton," 127.

7. On the other hand, individual titles at the head of each book are entirely in caps (e.g., **PARADISE LOST. / BOOK I. /** and so on).

8. Only book 7 is missing the usual tag, "The End of . . ."—whether by calculation or oversight is uncertain (see sig. Ee).

9. Line 881 is designated line 880, and from this point on the numbering of lines for book 10 is short by one line. Hence, line 1,540 is actually 1,541. The longest books have also been the most forbidding. In contrast, the shortest books of the poem have registered the greatest impact and still provoke raging controversy: the 798 lines of book 1 and the 751 (actually 742 lines) of book 3 (again because of misnumbering beginning at line 610, actually 600, and continued when line 651 is numbered 650).

10. See John Spencer, *A Discourse Concerning Prodigies . . . The Second Edition . . . To which is added a short Treatise concerning Vulgar Prophecies* (London, 1665), 55, 2.

11. Ibid., 71.

12. Ibid., 75, 110, 73.

13. See *Paradise Lost, in Twelve Books: Together with Paradise Regain'd in Four Books* (Dublin, 1724). Previously, as Shawcross notes, Milton's vast design, this time embracing the final trilogy of poems, was recognized in a volume "created by adding unsold copies of the 1688 *Paradise Regain'd* and *Samson Agonistes* to the 1695 *Paradise Lost*"; see Shawcross, *Milton*, 109.

14. Richardson, "Life of the Author," 271.

15. As adopted and adapted from Richardson, "Life of the Author," 272. See also Stephen Orgel, "Afterword: Records of a Culture," in Andersen and Sauer, *Books and Readers in Early Modern England*, 283.

16. Richardson, "Life of the Author," 239.

17. Ibid., 310. For a recent adoption of such a position, see John K. Hale, "*Paradise Lost, A Poem in Twelve Books*—or is it Ten?" in Marr and Ackerley, *Milton as Multilingual*, 193–209, as well as the counterargument of Maren-Sofie Røstvig, whose position is that Milton mismanaged the revision of *Paradise Lost* and that, therefore, we should "return to the first edition as the authoritative text" (Røstvig quoted by Hale, 195).

18. For this conversation, see the online discussion sponsored by the University of Richmond: Roy Flannagan, Joad Raymond, and Peter

Lindenbaum, June 2, 1999, and Flannagan, June 9, 1999. Compare Christopher Grose, "*Theatrum Libri:* Burton's *Anatomy of Melancholy* and the Failure of Encyclopedic Form," in Andersen and Sauer, *Books and Readers in Early Modern England,* concerning "the co-originality of the book proper and seeming prolegomenal apparatus, as in the proemeia of *Paradise Lost*" (82–83). To Flannagan's remark, quoted above in the text of this essay, should be added the insight of Sabrina A. Baron, "Licensing Readers, Licensing Authorities in Seventeenth-Century England," in ibid., that the unadorned, "underinformed title page . . . [is] a smoke screen behind which to conduct political and religious battles" (224).

19. See Shawcross, *Milton,* 79–80, no. 299 (edition 1, issue 4).

20. All quotations in this paragraph from Flannagan, Raymond, and Lindenbaum, online discussion, June 2, 1999.

21. McGann, "How to Read a Book," 36.

22. Adrian Johns (paraphrasing Roger Chartier), *The Nature of the Book: Print and Knowledge in the Making* (Chicago: University of Chicago Press, 1998), 57.

23. See the superb exploration of many of these issues in relation to one frontispiece by Stephen B. Dobranski, "Burghley's Emblem and the Heart of Milton's *Pro Populo Anglicano Defensio,*" *Milton Quarterly* 44 (May 2000): 33–48.

24. Johns, *The Nature of the Book,* 117; see also 127–28. For interesting speculations on Milton and his printers, see Baron, "Licensing Readers, " 217–42.

25. Mark Bland, "The Appearance of the Text in Early Modern England," in *Text: An Interdisciplinary Annual of Textual Studies,* ed. W. Speed Hill and Edward M. Burns, vol. 11 (Ann Arbor: University of Michigan Press, 1998), 100; and Roy Flannagan, ed., *The Riverside Milton* (Boston: Houghton Mifflin, 1998), 1135.

26. Peter Levi, *Eden Renewed: The Public and Private Life of John Milton* (New York: St. Martin's Press, 1996), 95; compare 45.

27. Noting that "Milton . . . was not a popular man," R. G. Moyles, *The Text of "Paradise Lost": A Study in Editorial Procedure* (Toronto: University of Toronto Press, 1985), seconds David Masson's earlier suggestion, arguing that "many people, seeing the name JOHN MILTON on the title-page, would throw down the book with an exclamation of disgust" (14). While Moyles thinks this view "is most likely correct" and accounts for slow sales, he also conjectures that "maybe it was not Milton's name at all but the absence of any guide to what the poem contained which had slowed sales" (14). See also David Masson, *The Life of John Milton: Narrated in Connexion with the Political, Ecclesiastical, and Literary History of His Time,* 7 vols. (London, 1880), 6:623. Valuable perspectives on the conditions of writing in the age of Milton are afforded by Christopher Hill, "Censorship and English Literature," in *The Collected Writings of Christopher Hill,* volume 1, *Writing and Revolution in Seventeenth Century England* (Amherst: University of Massachusetts Press, 1985), 32–71, and also 133–87; and Annabel Patterson, *Censorship and Interpretation: The Conditions of Writing and Reading in Early Modern England* (Madison: University of

Wisconsin Press, 1984), esp. 111–17, 176–80; and also Patterson, *Reading between the Lines* (Madison: University of Wisconsin Press, 1993), esp. 36–56, 244–75, 276–97.

28. Johns, *The Nature of the Book*, 147.

29. Nicholas von Maltzahn, "Milton's Readers," in *The Cambridge Companion to Milton*, 2nd ed., ed. Dennis Danielson (Cambridge: Cambridge University Press, 1999), 240.

30. See Sharon Achinstein, "Milton's Spectre in the Restoration: Marvell, Dryden, and Literary Enthusiasm," *Huntington Library Quarterly* 59, no. 1 (1997): 3. See also Achinstein, *Literature and Dissent in Milton's England* (Cambridge: Cambridge University Press, 2003), esp. 172–81.

31. Johns, *The Nature of the Book*, 134–35.

32. Ibid., 100.

33. Robert J. Griffin, "Authorship and Anonymity," *New Literary History* 30 (Autumn 1999): 888, 885. See also Anne Ferry, "*Anonymity*: The Literary History of a Word," *New Literary History* 33 (Spring 2002): 193–214.

34. See John T. Shawcross, both "The Balanced Structure of *Paradise Lost*," *Studies in Philology* 62 (January 1965): 696–718, and "The Son in His Ascendance: A Reading of *Paradise Lost*," *Modern Language Quarterly* 27 (December 1966): 288–301. See also by Shawcross, *With Mortal Voice: The Creation of "Paradise Lost"* (Lexington: University Press of Kentucky, 1982), esp. 42–55.

35. Anne Middleton, "Life in the Margins, or What's an Annotation to Do?" in Oliphant and Bradford, *New Directions in Textual Studies*, 168. See also Stephen B. Dobranski, "Samson and the Omissa," *Studies in English Literature 1500–1900* 36 (Winter 1996): 162–63, as well as Dobranski, "Text and Context for *Paradise Regain'd* and *Samson Agonistes*," in *Altering Eyes: New Perspectives on "Samson Agonistes*," ed. Mark R. Kelley and Joseph Wittreich (Newark: University of Delaware Press, 2002), 30–53.

36. Spencer, *A Discourse*, [A3v], 132, 134.

37. Thomas Newton, ed., *Paradise Lost. A Poem, In Twelve Books*, 9th ed., 2 vols. (London, 1790), 1:A2.

38. Peter Lindenbaum, "John Milton and the Republican Mode of Literary Production," in *Critical Essays on John Milton*, ed. Christopher Kendrick (New York: G. K. Hall, 1995), 151.

39. Newton, ed., *Paradise Lost*, 1:A2v, A4.

40. See John Dryden, "The Authors Apology," in *The State of Innocence, and Fall of Man: An Opera* (London, 1677), b, [bv], [c2v].

41. Nat[haniel] Lee, "*To Mr. DRYDEN, on his Poem of Paradice*," in ibid., [A4v], [A4].

42. See *Paradise Lost. A Poem in Twelve Books*, 4th ed. (London, 1688), frontispiece portrait.

43. Lindenbaum, "John Milton and the Republican Mode," 150. The dedication "To the Right Honourable / *John* Lord *Sommers*, / Baron of *Evesham*" first appeared in *Paradise Lost . . . The Seventh Edition* (London, 1705), A-[Av].

44. Andrew Marvell, "On Mr Milton's *Paradise Lost*," in *The Poems of Andrew Marvell*, ed. Nigel Smith (London: Pearson Longman, 2003), 184, ll. 43–44.

45. Heather Dubrow, "The Masquing of Genre in *Comus*," *Milton Studies*, vol. 44, ed. Albert C. Labriola (Pittsburgh: University of Pittsburgh Press, 2005), 65.

46. Flannagan, *The Riverside Milton*, 334.

47. See von Maltzahn, "Milton's Readers," 246.

48. Bland, "The Appearance of the Text," 101.

49. "Samuel Taylor Coleridge," entry 186, in Wittreich, *The Romantics on Milton*, 211. Writing his book as a corrective to Milton's representations of the devils in *Paradise Lost*, Defoe anticipates, and probably provokes, Coleridge's own complaint; see Daniel Defoe, *The Political History of the Devil, as well Ancient as Modern* (London, 1726), 27.

50. William Wordsworth's words from "The Recluse: Part First" are particularly apt; see *The Poetical Works of Wordsworth*, ed. Paul D. Sheats (Boston: Houghton Mifflin, 1982), 231, l. 794.

51. S. Margaret Fuller, "The Prose Works of Milton," in *Papers on Literature and Art* (New York: Wiley and Putnam, 1846), 39.

52. Both issues of the first edition from which I have been quoting read: "*He sends his Son to Judge the Transgressors*" (a2); another issue of the first edition also in the New York Public Library (identified as title page 8 by the New York Public Library and as "Issue 6" by Shawcross, *Milton*, 80), changes "Son" to "Angels": "*He sends his Angels to judge the Transgressors*." See **Paradise lost / A / POEM / IN TEN BOOKS**. / [bar] / The Author / *JOHN MILTON*. / [bar] / *LONDON*, / Printed by *S. Simmons*, and are to be sold by / *T. Helder*, at the *Angel* in *Little Brittain*, / 1669. This might be called "the Angel issue" of the first edition inasmuch as, unlike other title pages, the word "Angel" appears here in italic and then, mysteriously, in the argument to book 9.

53. In private correspondence, John Rogers, Yale University, wrote to me: "there were Socinians, like Jonas Schlichting, who held a higher Christology than his comrades (and who were therefore much more like Milton). You could say that they flirted with the higher Christology of Arianism. Schlichting's Christ had a preexistence in heaven, and may actually have been an angel himself, who got himself promoted above the others. My book will be arguing that the semi-Arian Socinians like Schlichting were important for Milton; and in fact may have supplied something like a theological narrative that Milton would use to write the Exaltation of the Son in Book 5." To which I would add that something of this heresy may be hidden in the description of Satan (cited in the text above) as of the first, if not *the* first archangel.

54. E. M. W. Tillyard, *The Epic Strain in the English Novel* (London: Chatto and Windus, 1958), 15.

55. Achinstein, "Milton's Spectre in the Restoration," 8; compare 28.

56. So one of Dryden's contemporaries seems to have thought: "The

very same Spirit of Contradiction seized me when I undertook to clear Milton's Paradice of Weeds." These words derive from a conversation imagined by Thomas Brown, and the words are spoken by Mr. Bays (who is supposedly John Dryden); see *The Reasons of Mr. Bays changing his religion. Considered in a dialogue between Crites, Eugenius, and Mr. Bays* (London, 1688), 18.

Notes to Dobranski, *"Simmons's Shell Game"*

1. In addition, the third title page of *Paradise Lost* (fig. 3) survives in a variant state, containing a minor though significant correction, which I discuss below. Here and throughout this essay, I refer to Samuel Simmons as both the epic's printer and publisher, the latter term signifying that he financed the book's production and had it entered in the Stationers' *Register* as his own copy.

2. See Fredson Bowers, *Principles of Bibliographical Description* (Princeton: Princeton University Press, 1949), 37–42. As Bowers concedes, "No problem offers more traps for the bibliographer than the classification of books by edition, issue, and state" (38).

3. William Thomas Lowndes, *The Bibliographer's Manual of English Literature,* 8 vols., revised by Henry G. Bohn (London: Bohn, 1857–64), 4:1557–58; and David Masson, *The Life of John Milton,* 7 vols. (1877–96; rpt. Gloucester, Mass.: Peter Smith, 1946), 6:622. See also the discussion of the first edition's title pages in George C. Williamson, *The Portraits, Prints, and Writings of John Milton, Exhibited at Christ's College, Cambridge* (Cambridge: Cambridge University Press, 1908), 96–97.

4. The insertion of the period appears to have been a correction: while setting the 1668 title page, the compositor not only changed the poet's attribution from *"JOHN MILTON"* to *"J. M."* but also deleted the word "Written" and replaced "By" with "The Author". The resulting title page, instead of containing, as formerly, one complete thought, "A POEM Written in TEN BOOKS By *JOHN MILTON"* (figs. 1–2), now reads, "A POEM IN TEN BOOKS The Author *J. M."* (fig. 3). The period after "BOOKS" was thus added as a necessary separation between these two syntactical units, "A POEM IN TEN BOOKS. The Author *J. M."* All of the subsequent title pages (figs. 4–6) also accordingly include a period after "BOOKS".

5. *A Milton Encyclopedia,* ed. William B. Hunter et al., 9 vols. (Lewisburg, Pa.: Bucknell University Press, 1978–83), 6:53.

6. K. A. Coleridge, *A Descriptive Catalogue of the Milton Collection in the Alexander Turnbull Library, Wellington, New Zealand* (Oxford: Oxford University Press, 1980), 125–26; and R. G. Moyles, *The Text of "Paradise Lost": A Study in Editorial Procedure* (Toronto: University of Toronto Press, 1985), 4–15. Hugh Amory arrives at a similar conclusion but from a different direction. He suggests that *Paradise Lost's* first four title pages, two dated 1667 (see figs. 1 and 2) and two dated 1668 (see fig. 3), were all printed before the book was sold publicly so that they all qualify as variants of the first

issue. Amory ultimately asserts that the first edition had four issues and one (what he calls) "subissue." As I discuss below, I am not entirely convinced by this narrative of the first edition's printing. See Amory, "Things Unattempted Yet," *The Book Collector* 32 (Spring 1983): 41–66.

7. Harris Francis Fletcher, ed., *John Milton's Complete Poetical Works Reproduced in Photographic Facsimile*, 4 vols. (Urbana: University of Illinois Press, 1943–48), 2:3–5, 139–55; hereafter cited as *Facsimile*. See also Helen Darbishire, ed., *The Poetical Works of John Milton*, 2 vols. (Oxford: Clarendon Press, 1952–55), 1:xix–xxxv, 313–22.

8. John Milton, *Areopagitica*, in *Complete Prose Works of John Milton*, 8 vols., ed. Don M. Wolfe et al. (New Haven: Yale University Press, 1953–82), 2:524.

9. Joseph Hall, *Virgidemiarum* (London: Robert Dexter, 1597; STC 12716), sig. ^{2}E8r (book 5, satire 2); and Ben Jonson, "To My Booke-seller," in *The Workes of Benjamin Jonson* (London: William Stansby, 1616; STC 14751), sig. 3T1v (lines 7–8). By "cleft-sticks," Jonson apparently refers to narrow pieces of wood, "split or divided to a certain depth," in which title leaves could then be inserted (see *OED* s.v. "cleft"). For further references to the practice of posting title pages as advertisements, see Ronald B. McKerrow, *An Introduction to Bibliography for Literary Students* (Oxford: Clarendon Press, 1928), 90.

10. See Joseph Moxon, *Mechanick Exercises of the Whole Art of Printing (1683–4)*, ed. Herbert Davies and Harry Carter, 2nd ed. (London: Oxford University Press, 1962), 13; and Marjorie Plant, *The English Book Trade: An Economic History of the Making and Sale of Books*, 2nd ed. (London: Allen and Unwin, 1965), 248–49.

11. Moxon, *Mechanick Exercises*, 211–13, 214.

12. George Wither, *The Schollers Purgatory* (London: G. Wood, 1624; STC 25919), sig. H5r, H5v.

13. Anthony Nixon, *Londons Dove* (London: Joseph Hunt, 1612; STC 18588), sig. A2r; and Samuel Rowley, *When You See Me, You Know Me* (London: Nathaniel Butter, 1613; STC 21418), sig. A1r.

14. Milton, *Colasterion* (London: [Matthew Simmons?], 1645; Wing M2099), sig. A2r; and Milton, *Tetrachordon* (London: [Thomas Paine and Matthew Simmons?], 1645; Wing M2184), sig. A1r.

15. See Wilhelm Creizenach, *The English Drama in the Age of Shakespeare* (New York: Russell and Russell, 1967), 236.

16. The contract is transcribed in J. Milton French, ed., *The Life Records of John Milton*, 5 vols. (New Brunswick, N.J.: Rutgers University Press, 1956), 4:429–31. Here and throughout this essay I use the uppercase "Stationer" to signify Simmons's status as a member of the Stationers' Company.

17. The Printing Act of 1662, based on the 1637 Star Chamber Decree, required a book to be complete before it was entered and licensed. The act specifically stipulates that a book must include "all and every the Titles, Epistles, Prefaces, Proems, Preambles, Introductions, Tables, Dedications, and other matters and things thereunto annexed." See appendix, *The Statutes at Large*, vol. 9, ed. Owen Ruffhead (London: Mark Basket, 1765), sig.

Bb3v–Cc2v; for information about the manuscript of *Paradise Lost*, see Helen Darbishire, ed., *The Manuscript of Milton's "Paradise Lost" Book I* (Oxford: Clarendon Press, 1931).

18. On Milton's collaborative relationship with printers and booksellers, see Dobranski, *Milton, Authorship, and the Book Trade* (Cambridge: Cambridge University Press, 1999).

19. Milton, *Paradise Lost* (London: Samuel Simmons, 1667; Wing M2136–M2143), sig. A1r (book 1, lines 1–2).

20. Three title pages are found bound with the 1688 text, one stating, "for Richard Bently," another "for Jacob Tonson," and a third reading, "for Richard Bently . . . and Jacob Tonson." See Coleridge, *A Descriptive Catalogue*, 130–31.

21. Milton, *Paradise Lost*, sig. A1v (book 1, line 16).

22. D. F. McKenzie provides a list of the Simmons family's publishing activities in "The Economies of Print, 1550–1750: Scales of Production and Conditions of Constraint," *Produzione e Commercio della Carta e del Libro secc. XIII–XVIII*, Istituto Internazionale di Storia Economica, "F. Dantini" Prato, Serie II—Atti delle "Settimane di Studi" e altri Convegni 23 (April 15–20, 1991), 389–425.

23. Milton, *Accedence Commenc't Grammar* (London: Samuel Simmons, 1669; Wing M2088a, M2088), sig. A1r.

24. Milton, *A Maske Presented at Ludlow Castle* (London: Humphrey Robinson, 1637; STC 17937), sig. A1r.

25. Milton, *Poems* (London: Humphrey Moseley, 1645; Wing M2160), sig. a2r.

26. See, for example, John Barnard, "Bibliographical Context and the Critic," *TEXT* 3 (1987): 27–46; and Hugh Wilson, "The Publication of *Paradise Lost*, the Occasion of the First Edition: Censorship and Resistance," in *Milton Studies*, vol. 37, ed. Albert C. Labriola (Pittsburgh: University of Pittsburgh Press, 1999), 18–41, esp. 31, 40 n. 96.

27. Masson, *The Life of John Milton*, 6:623; and Fletcher, *Facsimile*, 2:165.

28. The entry instead refers to Simmons, the licenser Thomas Tomkins, and the warden of the Stationers' Company, Richard Royston. For information on the partial manuscript, see Darbishire, *The Manuscript of Milton's "Paradise Lost" Book I.*

29. Barbara K. Lewalski, *The Life of John Milton* (Oxford: Blackwell, 2000), 456. This possibility is also raised by Moyles, *The Text of "Paradise Lost,"* 14; and see Lawrence W. Hyman, "The Publication of *Paradise Lost*: 1667–1674," *Journal of Historical Studies* 1 (1967): 50–64.

30. James H. Pershing, "The Different States of the First Edition of *Paradise Lost*," *The Library*, 4th series, 22 (1942): 34–66.

31. Amory, "Things Unattempted Yet," 50. While I agree with McKenzie, who argues in his unpublished Lyell Lectures (1988) that the use of an author's initials "was common practice and hardly made the work anonymous," I would not go so far as to suggest that this monogram exclusively identifies Milton. According to my count from the Wing Catalogue, more

than 63 authors with the initials "J. M." and "I. M." were having their works published in England between 1642 and 1662; if we take into account that authors sometimes had their initials transposed, the number of possible authors would probably double. On the use of initials in Renaissance publications, see Franklin B. Williams Jr., "An Initiation into Initials," *Studies in Bibliography* 9 (1957): 163–78.

32. Amory, "Things Unattempted Yet," 51.

33. See McKenzie's unpublished Lyell Lectures (1998) and W. W. Greg, review of *John Milton's Complete Poetical Works Reproduced in Photographic Facsimile* by Harris Francis Fletcher, *Modern Language Review* 42 (1947): 133–37. Wilson, "The Publication of *Paradise Lost,*" speculates that Simmons replaced Milton's full name with the initials "J. M." because of "renewed repression that began in the spring of 1668"; only after the poem had, without incident, "achieved a measure of recognition" could "Milton's full name . . . safely appear on the title page again" (40–41). Such a hypothesis ignores, however, that the poem had been officially licensed and entered in the Stationers' *Register*. Legally, Simmons had nothing to fear.

34. "Undated Petitions," in *Calendar of State Papers, Domestic Series, October 1668 to December 1669*, ed. Mary Anne Everett Green (London, 1894), 130.

35. Some Milton critics have underestimated the success of *Paradise Lost*'s first edition by assuming that Simmons published Milton's poem in late August, shortly after entering it in the Stationers *Register* (see, for example, Masson, *Life*, 6:516). But even if Simmons began work on the book on April 27, 1667, the same day he and Milton signed their contract, the printer would not have finished printing the poem until the middle of November. Based on D. F. McKenzie's estimate of a seventeenth century printer's typical output—and if we take into account that Simmons's shop was concurrently working on other texts—the printer probably completed an average of one and a half sheets each week. At that rate, *Paradise Lost*'s 43 sheets would have been finished more than 28 weeks later, some time in the middle of November. Apparently all these copies of the first edition were then sold by April 26, 1669, the day on which, according to the terms of their original agreement, Simmons paid Milton £5 for the second edition. For the surviving receipt of this payment, see French, *The Life Records of John Milton*, 4:448; for printers' estimated rates of production, see D. F. McKenzie, "Printers of the Mind: Some Notes on Bibliographical Theories and Printing-House Practices," *Studies in Bibliography* 22 (1969): 1–76, esp. 15; and for Simmons's other books in these years, see McKenzie, "The Economies of Print," 424–25. I discuss the quantity of complimentary copies that Milton received in Dobranski, *Milton, Authorship, and the Book Trade*, 208.

36. French, *The Life Records of John Milton*, 4:438.

37. Moxon, *Mechanick Exercises*, 214.

38. Robert Howard, *Five New Plays* (Wing H2992, H2992A, H2993, H2994).

39. Abraham Cowley, *Works* (Wing C6649–C6660).

40. Another title page for Cowley's *Works*, also dated 1681, restores all

these changes, but prints the words "Original Copies" back in the larger, roman type (and omits the period after "Mr" preceding Cowley's name).

41. I also make this argument in Dobranski, *Milton, Authorship, and the Book Trade,* 38–39.

42. Edward Arber, ed., *The Term Catalogues, 1668–1709,* 3 vols. (London: Arber, 1903–06), 1:159–60.

43. Samuel Simmons's father, Matthew Simmons, for example, printed two of Milton's government tracts, *Articles of Peace* (May 1649) and *Eikonoklastes* (October 1649), both of which were "Published by Authority," according to their title pages. Interestingly, *Eikon Basilike* had also been entered to Matthew Simmons in the Stationers' *Register* on March 16, 1649, but was then crossed out by him in person on August 6, 1651.

44. The first printing of the first edition (Pforz 716) collates as follows: 4°: π²A-Z⁴Aa-Tt⁴Vv²; 172 leaves. The second printing of the first edition contains two inserted gatherings of preliminaries, A and a, which contain "The Argument," Simmons's note, the defense of the verse, and the errata. One of the copies of the second printing that I examined (Pforz 717) retained the original title page and removed the first leaf of gathering A. The collation reads as follows: 4°: π²A⁴(-A1)a⁴A-Z⁴Aa-Tt⁴Vv²; 182 leaves. Another copy that I examined (Pforz 718) canceled the original title page and replaced it with the first leaf of gathering A. The collation reads as follows: 4°: A⁴a⁴A-Z⁴Aa-Tt⁴Vv²; 182 leaves. This latter copy contains "The Printer to the Reader" (A2). All of these copies are held in the Pforzheimer Collection at the Harry Ransom Humanities Research Center at the University of Texas at Austin.

45. Some copies omit Simmons's note and some contain a shorter version: "*Courteous Reader,* There was no Argument at first intended to the Book, but for the satisfaction of many that have desired it, is procured [*sic*]. *S. Simmons.*" That this version of the note is a little garbled—". . . have desired it, is procured"—may indicate that the longer version constitutes a correction. See Fletcher, *Facsimile,* 2:178–79.

46. See Helen Darbishire, "The Printing of the First Edition of *Paradise Lost,*" *Review of English Studies* 17 (1941): 415–27.

47. Peter Lindenbaum, "Milton's Contract," in *The Construction of Authorship,* ed. Martha Woodmansee and Peter Jaszi (Durham, N.C.: Duke University Press, 1994), 176–90.

48. Nor was Simmons merely accommodating the opening ornamental initial, for none of the opening lines in none of the other ten books are similarly spaced; elsewhere, when the compositor needs to extend a line of verse beyond the margin, the extra words are right-justified.

49. Milton, *Paradise Lost,* 2nd ed. (London: Samuel Simmons, 1674; Wing M2144), sig. A1r.

50. Milton, *Paradise Regain'd . . . To which is added Samson Agonistes* (London: John Starkey, 1671; Wing M2152), sig. A1r, I1r.

51. Roger Chartier, *The Order of Books,* trans. Lydia G. Cochrane (Stanford: Stanford University Press, 1994), 37–39. On these changing cultural conditions and authors' increased status—economically, legally, and practically—see Dobranski, *Readers and Authorship in Early Modern England* (Cambridge: Cambridge University Press, 2005), 6–8.

Notes to Guibbory, *"Milton's 1667* Paradise Lost *in Its Historical and Literary Contexts"*

1. Hugh Wilson, "The Publication of *Paradise Lost,* the Occasion of the First Edition: Censorship and Resistance," in *Milton Studies,* vol. 37, ed. Albert C. Labriola (Pittsburgh: University of Pittsburgh Press, 1999), 18–41.

2. Wilson briefly but suggestively notes the "contrast between Waller and Dryden on the one hand" and "Marvell and Milton on the other" in order to place *Paradise Lost* (ibid., 29–30).

3. John Milton, *Complete Poems and Major Prose,* ed. Merritt Y. Hughes (New York: Odyssey, 1957), 398–99.

4. Edmund Waller, *To the King Upon His Majesties Happy Return* (printed for Richard Marriot, 1660), 3.

5. Abraham Cowley, *Ode upon the Blessed Restoration and Returne of His Sacred Majestie, Charls the Second* (for Henry Herringman, 1660), 8, 18, 11.

6. Nicholas von Maltzahn, "Laureate, Republican, Calvinist: An Early Response to Milton and *Paradise Lost* (1667)," in *Milton Studies,* vol. 29, ed. Albert C. Labriola (Pittsburgh: University of Pittsburgh Press, 1993), 181–98; quotation, 189.

7. "The Printer to his MAIESTY," *Britannia Rediviva* (Oxford: A. and L. Lichfield, 1660).

8. Laura Lunger Knoppers, *Historicizing Milton: Spectacle, Power, and Poetry in Restoration England* (Athens: University of Georgia Press, 1994), 68. Knoppers shows how Milton's poems "register the power and problematics of monarchical spectacle in the Restoration," challenging and replacing "the spectacles of state" (10). N. H. Keeble, *The Literary Culture of Nonconformity in Later Seventeenth-Century England* (Athens: University of Georgia Press, 1987), discusses Milton in the context of Restoration nonconformity.

9. David N. Griffiths, *The Bibliography of the Book of Common Prayer, 1549–1999* (London: The British Library, Oak Knoll Press, 2002), 8.

10. Ibid., 108–11.

11. Peter Heylyn, *Cyprianus Anglicanus; or, The History of the Life and Death of the Most Reverend and renowned prelate William [Laud]* (1668). A second edition appeared in 1671.

12. Richard Hooker, "To the Kings Most Excellent Majestie Charls the II," *Of the Lawes of Ecclesiastical Politie. Eight Bookes by Richard Hooker* (London: Printed for Andrew Crooke, 1661).

13. Sharon Achinstein, *Literature and Dissent in Milton's England* (Cambridge: Cambridge University Press, 2003), suggests that, particularly in the figure of Abdiel, Milton's *Paradise Lost* defends "dissent," expressing the view of the dissenters in the Restoration (120–22).

14. Karen L. Edwards, *Milton and the Natural World* (Cambridge: Cambridge University Press, 1999), 7, 47, and generally chap. 2, 40–63; Stephen M. Fallon, *Milton Among the Philosophers: Poetry and Materialism in Seventeenth-Century England* (Ithaca, N.Y.: Cornell University Press, 1991);

John Rogers, *The Matter of Revolution: Science, Poetry, and Politics in the Age of Milton* (Ithaca, N.Y.: Cornell University Press, 1996), 104.

15. Robert Boyle, *The Origine of Formes and Qualities (According to the Corpuscular Philosophy) Illustrated by considerations and Experiments*, 2nd ed. (1667), 64.

16. Ken Hiltner, *Milton and Ecology* (Cambridge: Cambridge University Press, 2003), esp. chaps. 2–3 (30–54) and 9 (125–34).

17. Robert Hooke, "To the King, The Epistle Dedicatory," *Micrographia; or, Some Physiological Descriptions of Minute Bodies Made by Magnifying Glasses* (1667).

18. Hooke, "To the Royal Society," ibid.

19. Hooke, "The Preface," ibid., sig. a [1r], a [4r].

20. Margaret Cavendish, *Observations upon Experimental Philosophy. To which is added, The Description of a New Blazing World* (1666), "To His Grace the Duke of Newcastle," sig. b[1r]–b[1v], "The Preface to the Ensuing Treatise," sign. C[2r]. Elizabeth Spiller, *Science, Reading, and Renaissance Literature: The Art of Making Knowledge, 1580–1670* (Cambridge: Cambridge University Press, 2004), rightly argues that the first part of Cavendish's *Observations* is "an unmistakably direct response to Robert Hooke's *Micrographia*," but she "effaces him as a philosopher by never mentioning him by name," rejecting the mechanistic model in favor of the imaginative model of fiction presented in her *New Blazing World* (151–52, 176).

21. Thomas Sprat, *The History of the Royal-Society of London, for the Improving of Natural Knowledge* (London, 1667), frontispiece, and "To the King."

22. It is significant that Dryden too was attracted to the progressive ideology of those connected with the Royal Society. His poem, "To My honor'd Friend, Dr. Charleton," was printed in the prefatory material for Walter Charleton's *Chorea Gigantum* (on Stonehenge) (1663). Charleton was one of the first members of the Royal Society (he was elected in May 1661), and Dryden's poem to him anticipates Cowley's more famous "Ode to the Royal Society" in praising Bacon and the liberation from Aristotle.

23. Wilson, "The Publication of *Paradise Lost*," 29.

24. James Anderson Winn, *John Dryden and His World* (New Haven: Yale University Press, 1987), 81–82. Wilson, "The Publication of *Paradise Lost*," notes the contrast with Dryden's *Annus Mirabilis*, but does not pursue it at length.

25. John Dryden, "An Account of the ensuing Poem, in a letter to the Honourable Sir Robert Howard," *Annus Mirabilis: The Year of Wonders, 1666* (1667).

26. *Areopagitica*, in Hughes, *Complete Poems and Major Prose*, 745.

27. Dryden, "To the Metropolis," *Annus Mirabilis*, sig. A2v.

28. Hughes, *Complete Poems and Major Prose*, 898.

29. See the title pages of *Annus Mirabilis* (London, 1688) and Milton's *Paradise Lost* (1688).

Notes to DuRocher, "The Emperor's New Clothes"

1. Nancy Lee-Riffe, "Milton and Charles II," *Notes and Queries* 11 (March 1964): 93–94. See also J. Milton French, *The Life Records of John Milton*, 5 vols. (1950; rpt. New York: Gordian Press, 1966), 4:389–91.

2. Lee-Riffe, "Milton and Charles II," 94.

3. The Latin text of the *Defensio secunda* is from *The Works of John Milton*, 18 vols., ed. Frank Allan Patterson et al. (New York: Columbia University Press, 1931–40), 8:138. The English version is from *Complete Prose Works of John Milton*, 8 vols., ed. Don M. Wolfe et al. (New Haven: Yale University Press, 1953–82), 4:628. Unless otherwise indicated, all references to Milton's prose are to this edition, cited as YP with volume and page number. All references to Milton's poetry are to *John Milton: Complete Poems and Major Prose*, ed. Merritt Y. Hughes (Indianapolis: Odyssey Press, 1957). Fellowes's translation is reprinted in Hughes, *Complete Poems and Major Prose*, 832.

4. Estella Schoenberg, "The Face of Satan, 1688," in *Ringing the Bell Backward: The Proceedings of the First International Milton Symposium*, ed. Ronald D. Shafer (Indiana, Pa.: Indiana University Press, 1982), 56–57.

5. My interpretation assumes that Milton was responding to events in the English court beginning in October 1666; therefore, a fresh look at when Milton completed *Paradise Lost* is in order. One must be careful to distinguish scholarly assumptions in this regard from the documentary record. Although the complete manuscript of the poem is lost, a fair copy of book 1 survives, and it is currently in the Morgan Library in New York City. Noting that this manuscript contains printer's symbols used in the process of preparing the copy for pagination, James Holly Hanford and James G. Taaffe, *A Milton Handbook*, 5th ed. (New York: Meredith, 1970), 160–61, assume that the text of the 1667 edition was set from this copy. Helen Darbishire, *The Manuscript of Milton's "Paradise Lost," Book I* (Oxford: Clarendon Press, 1931), makes the assumption that "if this first book was part of the copy of *Paradise Lost* which Milton gave to Elwood [sic] at Chalfont St. Giles 'to take home and read at his leisure', then it must have been finished before the late summer of 1665" (ix), and on that assumption dated the transcript of book 1 as 1665. Barbara Lewalski, *The Life of John Milton: A Critical Biography*, rev. ed. (Oxford: Blackwell, 2003), 444, echoes this assumption, adding further speculation: "Apparently, Milton had a draft of *Paradise Lost* in hand by August, 1665, though he probably continued working on it at Chalfont and in London until he gave it to the printer 18 months later." Lewalski's more specific date of "August, 1665" is speculative, and is presumably based on Thomas Ellwood's imprisonment for about a month during July 1665. Certainly Milton presented Ellwood with a manuscript of the poem to read at Chalfont St. Giles, and we know that Milton stayed there, for the most part, from June 1665 through February 1666. What Ellwood read, however, may just as well have been an earlier version of the poem than the final one, a version lacking authorial changes made after he read the text. Granting that Ellwood read a draft of the epic sometime during the late

summer of 1665, I see nothing in the documentary record that would have prevented Milton from continuing to revise his manuscript after that reading.

My essay argues that Milton was responding to events at court beginning in October 1666. If I am correct, Milton must have continued to revise the manuscript of *Paradise Lost* beyond Lewalski's speculative date of August 1665. I see no evidence contradicting the claim that the surviving manuscript of book 1 was the author's final copy, the text Milton held and revised until he submitted it to the printer in April 1667. After all, apart from its marginalia, the surviving manuscript differs only in spelling and accidentals like punctuation and capitalization from the first edition published in 1667. This scenario would explain the inclusion in the surviving manuscript, as in the first edition, of topical references to events in October 1666.

Further support for my claim that Milton continued to work on *Paradise Lost*—in particular on parts of books 1 and 2 essential to my argument—beyond 1665 and through October 1666 comes from Allan H. Gilbert, *On the Composition of "Paradise Lost"* (New York: Octagon, 1966), 151–55. In a section entitled "A Table Showing Sequence in Composition," Gilbert proposes what is eminently logical upon reflection, that certain sections of the poem must have been composed long before others, and that completion of such a monumental work no doubt occurred through several rounds of revision conducted over many years. Gilbert is careful to call his table "tentative rather than absolute," and certainly it should be taken in that spirit. Gilbert identifies six groups or parts of the poem according to sequence of composition, beginning with the lines composed for a tragedy or tragedies based on the Fall. For my purposes, the relevant groups are the last two: Group Five: "The Independent Epic (parts not suggested in the plans for tragedies and probably not planned until the epic form was settled on" [154]); and Group Six: "The Epic Complete (parts substituted for earlier passages or inserted when the poem seemed finished" [155]). The point is that all of the passages discussed in my essay fall within these latter two categories. Considered within the overall economy of the epic, then, nothing in the poem is disturbed if we view Milton, sometime after October 7, 1666, adding new lines or revising already composed lines about Satan that might reflect the king's new fashion. And, as I hope to show, much is gained.

Finally, William Riley Parker's assessment of the dating questions in *Milton: A Biography*, 2nd ed., ed. Gordon Campbell (Oxford: Clarendon Press, 1996), 2:1100, is sobering and salutary: "When was *Paradise Lost* completed and when was *Paradise Regained* begun? We still do not know, and may never know." For the present, the best discussion of the dating issue remains John Shawcross's trenchantly factual "Appendix: The Dates of Composition" to his book, *With Mortal Voice: The Creation of "Paradise Lost"* (Lexington: University Press of Kentucky, 1982), 173–77, on which my argument depends.

6. John Toland, *Life of John Milton* (1698), told of the licenser who nearly suppressed the whole poem for Milton's "Imaginary Treason" in these lines. For Toland's life, see Helen Darbishire, *The Early Lives of Milton* (1932; rpt.

London: Constable, 1965), 170. For further discussion of these lines, particularly regarding Milton's "oblique, careful" poetic strategy under the circumstances, see Michael Wilding, *Dragons Teeth: Literature in the English Revolution* (Oxford: Clarendon Press, 1987), 237–38; and Nicholas von Maltzahn, "The First Reception of *Paradise Lost* (1667)," *Review of English Studies* 47 (1996): 479–501.

7. Annabel Patterson, *Censorship and Interpretation: The Conditions of Writing and Reading in Early Modern England* (Madison: The University of Wisconsin Press, 1984). One principle Patterson articulates is especially relevant here, as it suggests a further reason why Milton might have decided not to remove any allusions to Charles II's appearance in the 1660s from the later, 1674 edition of *Paradise Lost*. Patterson argues that writing under censorship develops habits that a writer is unlikely to abandon when censorship is lifted: "The habits of mind, the arts of difficulty, developed out of political necessity are seen to retain their value when the constraints that produced them are removed. What we witness here is the birth of the most characteristically 'modern' idea of fiction, that it ought to be artfully difficult" (197).

8. My discussion of Charles's vest is indebted chiefly to Esmond S. de Beer, for his pioneering essay, "King Charles II's Own Fashion: An Episode in Anglo-French Relations 1666–70," *Journal of the Warburg Institute* 2 (October 1938): 105–15; and secondly to Diane De Marly, for her demonstration of the vest's theatrical aspect in "King Charles II's Own Fashion: The Theatrical Origins of the English Vest," *Journal of the Warburg and Courtauld Institutes* 37 (1974): 378–82. Both de Beer and De Marly pursue questions about the outfit raised by Francis M. Kelly, "A Comely Vest After the Persian Mode," *The Connoisseur* 88 (1931): 96–99. My slight divergences from these scholars' views appear in the text.

9. All references to the diarists are to the following editions, and are cited by entry date: Samuel Pepys, *Diary*, 11 vols., ed. Robert Latham and William Matthews (Berkeley and Los Angeles: University of California Press, 1970); John Evelyn, *Diary of John Evelyn*, 6 vols., ed. E. S. de Beer (Oxford: Clarendon Press, 1955).

10. State Papers, Domestic, vol. 174, no. 139; cited in de Beer, "King Charles II's Own Fashion," 106.

11. BM, Add. MS. 10117, 179–179r–v; cited in ibid., 106.

12. Francis M. Kelly, "A Comely Vest after the Persian Mode," *The Connoisseur* 88 (1931): 98–99, analyzes Montague's sketch and accounts for Montague's late date of November 1666 as possibly reflecting that the vest was modified a few weeks after its initial appearance.

13. De Beer, 115.

14. Both de Beer, ibid., 111, and De Marly, "King Charles II's Own Fashion," 378, note that no French sources have been found to corroborate this story. Because the joke is on the English, however, it seems unlikely that the true-blue royalist Pepys would simply fabricate it.

15. De Beer, "King Charles II's Own Fashion," 110.

16. See Laura Lunger Knoppers, "The Politics of Portraiture: Oliver

Cromwell and the Plain Style," *Renaissance Quarterly* 51 (Winter 1998): 1282–1319.

17. De Marly, "King Charles II's Own Fashion," 378. The intrigue between the English and French kings that resulted in the secret Treaty of Dover, particularly as it involved Charles's beloved sister, Henriette, may provide part of the explanation for Charles's rejection of the French style in 1666 and his reversion to it after 1670. In 1662, Henriette married Philip, Duc d'Orleans, and by all accounts she was most unhappy in the marriage. According to David Masson, *Life of John Milton* (New York: Peter Smith, 1946), 6:571, Henriette, "Charles's favourite and only remaining sister," as the Duchess of Orleans, was "the special link of communication between king and king" for their negotiations at Dover. The terms of the treaty provided Charles with ready money and Louis with English troops for the French war with the Dutch. A few days after the treaty had been signed, Henriette returned to her husband; very shortly thereafter, news reached Charles of her sudden death in France on June 20. Rumors circulated that Henriette's husband had poisoned her. Masson writes, "Charles was greatly shaken" (6:578) by this tragedy. Could the king's sister's unhappy French marriage have led to his initial rejection of French ways, and his return to French fashion signaled his renewed acceptance of dependency on France after 1670? For Masson's account of these events, see 6:570–81.

18. De Beer, "King Charles II's Own Fashion," 111.

19. Ibid., 108.

20. Edward Chamberlayne, *Angliae Notitia*, 25–26; cited in de Beer, ibid., 108.

21. Stevie Davies, *Images of Kingship in "Paradise Lost": Milton's Politics and Christian Liberty* (Columbia: University of Missouri Press, 1983), 67–68.

22. De Marly, "King Charles II's Own Fashion," 381.

23. For a discussion of the provenance and date of the satire, see H. M. Margoliouth, ed., *The Poems & Letters of Andrew Marvell*, 2 vols., 2nd ed. (1952; rpt., Oxford: Oxford University Press, 1967), 286–88; and Warren L. Chernaik, *The Poet's Time: Politics and Religion in the Work of Andrew Marvell* (Cambridge: Cambridge University Press, 1983), 212–14. A version of the poem entitled "A Prophetick Lampoon, Made Anno 1659, By his Grace George Duke of Buckingham," appears to be fictitious according to both date and author (see Chernaik, 213), but uncertainty remains about who first composed the poem and when he or they wrote it. Yale MS. Osborn b. 54 includes a six-stanza version of the poem, dating from 1667. An early complete text, found in British Library MS. Add. 18220, contains the six-line introduction (as in Margoliouth's printed text) and eleven stanzas, including the one describing the king's vest. Although the poem was first published under Marvell's name in the *State Poems* of 1697, the evidence that Margoliouth examines indicates that the latest date for its composition was 1670; on that basis, he ascribes the poem to Marvell as of that date. Having reviewed the manuscript evidence, Chernaik concludes that "there is no inherent improbability in Marvell's authorship of an early version of 'The Kings Vowes' written in 1668–70" (214).

Considering this satire's relationship with the 1667 edition of *Paradise Lost*, we can readily imagine two possible scenarios for poetic influence. In the first, Marvell may have read Milton's draft (or the first edition) of *Paradise Lost*, and it inspired the younger poet's satire. In the second, Marvell could have shared *his* draft of his new verses about the vest for "The King's Vowes" with Milton, and it inspired the epic poet as he added the finishing touches to the epic before its went to press in 1667. A third possibility, pointed out by John Shawcross in correspondence, is that the influence may have gone both ways. In other words, both writers may have seen early versions of the other's work, then composed their final verses. Certainly Marvell's connections with the court in the 1660s would have made him the conveyer of the news of the king's new fashion to Milton rather than the other way around.

In addition to Marvell, Milton had other means of access to court news. One of these was his nephew Edward Phillips, who was employed by Evelyn from October 1663 through February 1665 and possibly later, and who was tutor to Philip Hebert, afterwards seventh Earl of Pembroke, through Evelyn's recommendation, from March 1665–70 (*DNB* 1:1037–38). Significantly for my argument, Phillips was one of his uncle's chief amanuenses for the manuscript of *Paradise Lost*.

24. Milton is here echoing and rebutting Lord Ormond's charge that Parliament's aim is "to set up first an elective Kingdome, and after that a perfet Turkish tyranny" (YP 3:312). Milton again implies that Charles I's government was a Turkish tyranny in *Eikonoklastes* (1649), chapters 10 and 27 (YP 3:448, 574). For a full discussion of Milton's allusions to Charles I, including the possibility that Milton was depicting Charles I in the portrayal of Satan in *Paradise Lost*, see Joan Bennett, *Reviving Liberty: Radical Christian Humanism in Milton's Great Poems* (Cambridge, Mass.: Harvard University Press, 1989), 33–58. In particular, Bennett seeks to demonstrate that Milton uses sun imagery to link Satan with Charles I's political arguments upholding the divine right of kings. In making her case, however, Bennett at times adduces evidence that actually supports the association between Satan and Charles II. For example, in discussing the simile of Satan as an eclipsed sun in book 1, 594–99, Bennett writes, "Charles II's censor, presumably reading the poem with the royalist king / sun symbolism in mind, is said to have taken these lines as a threat to the new king, veiled in the traditional interpretation of an eclipse by monarchs who think of themselves as ruling on earth as the sun rules the heavens" (37). Bennett's apt reading of these lines as a threat to Charles II supports my interpretation.

25. Davies, *Images of Kingship in "Paradise Lost,"* 68–71, points out that as a result of the 1622 capture, Ormus had fallen from its height of splendor and importance as a trading port. With that fall in mind, Davies maintains, Milton uses this poetic emblem of faded glory to reassure readers of Satan's decline.

26. See Alastair Fowler's note on *"Barbaric"* in his edition of *Paradise Lost* (London: Longman, 1968), 91.

27. John Ogilby, *The Entertainment of His Most Excellent Majestie*

Charles II (London, 1662), a facsimile with introduction by Ronald Knowles (Binghamton, N.Y.: Medieval and Renaissance Texts and Studies, 1988).

28. John Ogilby, *The Relation of His Majesties Entertainment* (1661), 10, cited in Blair Hoxby, *Mammon's Music: Literature and Economics in the Age of Milton* (New Haven: Yale University Press, 2002), 99–100.

29. David Quint, *Epic and Empire: Politics and Generic Form from Virgil to Milton.* (Princeton, N.J.: Princeton University Press, 1993), 281. See also J. Martin Evans, *Milton's Imperial Epic: "Paradise Lost" and the Discourse of Colonialism* (Ithaca, N.Y.: Cornell University Press, 1996).

30. Quint, *Epic and Empire,* 248.

31. Davies, *Images of Kingship in "Paradise Lost,"* 81–86.

32. For Johnson's critique, see "Milton," *Lives of the English Poets,* reprinted in *Samuel Johnson's Literary Criticism,* ed. R. D. Stock (Lincoln: University of Nebraska Press, 1974), 224–25. C. S. Lewis, "The Mistake About Milton's Angels," *A Preface to "Paradise Lost"* (London: Oxford University Press, 1942), 108–15. Stephen M. Fallon, *Milton Among the Philosophers: Poetry and Materialism in Seventeenth-Century England* (Ithaca, N.Y.: Cornell University Press, 1991); John Rogers, *The Matter of Revolution: Science, Poetry, and Politics in the Age of Milton* (Ithaca, N.Y.: Cornell University Press, 1996), 103–76.

33. Stanley Fish, *How Milton Works* (Cambridge, Mass.: Harvard University Press, 2002), 39–40, discusses the display of angelic service in the Nativity poem. On the faithful angels' service and appearance in the epic, see Boyd Berry, *Process of Speech: Puritan Religious Writing and "Paradise Lost"* (Baltimore: Johns Hopkins University Press, 1976), 177–90.

34. Fowler, *Paradise Lost,* 575.

35. See Schoenberg, "The Face of Satan, 1688," 46–59. Stella Revard's "Response," in Shafer, *Ringing the Bell Backward,* 60–61, suggests that the vaguely Roman character of these illustrations points to the poem's subtle, underlying political agenda.

36. Merritt Y. Hughes, "Satan and the 'Myth' of the Tyrant," *Essays in English Literature from the Renaissance to the Victorian Age Presented to A. S. P. Woodhouse* (Toronto: University of Toronto Press, 1964), 129.

Notes to Knoppers, "Now let us play"

1. Samuel Pepys, *The Diary of Samuel Pepys,* 11 vols., ed. Robert Latham and William Matthews (Berkeley and Los Angeles: University of California Press, 1970–83), 8:240. Further citations will be noted parenthetically in the text by volume and page number.

2. On the gardens and royal parks, see Jacob Larwood, *The Story of the London Parks* (London: Chatto & Windus, 1881); Liza Picard, "Gardens, Parks, and Open Spaces," *Restoration London* (New York: St. Martin's Press, 1998), 54–63; and David Kerr Cameron, "Gardens of Dalliance and Delight," *London's Pleasures: From Restoration to Regency* (Gloucestershire: Sutton, 2001), 45–61. Specifically on Vauxhall, see James Granville Southworth,

Vauxhall Gardens: A Chapter in the Social History of England (New York: Columbia University Press, 1941).

3. The classic text is J. H. Plumb, *The Commercialization of Leisure in Eighteenth Century England* (Reading: University of Reading, 1973). See also Roy Porter, "Material Pleasures in the Consumer Society," in *Pleasure in the Eighteenth Century,* ed. Roy Porter and Marie Mulvey Roberts (New York: New York University Press, 1996), 19–35.

4. Cynthia Wall, *The Literary and Cultural Spaces of Restoration London* (Cambridge: Cambridge University Press, 1998), 148–67, treats the parks as refuge or safe space. David Roberts, "Caesar's Gift: Playing the Park in the Late Seventeenth Century," *English Literary History* 71 (2004): 115–39, argues in response that the spaces of the parks were politically fraught: established under a royal milieu, disrupted in the Interregnum, and reappropriated under the restored monarchy, before being variously staged in Restoration drama. See also J. F. Merritt, ed., *Imagining Early Modern London: Perceptions and Portrayals of the City from Stow to Strype, 1598–1720* (Cambridge: Cambridge University Press, 2001), which includes an essay specifically on the parks: Laura Williams, "'To recreate and refresh their dulled spirites in the sweet and wholesome ayre': Green Space and the Growth of the City," 185–216.

5. On the social production of space, see Henri Lefebvre, *The Production of Space* (Oxford: Blackwell, 1991).

6. On literary sources, see A. Bartlett Giamatti, *The Earthly Paradise and the Renaissance Epic* (Princeton, N.J.: Princeton University Press, 1966). John Dixon Hunt, "Milton and the Making of the English Landscape Garden," in *Milton Studies,* vol. 15, ed. James D. Simmonds (Pittsburgh: University of Pittsburgh Press, 1981), 81–105, argues that the descriptions of Milton's Eden derive from Italian examples, while Charlotte Otten, "'My Native Element': Milton's Paradise and English Gardens," in *Milton Studies,* vol. 5, ed. James D. Simmonds (Pittsburgh: University of Pittsburgh Press, 1973), 249–67, demonstrates links with native English gardening practices. Rebecca Bushnell, *Green Desire: Imagining Early Modern English Gardens* (Ithaca, N.Y.: Cornell University Press, 2003), 94–96, includes Milton's Adam and Eve in her discussion of seventeenth century gardening manuals. None of these studies looks at the poem's contemporary milieu, especially the charged meanings of pleasure gardens in the Restoration, although Hunt does maintain that the derivation of the grotto, for example, from Italian gardens is a rebuttal to the French styles in fashion under Charles II.

7. Discussions of labor in the poem have, for the most part, situated Milton in a broad shift from feudalism to capitalism, largely ignoring the fact that Adam and Eve are gardening. Teresa Michals, "'Sweet gardening labour': Merit and Hierarchy in *Paradise Lost,*" *Exemplaria* 7, no. 2 (1995): 499–514, argues that the poem's gardening scenes attempt to negotiate the tensions between feudalism and capitalism, foregrounded in the figure of Eve. Kevis Goodman, "'Wasted Labor?' Milton's Eve, the Poet's Work, and the Challenge of Sympathy," *English Literary History* 64 (1997): 415–46, sees Eve's arguments for gardening alone as the beginning of alienated labor. See also Marshall

Grossman, "The Fruits of One's Labor in Miltonic Practice and Marxian Theory," *English Literary History* 59 (1992): 77–105. The major exception to this neglect of gardening per se is Barbara Kiefer Lewalski, "Innocence and Experience in Milton's Eden," in *New Essays on "Paradise Lost,"* ed. Thomas Kranidas, 86–117 (Berkeley and Los Angeles: University of California Press, 1971), an important reading of Adam and Eve's gardening as a developmental process emblematic of their need to prune and curb their own excessive impulses and desires.

8. Scholars have noted the stress on pleasure in the poem, but not primarily in relation to labor. For example, Steven Zwicker, *Lines of Authority: Politics and English Literary Culture, 1649–1689* (Ithaca, N.Y.: Cornell University Press, 1993), 90–129, traces how pleasure is variously praised as abundance and sexual delight or linked with degeneration, luxury, and decadence in Restoration works by Milton, Marvell, and Dryden.

9. Balthasar de Monconys, *Journal des Voyages,* vol. 2, *Voyage d'Angleterre* (Lyon, 1665–66), 16–17; Southworth, *Vauxhall Gardens,* 9–10.

10. See Mark Mcdayter, "Poetic Gardens and Political Myths: The Renewal of St. James's Park in the Restoration," *Journal of Garden History* 15, no. 3 (1995): 135–48.

11. *The Diary of John Evelyn,* ed. E. S. De Beer (Oxford: Clarendon Press, 1955), 3:573.

12. James Grantham Turner, "Pepys and the Private Parts of Monarchy," in *Culture and Society in the Stuart Restoration: Literature, Drama, History,* ed. Gerald MacLean (Cambridge: Cambridge University Press, 1995), 95–110.

13. Gilbert Burnet, *Bishop Burnet's History of His Own Time* (London: William S. Orr, 1850), 236.

14. *Milton: A Biography,* ed. William Riley Parker, rev. ed. Gordon Campbell (Oxford: Clarendon Press, 1996), 1:400.

15. All quotations from *Paradise Lost* are from the 1667 edition, as reproduced in facsimile by Harris Francis Fletcher, *John Milton's Complete Poetical Works,* vol. 2, *The First Edition of Paradise Lost* (Urbana: The University of Illinois Press, 1945). Book and line numbers will be given parenthetically in the text.

16. On Satan's envious and sexualized reaction to Adam and Eve in Eden, see John Shawcross, *John Milton: The Self and the World* (Lexington: The University Press of Kentucky, 1993), 183–85.

17. Lewalski, "Innocence and Experience," stresses the educative function and emblematic nature of Adam and Eve's labor, although she does note the extensiveness of the task. John R. Knott, "Milton's Wild Garden," *Studies in Philology* 102, no. 1 (2005): 66–82, traces the wildness and wantonness of the garden in rich detail. Knott notes the contradiction between the mandate to labor and the overwhelming profusion of the garden, but then retreats from this insight by arguing that "wildness" itself must be revalued as (at least sometimes) positive and hence that Adam and Eve need not worry so much about curbing the wild. I would maintain that the gardening *is* overwhelming, as a test of faith and obedience for Adam and Eve.

18. On the phallic serpent, see Shawcross, *John Milton,* 202–03.

19. For Lewalski, "Innocence and Experience," Adam and Eve's gardening of themselves and of the literal plants, flowers, and trees "is unlaborious but it is absolutely necessary, and it increases daily in complexity and challenge" (93). I retain the focus on the educative function of gardening, drawn from Lewalski's essay, but point to the overwhelming and nonprogressive aspects of the task, with consequences both for the themes of Milton's poem and its resonances in 1667.

20. William Empson, *Milton's God* (London: Chatto & Windus, 1965), chapter 4.

Notes to Hampton, "'[N]ew Laws thou see'st impos'd'"

I wish to thank John Shawcross and Michael Lieb for their "incessant labor to cull out, and sort asunder" the relative merits and shortfalls of my own work, as well as for their enduring commitment to a younger generation of Milton scholars.

1. Anonymous, *The last Speech and Prayer with other passages of Thomas Venner The Chief Incourager and Promoter of the late Horrid Rebellion* (London: 1660 / 1), 3–4, 8.

2. Bernard Capp, "The Fifth Monarchists and Popular Millenarianism," *Radical Religion in the English Revolution*, ed. J. F. McGregor and Barry Reay (Oxford: Oxford University Press, 1984), 165–90; quotation from 175. Capp more fully discusses the movement in *The Fifth Monarchy Men: A Study in Seventeenth-Century Millenarianism* (London: Faber and Faber, 1972). For more on Venner's rebellion and its aftermath, see Richard L. Greaves, *Deliver Us from Evil: The Radical Underground in Britain, 1660–1663* (New York: Oxford University Press, 1986), chapter 1; quotations from 57–65, 49.

3. All quotations from *Paradise Lost* are from the 1667 edition (London), available at Early English Books Online (EEBO), http://eebo.chadwyck.com; all other quotations from the poetry are from *John Milton: Complete Poems and Major Prose*, ed. Merritt Y. Hughes (New York: Macmillan, 1957). Subsequently, all quotations of Milton's prose are from the *Complete Prose Works of John Milton*, 8 vols., ed. Don M. Wolfe, et al. (New Haven: Yale University Press, 1953–82), hereafter cited by volume and page number as YP.

4. David Loewenstein, *Representing Revolution in Milton and His Contemporaries: Religion, Politics, and Polemics in Radical Puritanism* (Cambridge: Cambridge University Press, 2001), 10.

5. Thomas Edwards, *Gangraena; or, A Catalogue and Discovery of many of the Errours, Heresies, Blasphemies and pernicious Practices of the Sectaries of this time* (London, 1646), 1.3.113–14; see also Ephraim Pagitt, *Heresiography; or, A Description of the Heretickes and Sectaries* (London, 1654).

6. For more on these developments and an assessment of this year of transition, see Brian Manning, *1649: The Crisis of the English Revolution* (Chicago: Bookmarks, 1992).

7. George Savile, Marquis of Halifax, *A Letter to a Dissenter Upon occasion of His Majesties late Declaration of Indulgence* (London, 1687), 6, 2. See Robert Ferguson, *A Representation of the Threatning Dangers, impending over Protestants* (Edinburgh, 1687), a heated pamphlet intended to bolster Protestant unity against the Catholic king. For more on James II's policies toward nonconformity, see N. H. Keeble, *The Literary Culture of Nonconformity in Later Seventeenth-Century England* (Athens: University of Georgia Press, 1987), chapter 1.

8. See, for instance, Kristen Poole, *Radical Religion from Shakespeare to Milton: Figures of Nonconformity in Early Modern England* (Cambridge: Cambridge University Press, 2000), chapter 4. See also Ann Hughes, "Approaches to Presbyterian Print Culture: Thomas Edwards's *Gangraena* as a Source," in *Books and Readers in Early Modern England*, ed. Jennifer Andersen and Elizabeth Sauer (Philadelphia: University of Pennsylvania Press, 2002), 96–116.

9. For more on the centrality of religious issues to the politics of the Restoration settlement, see Tim Harris, Paul Seaward, and Mark Goldie, eds., *The Politics of Religion in Restoration England* (Oxford: Blackwell, 1990).

10. Paul Seaward, *The Restoration* (New York: St. Martin's Press, 1991), 59–60.

11. John Miller, *After the Civil Wars: English Politics and Government in the Reign of Charles II* (New York: Longman, 2000), 133, 145–46.

12. Seaward, *The Restoration*, 60, 42; Barry Reay, "Quakerism and Society," in McGregor and Reay, *Radical Religion in the English Revolution*, 141–42.

13. The best book on Nayler is Leo Damrosch, *The Sorrows of the Quaker Jesus: James Nayler and the Puritan Crackdown on the Free Spirit* (Cambridge, Mass.: Harvard University Press, 1996). The Derwentdale Plot is discussed in Greaves, *Deliver Us from Evil*, chapter 6.

14. Barry Reay, "The Quakers, 1659, and the Restoration of the Monarchy," *History* 63 (1978): 193–213.

15. Quoted in Barry Reay, "Quakerism and Society," in McGregor and Reay, *Radical Religion in the English Revolution*, 164.

16. Ronald Hutton, *Charles the Second, King of England, Scotland, and Ireland* (Oxford: Clarendon Press, 1989), 181. For more on this distinction in the 1660s, see Keeble, *The Literary Culture of Nonconformity*, 33–45. Independents, Quakers, and Baptists were comfortable with being labeled as "dissenters." But Presbyterians who hoped for comprehension within the Church of England consistently identified themselves as "nonconformists"— those who desire the national church, but who may demur on some ceremonies. Episcopal authorities, however, perceived no distinction.

17. The Declaration of Breda is reprinted in *English Historical Documents, 1660–1714*, ed. Andrew Browning (London: Eyre and Spottiswoode, 1953), 57–58.

18. N. H. Keeble, *The Restoration: England in the 1660s* (Oxford: Blackwell, 2002), 112.

19. Bodleian Library MS Carte 45, fol. 151; quoted in John Spurr, *The*

Restoration Church of England, 1646–1689 (New Haven: Yale University Press, 1991), 47.

20. Keeble, *The Restoration*, 122–23.

21. Quoted in Hutton, *Charles the Second*, 180.

22. These acts are partially reprinted in *Documents of the Christian Church*, 3rd ed., ed. Henry Bettenson and Chris Maunder (Oxford: Oxford University Press, 1999), 331–36.

23. Miller, *After the Civil Wars*, 171.

24. Keeble, *The Restoration*, 142.

25. Act of Uniformity quoted in Keeble, *The Restoration*, 117–18.

26. Miller, *After the Civil Wars*, 187; Seaward, *The Restoration*, 56.

27. Blair Worden, "The Question of Secularization," in *A Nation Transformed: England after the Restoration*, ed. Alan Houston and Steve Pincus (Cambridge: Cambridge University Press, 2001), 20–70; quotation from 30, emphasis added.

28. Michael Lieb discusses divine Sabbath rest in *Poetics of the Holy: A Reading of "Paradise Lost"* (Chapel Hill: University of North Carolina Press, 1981). On Satan as restless reader in the poem, see Bryan Adams Hampton, "Milton's Parable of Misreading: Navigating the Contextual Waters of the 'night-founder'd Skiff' in *Paradise Lost*, 1.192–209," in *Milton Studies*, vol. 43, ed. Albert C. Labriola (Pittsburgh: University of Pittsburgh Press, 2004), 86–110.

29. Keeble, *The Literary Culture of Nonconformity*, 45. For an extended discussion of Milton and his contemporaries on the subject of the Sabbath, see Boyd M. Berry, *Process of Speech: Puritan Religious Writing and "Paradise Lost"* (Baltimore: Johns Hopkins University Press, 1976), chapters 5–7.

30. Keeble, *The Restoration*, 181. The *Book of Sports* is partially reprinted in Bettensen and Maunder, *Documents of the Christian Church*, 313–16.

31. William Perkins, *The Workes of That Famous and Worthy Minister of Christ in the Universitie of Cambridge, Mr William Perkins*, 3 vols. (Cambridge, 1608–13), 2:109–11, 1:775.

32. James Nayler, *A Salutation to the Seed of God* (London, 1656), 20.

33. See Sharon Achinstein, *Literature and Dissent in Milton's England* (Cambridge: Cambridge University Press, 2003). Achinstein observes that while many of the established clergy busily appeal to the reasonableness of doctrine, some dissenters and enthusiasts consistently deny that the claims of reason were even valid or necessarily comprehensive for understanding the phenomenology of religious experience (169).

34. Gary S. De Krey, "Radicals, Reformers, and Republicans: Academic Language and Political Discourse in Restoration London," in *A Nation Transformed: England after the Restoration*, ed. Alan Houston and Steve Pincus (Cambridge: Cambridge University Press, 2001), 71–99; quotation at 81. See also his "Rethinking the Restoration: Dissenting Cases of Conscience, 1667–1672," *Historical Journal* 38, no. 1 (1995): 53–83.

35. George Fox, *Newes Coming up out of the North, Sounding towards the South* (London, 1654), 31; *The Vials of the Wrath of God* (London, 1655), 8. William Prynne, *The Quakers Unmasked* (London, 1655), 36. For

a sustained analysis of Fox's revolutionary rhetoric, see Loewenstein, *Representing Revolution,* chapter 4.

36. Worden, "The Question of Secularization," 31.

37. Poole, *Radical Religion from Shakespeare to Milton,* 107–08.

38. John Humfrey, *A Case of Conscience* (London, 1669), 29–30; quoted in De Krey, "Radicals, Reformers, and Republicans," 82.

39. Edwards, *Gangraena,* 1.123.

40. *Acts and Ordinances of the Interregnum, 1642–1660,* 3 vols., ed. C. H. Firth and R. S. Rait (London: H. M. Stationery Office, 1911), 2:409–12.

41. For more on the Church of England's relationship to these synods, especially in the Elizabethan era, see Patrick Collinson, *The Elizabethan Puritan Movement* (Berkeley and Los Angeles: University of California Press, 1967).

42. This shift is also noted in passing by Keeble, *The Restoration,* 134.

Notes to Donnelly, "Poetic Justice"

1. See, for example, Alastair Fowler's introduction to *Paradise Lost,* in *The Poems of John Milton,* ed. John Carey and Alastair Fowler (London: Longmans, 1968), 440–43; Maren-Sofie Røstvig, *Configurations: A Topomorphic Approach to Renaissance Poetry* (Oslo-Copenhagen-Stockholm: Scandinavian University Press, 1994), 461–534; John T. Shawcross, *With Mortal Voice: The Creation of "Paradise Lost"* (Lexington: University of Kentucky Press, 1982), 56–67. Building upon such numerological and structural arguments, Michael Lieb, "Encoding the Occult: Milton and the Traditions of *Merkabah* Speculation in the Renaissance," in *Milton Studies,* vol. 37, ed. Albert C. Labriola (Pittsburgh: University of Pittsburgh Press, 1999), argues that the ten-book edition of *Paradise Lost* foregrounds the "elements of Neoplatonism customarily associated with *Merkabah* speculation in the early modern period" (68). While not denying that Milton was influenced by interpretations of Ezekiel's vision, such as the kabbalistic "Work of the Chariot [*maaseh merkabah*]," the argument here offers a further intertextual explanation for Milton's locating the apex of his poem in the Son's victory in book 6. Although such symmetry might be expected in any two writers so deeply influenced by Pythagorean number theory, I contend that Milton engages Plato's text directly through that structural symmetry. The exceptions to such numerological emphases would include Arthur E. Barker, "Structural and Doctrinal Pattern in Milton's Later Poems," in *Essays in English Literature from the Renaissance to the Victorian Age,* ed. Millar MacLure and F. W. Watt (Toronto: University of Toronto Press, 1964), 169–94, which argues for a ten-book tragic structure based on Davenant's *Gondibert* (compare Shawcross, *With Mortal Voice,* 64) and David Norbrook's case for a parallel with Lucan's *Pharsalia,* in *Writing the English Republic: Poetry, Rhetoric and Politics, 1627–1660* (Cambridge: Cambridge University Press, 1999), 438–67.

2. John Hale, "*Paradise Lost:* A Poem in Twelve Books, or Is It Ten?" *Philological Quarterly* 74 (1995): 146, considers Milton's possible reasons

for shifting from a ten-book to a twelve-book structure and attributes the change largely to Milton's ongoing revision of his own textual corpus generally and to a "wider Virgilianizing," in view of Virgil's "Augustan-normative" status (138–47). As Norbrook, *Writing the English Republic*, points out, drawing upon Hale's observations, one difficulty with those numerological claims that depend upon the number of lines in the first edition of *Paradise Lost* is that Milton's blindness could have made it difficult for him to know the exact number of total lines in the poem, given that even the printer misnumbered them (443n28; compare Hale, "*Paradise Lost*," 134–47). But see the evidence concerning the misnumbering and addition of lines in the second edition of the poem discussed by William B. Hunter, "The Centre of *Paradise Lost*," *English Language Notes* 7 (1969): 32–34. As Hunter points out, although the printer may have misnumbered some lines, the lines of the poem that survive in manuscript form are indeed numbered correctly. Shawcross, *With Mortal Voice*, suggests that Milton's accommodations to popular Virgilian tastes were partially driven by concerns regarding sales of the epic (64–65), although Nicholas von Maltzahn, "The First Reception of *Paradise Lost* (1667)," *Review of English Studies* 47 (1996), has since argued that "the first edition sold more quickly than has been supposed" (487).

3. Norbrook, *Writing the English Republic*, 493; compare 438–67.

4. In what follows, all *Paradise Lost* book numbers, as with all quotations and citations, are from John Milton, *Paradise Lost, A Poem Written in Ten Books* (London, 1667; reprint, Menston: Scolar Press, 1968), cited parenthetically hereafter as *PL*, followed by book and line number. Citations and quotations of Milton's prose are from *Complete Prose Works of John Milton*, 8 vols., ed. Don Wolfe et al. (New Haven: Yale University Press, 1953–82), hereafter cited as *YP*, followed by volume and page number.

5. There is, of course, a strictly numerological answer to this particular question. As Shawcross, *With Mortal Voice*, points out, "since, according to Philo and Pythagoras, six was the first perfect number between one and ten (as it is the sum and product of 1, 2, 3), Milton placed the middle of his poem within that book" (58). The specific engagement of Plato's *Republic* in *Paradise Lost* further corroborates Milton's relationship to such traditions of Pythagorean-Platonist numerological theory and suggests answers to questions that do not arise for numerological analyses.

6. Various critics have observed Platonist and or Neoplatonist themes in Milton's early and late prose and poetry. See, for example, Herbert Agar, *Milton and Plato* (Princeton: Princeton University Press, 1928); Anna Baldwin, "Platonic Ascents and Descents in Milton," in *Platonism and the English Imagination*, ed. Anna Baldwin and Sarah Hutton (Cambridge: Cambridge University Press, 1994), 151–62; John Spencer Hill, *Infinity, Faith, and Time: Christian Humanism and Renaissance Literature* (Montreal: McGill-Queen's University Press, 1997); Stephen M. Fallon, *Milton Among the Philosophers: Poetry and Materialism in Seventeenth Century England* (Ithaca, N.Y.: Cornell University Press, 1991), 81–84; Irene Samuel, *Plato and Milton* (Ithaca, N.Y.: Cornell University Press, 1947). None of these

studies, however, considers the ten-book arrangement of the 1667 *Paradise Lost* as a direct engagement of the *Republic*.

7. Samuel, *Plato and Milton*, 27.

8. Throughout this essay, I use the adjective "Platonist" to designate the wide-range of traditions that have offered interpretations of Plato's texts, from antiquity through the Renaissance. I use the term "Platonic" to designate a text or to indicate my claims regarding what a given text of Plato's could imply. Likewise, my distinction throughout between "Plato" and "Socrates" should not be taken to imply that they necessarily disagree on a given point. To insist that a given claim belongs properly to Socrates merely indicates that I am making a point regarding the explicit claims of the text in that passage, rather than attempting to draw out implications.

9. Thomas H. Luxon, "Milton's Wedded Love: Not About Sex (As We Know It)," in *Milton Studies*, vol. 40, ed. Albert C. Labriola (Pittsburgh: University of Pittsburgh Press, 2001), 43.

10. Ibid., 43.

11. I shall not attempt here to determine the relative extent to which Milton was influenced by, for example, the Platonism of Nicholas of Cusa, Marsilio Ficino, or by the more local English influences of John Colet or Edmund Spenser, or the longstanding traditions of English Augustinianism, or the more recent work of the so-called Cambridge Platonists. Beyond the wide influence of themes generally associated with Platonism, Milton's letter to Charles Diodati, November(?) 23, 1637, seems to mark an important shift in his direct engagement of Plato. His early use of generally Platonist themes (as in *Comus*) apparently drew upon "commonplaces of school and society" and required no specific knowledge of a given text, whereas the precise allusions to Plato's *Phaedrus* in the 1637 letter arguably depend upon a direct engagement of the passage (Samuel, *Plato and Milton*, 9–11; compare YP 1:327). As we shall also see, Milton apparently read some parts, if not all, of the *Republic* in Greek, and most likely had access, at the very least, to Ficino's translated *Opera Omnia* in Latin.

12. Efterpi Mitsi, "The 'Popular Philosopher': Plato, Poetry, and Food in Tudor Aesthetics," *Early Modern Literary Studies* 9, no. 2 (2003), 2.16; available at http://extra.shu.ac.uk/emls/09-2/mitsfood.html.

13. Longinus, *On the Sublime / Peri Hupsous*, rev. ed., ed. and trans. W. Hamilton Fyfe, revised by Donald Russell (Cambridge, Mass.: Harvard University Press, 1995), books 12–15; compare books 32–33. For example, "Was Herodotus alone Homeric in the highest degree? No, there was Stesichorus at a still earlier date and Archilocus too, and above all others Plato" (13.3).

14. As I will discuss later, Milton acknowledges the obvious opposition of Socrates to some forms of poetry and to the Sophists, but Milton never imagines rhetoric and philosophy as offering opposing ontologies. In this respect, it is important not to confuse the disagreement between Socrates and Sophists like Thrasymachus with later intellectual conflicts, like that between Petrarch and Scholastic logicians. The early modern disputes between "rhetoric" and "dialectic" in general were not concerned with the

same root issues broached by Socrates and the Sophists. Literary humanists like Petrarch and Thomas More were critical of Scholastic dialectic specifically when it was claimed as an end in itself and when it failed to allow
for accommodations to the circumstance of a nonacademic audience. See,
respectively, Francesco Petrarch, "To Tomasso da Messina," in *Familiar
Letters*, ed. and trans. James Harvey Robinson, in *Petrarch: The First Modern
Scholar and Man of Letters* (New York: Putnam, 1898), 219–22; available
at http://history.hanover.edu/texts/petrarch/pet08.html; and Thomas More,
Utopia, trans. Clarence H. Miller (New Haven: Yale University Press, 2001),
41–50. In More's case, he implicitly sets "Plato" in direct opposition to the
disputatious ethos of Scholastic dialectic. In general, humanists like Petrarch,
Erasmus, and More saw dialectic as a potentially useful tool that, when mistaken for the whole of wisdom, actually made its professional practitioners into obstacles to the true "love of wisdom," or *philosophia*, in a Platonist
sense. This point would not bear stating except for the fact that Stanley Fish,
following Richard Lanham, has deployed the term "rhetoric" as though it
were tautologically defined by being anti-Platonist or "anti-philosophic,"
as though "rhetoric" and "metaphysics" were synonyms for "pragmatism"
and "idealism," respectively. See Stanley Fish, "Rhetoric," *Doing What Comes
Naturally: Change, Rhetoric, and the Practice of Theory in Literary and Legal
Studies* (Oxford: Oxford University Press, 1989), 471–85; and Richard A.
Lanham, *The Motives of Eloquence: Literary Rhetoric in the Renaissance*
(New Haven: Yale University Press, 1976), 1–35. Not only does such a view
fail to acknowledge the central place of rhetorical irony in Plato's writing,
but it also effectively makes the Thrasymachean ontology merely a synonym
for the whole of "rhetoric," rather than viewing it as one possible rhetorical stance. As Fish's argument shows (473–74), the attempt to narrate a binary
opposition between so-called "rhetoric" and "philosophy" requires, among
other things, simply dismissing the influence of Aristotle, Cicero, and
Augustine as irrelevant because they do not share the Thrasymachean
ontology and therefore unfairly (according to Fish) subsume rhetoric within
"philosophy," rather than vice versa.

15. See, for example, Plato's *Gorgias*, trans. Donald J. Zeyl, 464b–66a,
500a–08a, and *Phaedrus*, trans. Alexander Nehamas and Paul Woodruff,
266b–68e, in *Plato: Complete Works*, ed. John M. Cooper (Indianapolis:
Hackett, 1997).

16. Plato, *Politeia*, ed. John Burnet, *Platonis Opera*, vol. 4 (Oxford:
Clarendon, 1902), 403a–c. In what follows, quotations in English are from
Republic, trans. G. M. A. Grube, rev. C. D. C. Reeve (Indianapolis: Hackett,
1992). Citations from the *Republic* will be given parenthetically hereafter.

17. Such a view is also evident in, for example, *Of Education* (YP 1:396)

18. Milton did not apparently view the *Laws* as primarily a work of practical politics. When he first invokes the name of Plato, in this passage in
Areopagitica, Milton seems to be thinking of the *Republic*, but the rest of
the passage clearly seems to indicate details from the *Laws*. In a still later
part of the argument, however, Milton again seems to have the *Republic* in
mind (YP 1:526; *Republic*, 423–33). I suggest that Milton understood the *Laws*

to be just as "Utopian" as the *Republic,* despite explicit claims to the contrary in the *Laws.* Milton's treatment of these texts clearly suggests that he viewed them as involving similar strategies of indirection. Which is to say that, like More's *Utopia,* their primary function is not to propose a political program but to offer indirect criticism of existing political regimes. Trevor J. Saunders, in introducing his own translation of the *Laws* (New York: Penguin, 1970), describes Plato's text as "emphatic yet imprecise, elaborate yet careless, prolix yet curiously elliptical" (39), suggesting not only the plausibility of Milton's apparent view but also the striking stylistic similarities between the *Laws* and More's *Utopia.*

19. On poetry and music, see, for example, *Republic,* 376c–83c. Whether or not Plato's text ultimately implies that censorship is really a viable part of the practice of statecraft remains, of course, an open question, depending upon how one interprets the *Republic*'s central psyche-polis analogy. Nevertheless, there remains at the surface of Plato's text an explicit claim that imitative poets should be banned from the *kallipolis* (*Republic,* 605a–b). Milton had obviously encountered or imagined interlocutors who would attempt to deploy such explicit claims in order to argue for the practice of state censorship.

20. I have in mind here interpretations like that of Plato offered by a Straussian like Allan Bloom and that of *Paradise Lost* offered by a Romantic like Harold Bloom. Although the former Bloom is more coy than the latter regarding his views, he consistently suggests that, notwithstanding the rudeness of Thrasymachus, the core Thrasymachean insight regarding the nature of political power could be closer to Plato's teaching than might be initially supposed. See Allan Bloom, "Interpretive Essay," in *The Republic of Plato,* trans. Allan Bloom (New York: Basic Books, 1968), 305–436, esp. 325–39. Whether the presentation of either Thrasymachus in the *Republic* or Satan in *Paradise Lost* ultimately favors tacitly their account of reality need not be resolved here. Both Blooms would likely be loath to admit the striking physiognomic resemblances between their respective interpretations.

21. The explicit claims advanced by Machiavelli's *The Prince* reiterate three pivotal Thrasymachean claims: (1) that "justice" is ultimately reducible to the power to control by means of either cunning or coercion; (2) that the successful practice of politics depends upon the mere appearance of those conventional virtues that people typically praise; (3) that the practice of "justice" is not an end in itself but a means to extrinsic benefits. See, for example, Machiavelli, *The Prince,* 2nd ed., trans. Harvey C. Mansfield (Chicago: University of Chicago Press, 1998), chapters 6, 12, 18–21.

22. Critical treatments of Milton's engagement of Machiavelli include Victoria Kahn, *Machiavellian Rhetoric: From the Counter-Reformation to Milton* (Princeton: Princeton University Press, 1994), 169–235; Barbara Riebling, "Milton on Machiavelli: Representations of the State in *Paradise Lost,*" *Renaissance Quarterly* 49 (1996): 573–97; Paul Stevens, "Milton's 'Renunciation' of Cromwell: The Problem of Raleigh's Cabinet-Council," *Modern Philology* 99 (2001): 382–89; William Walker, "Human Nature in Republican Tradition and *Paradise Lost,*" *Early Modern Literary Studies* 10,

no. 1 (2004): 6.16–42; available at http://extra.shu.ac.uk/emls/10-1/walk-milt.htm.

23. Riebling, "Milton on Machiavelli," 574.

24. In what follows, as above, I deploy the term "Machiavel" to indicate a character who embodies the policies explicitly presented in *The Prince*, leaving unanswered the question whether Machiavelli himself is a "Machiavel." We shall thus not attempt to determine here whether Machiavelli's genuine views are more apparent (even relatively so) in *The Prince* or in those passages of *The Discourses* that seem to contradict *The Prince*; however, Milton's own apparent response to that question is notable. Milton's use of Machiavelli in his *Commonplace Book* clearly favors passages from *Discourses* that contradict or crucially qualify the advice given in *The Prince* (Stevens, "Milton's 'Renunciation' of Cromwell," 382–87). My further point is that the explicit position of the "Machiavel" depicted in *The Prince* is, as a matter of course, identical to that of Thrasymachus in key respects (see note 21 above).

25. Thrasymachus is mentioned by name in book 5 (450a–b), book 6 (498c–d), book 8 (545a), and book 9 (590d).

26. These differences between the end of book 2 and the beginning of book 3 are, of course, differences in emphasis, insofar as questions of poetic content and form are not finally subject to sharp distinction. Nevertheless, although both passages are ultimately concerned with inculcation of virtues, the end of book 2 is specifically concerned with the way that depictions of the gods, a particular kind of content, can undermine virtue. Likewise, although book 3 mentions poetic content, the distinction between narrative and dramatic modes of representation does not arise until that point.

27. This point becomes still more explicit after the infernal deliberations have ended, when the narrator observes that even "Devil with Devil damn'd / Firm concord hold, men onely disagree / Of creatures rational" (*PL* 2.496–98). The fact that demons preserve a kind of social contract for mutual benefit is consistent with Plato's implicit claim that social-contract theory presumes a Thrasymachean ontology. Compare Eric Voegelin, *Plato* (1958; reprint, Columbia: University of Missouri Press, 2000), 72–76. Milton offers his own version of something like a social-contract theory in *Tenure of Kings and Magistrates* (YP 3:198–201); however, Milton's account in *Tenure* is distinct from both that of Hobbes and Locke. Unlike Hobbes, Milton does not hypostasize the effects of the Fall; unlike Locke, Milton does not think the social contract antedates the Fall. The demonic social contract in *Paradise Lost* is, in this respect, arguably Hobbesian. Compare Fallon, *Milton Among the Philosophers*, 216–22.

28. Phillip J. Donnelly, "The *Teloi* of Genres: *Paradise Lost* and *De Doctrina Christiana*," in *Milton Studies*, vol. 39, ed. Albert C. Labriola (Pittsburgh: University of Pittsburgh Press, 2000), 85–93; compare Revelation 5, Zechariah 3:1–10, and Job 1–2.

29. The tendency to minimize the differences between Platonic and Christian teachings regarding sin, although warranted in many respects, can be misleading. For example, Voegelin, *Plato*, 122, discusses the account in

book 8 of the *Republic* regarding how the polis could ever go into decline: "the question cannot be answered directly because it concerns the mystery of iniquity, that is, the instability of the cosmic Form itself." Much depends here on whether "instability" is a synonym for "mutability," but in Milton's view such a statement would seem to treat a necessary but not sufficient cause for sin, temporal changeability, as though it were a consequence of sin. Compare Milton's point that a "mutable state" is a condition for sin, not its sufficient cause (YP 6:309).

30. The education of the philosopher-kings is quite different from that proposed for the lower class of "guardians" in books 2, 3, and the early parts of book 5 in the *Republic*. In this respect, Raphael's educational narratives and conversations, extending from the latter part of book 5 through to the end of book 7 in *Paradise Lost*, correspond precisely with the advanced and truly philosophic education of the philosopher-kings in Plato's text.

31. Although the illustration of the divided line and the sun analogy are both subsumed in the ensuing allegory of the cave, the sun analogy represents the metaphysical apex of the dialogue. The divided line helps to explain what the sun analogy represents, while the allegory of the cave describes the educational process that leads to a vision of the "sun" already described. Thus, although the dialogue continues to elaborate upon and develop the analogy of the sun, the argument does not ascend to a higher level of metaphysical speculation.

32. The analogy was widely used by ancient Christians to describe the unity of the Father and Son. Thus, for example, the Nicene Creed, following John 1:4–9, refers to the Son as "very light of light." Milton was also evidently familiar with Dante's elaborate poetic deployment of the analogy in the *Divine Comedy*. See, for example, *Paradise*, trans. Mark Musa (New York: Penguin, 1995), canto 10.46–51; compare 13.52–60.

33. The centrality of the Son also explains why Milton locates the initial exaltation of the Son in book 5 at the chronological origin of the epic (*PL* 5.577–615). The poem implies that the Son is the infinite and personal horizon of human intelligibility regarding the relation between God and Creation.

34. See Dennis Danielson, "Through the Telescope of Typology: What Adam Should Have Done," *Milton Quarterly* 23 (1989): 121–27.

35. One could argue, given Plato's general emphasis upon the identity of knowledge and moral virtue, that he would say there is no such thing as a "blameless error." But the passage in the *Republic* clearly implies such an evaluation when Socrates points out that the inevitable fall is rooted in temporal change: "everything that comes into being must decay" (546a). More importantly, although Plato would insist that a person truly knows the good only to the extent that one lives in accord with the good (hence all such "error" would be culpable), such an evaluation seems not to apply to an art like eugenics.

36. See, respectively, the examples of deceived Uriel (*PL* 3.630–735), mistaken Adam (5.95–128), and tempted Eve (5.31–121) or Abdiel (5.740–845).

37. In book 3 of the *Republic*, Socrates seems to distinguish between dramatic poetry, narrative poetry, and "mixed" (drama / narrative) poetry, using the term "imitation" to name the first kind (392d–98b). In that context, the *kallipolis* would seem to allow the actions of virtuous characters to be "imitated" using drama. In book 10, however, Socrates seems to use the term "imitative poetry" to include all dramatic and mixed poetry, identifying Homer as the most notorious culprit among such poets, and banning all poetry except "hymns to the gods and eulogies to good people" (607a).

38. This sentence merely summarizes the ostensible claims of the relevant passage in the *Republic* (595b–601a) and does not purport to describe, or impute to Socrates or Plato, a systematic or comprehensive "theory of forms."

39. In *An Apologie for Poetrie* (London, 1595), Sidney famously argues that the depictions of virtue in poetry can be based on direct knowledge of the forms, rather than imitating other temporal imitations of forms (whether of objects or virtues). Whether Milton was primarily influenced by Sidney's account, or by Aristotle's *Poetics*, or by Italian commentators on Aristotle's *Poetics*—as Mary Ann Radzinowicz suggests in *Toward "Samson Agonistes"* (Princeton: Princeton University Press, 1978), 11–12—Milton clearly does not subscribe to the explicit claims advanced in Socrates's ontological critique of poetry in the *Republic*. Nor should we presume that Socrates, much less Plato, subscribes to that argument on its own terms. For example, according to Voegelin, *Plato*, 133, if the critique is understood in the context of the "old quarrel" between philosophy and poetry, "the attack on mimetic poetry from Homer to the time of Socrates pronounces no more than the plain truth that the Age of the Myth is closed." Even such a quasi-Viconian reading, however, implicitly treats the argument as a kind of allegory for some other "plain truth" and does not accept the critique on its own explicit terms.

40. For a fuller account of how Michael's prophecy engages the specific virtue of charity, see Phillip J. Donnelly, *"Paradise Regained* as Rule of Charity: Religious Toleration and the End of Typology," in *Milton Studies*, vol. 43, ed. Albert C. Labriola (Pittsburgh: University of Pittsburgh Press, 2004), 173–83.

41. In one sense, *Paradise Lost* apparently aims to hold together two distinct views of eternity: the Father's view of time as an atemporal unity (*PL* 3.77–79) and Raphael's view that eternity is infinite duration (5.580–82). In *Artis Logicae Plenior Institutio*, Milton, writing in his own voice, seems to favor Raphael's view, but even in that context he is sufficiently circumspect, suggesting that he still has unresolved doubts regarding this topic (YP 8:248). In either case, Milton would have remained insistent that the ontological assumptions in Plato's *Republic* regarding the *relation* (or, rather, nonrelation) between time and eternity are flawed.

42. On the popularity of Virgil, see Hale, *"Paradise Lost*," 138–47; Shawcross, *With Mortal Voice*, 64–67. See also note 2 above. On irony, see Hale, 145; Norbrook, *Writing the English Republic*, 440–44.

Notes to Bryson, "The Mysterious Darkness of Unknowing"

1. Barbara Lewalski, *The Life of John Milton: A Critical Biography* (Oxford: Blackwell, 2000), writes of the difficulty the poem faced: "That Milton's poem was sent forth into the world bare and unaccommodated suggests that likely presenters and commenders had qualms about associating themselves with the rebel Milton's return to print" (456). The six different title pages under which the ten-book *Paradise Lost* appeared over the next three years are explained by Lewalski as "a strategy to make it more widely available, spread the risk, and promote sales" (456). John Shawcross, "The Life of Milton," in *The Cambridge Companion to Milton*, 1st ed., ed. Dennis Danielson (Cambridge: Cambridge University Press, 1989), also notes several possible difficulties the poem faced on the market: "*Paradise Lost* did not sell well for perhaps a number of reasons: its length, its subject, its blank verse, its narrative difficulty; the recovery of the times which was still going on; [and] the generally altered literary climate" (17).

2. Nicholas von Maltzahn, "The First Reception of *Paradise Lost* (1667)," *The Review of English Studies*, n.s. 47 (November 1996), notes that the spare quality of the first printing of *Paradise Lost* was considered highly (and detrimentally) unusual: "Citing booksellers' demands, a contemporary could observe generally that 'tis neither usual nor handsome, to leap immediately from the Title-Page to the matter'" (479).

3. Lewalski, *Life of John Milton*, 460.

4. Von Maltzahn, "First Reception," emphasizes that "the events of 1659–60 have been seen as crucial to Milton's production of *Paradise Lost*" but goes on to argue that "those of 1666–7 [are] crucial to the publication and first reception of the epic" (480).

5. Robert Elborough, *London's Calamity by Fire* (London: 1666), 19–20.

6. Thomas Vincent, *Gods Terrible Voice in the City*, 5th ed. (London, 1667), 9, 12.

7. Ibid., 109, 116, 143.

8. Ibid., 20, 23.

9. Lewalski, *Life of John Milton*, 452.

10. In his prose, such as the following from *A Defence of the People of England*, in *Complete Prose Works of John Milton*, 8 vols., ed. Don M. Wolfe et al. (New Haven: Yale University Press, 1953–82), hereafter cited as YP, Milton constructed a God in his own antimonarchical image: "A republican form of government . . . seemed to God more advantageous [than monarchy] for his chosen people" (4:344). In essence, Milton had once been positive that God was antimonarchical, just as positive as Salmasius had been that God was a monarch (and pro monarchy). In *Paradise Lost*, Milton creates doubt about such firmly delineated ideas and categories, picturing God as a tyrannical monarch, Satan as a republican hypocrite who himself aspires to monarchy, and the Son as a balancing figure that aspires to the end of heavenly monarchy—taking up the regal scepter, only to lay it down.

11. In "How to Avoid Speaking: Denials," in *Languages of the Unsayable*, ed. Sanford Budick and Wolfgang Iser (New York: Columbia University Press,

1996), 3–70, Derrida states, "negative theologies . . . are always concerned with disengaging a superessentiality beyond the finite categories of essence and existence, that is, of presence and always hastening to recall that God is refused the predicate of existence, only in order to acknowledge his superior, inconceivable, and ineffable mode of being" (63n). In my view, negative theology and deconstruction are remarkably similar in technique, though different in their final aim. To posit even something so nearly infinitely deferred as a God beyond God, or Jean Luc Marion's "God without Being" may involve a move more "positive" than Derrida—even in his final period—was able or willing to align himself with. Where negative theology might be described as an attempt to silence, or get beyond, language, deconstruction argues the impossibility of success in such an attempt.

12. All quotations of Dionysius are from *Pseudo-Dionysius: The Complete Works*, trans. Colm Luibheid (New York: Paulist Press, 1987). Such quotations are cited parenthetically as either *DN* (*Divine Names*) or *MT* (*Mystical Theology*).

13. The basic argument is this: Pseudo-Dionysius is "Pseudo" because, given the pervasive presence of the fifth century A.D. philosopher Proclus's ideas and language in the Dionysian texts, it is impossible that the Dionysius of *The Mystical Theology* is actually the Dionysius of Acts 17:34.

14. Proclus, *The Elements of Theology*, trans. E. R. Dodds, 2nd ed. (Oxford: Clarendon Press, 1963), 111.

15. "All that participates is inferior to the participated, and this latter to the unparticipated," or the One. "The unparticipated [the One], then, precedes the participated, and these the participants" (ibid., 29).

16. Oliver Davies and Denys Turner, introduction to *Silence and the Word: Negative Theology and Incarnation*, ed. Oliver Davies and Denys Turner (Cambridge: Cambridge University Press, 2002), 3.

17. Nicholas of Cusa, "On Learned Ignorance," *Nicholas of Cusa: Selected Spiritual Writings*, trans. H. Lawrence Bond (New York: Paulist Press, 1997), 126.

18. Michael Lieb, *The Visionary Mode: Biblical Prophecy, Hermeneutics, and Cultural Change* (Ithaca, N.Y.: Cornell University Press, 1991), 236–37.

19. Marion, *God Without Being*, 16, 18.

20. Ibid., 13, 14.

21. The *Mystical Theology* was published in 1653, in an English translation by John Everard, appended to Everard's *Some Gospel Treasures Opened*. It also appeared alone, in the same translation, under the title *The Mystical Divinity of Dionysius the Areopagite* in 1657. Though Milton could certainly have read Dionysius in Greek or Latin translation, the English translation made Dionysius available to a far wider audience, and enables a "fit" audience (though few) to have the background of ideas necessary to recognize apophatic ideas in *Paradise Lost*.

22. John Calvin, *Institutes of the Christian Religion*, 2 vols., trans. Ford Lewis Battles, ed. John T. McNeill (Philadelphia: Westminster Press, 1960), 164.

23. Dennis Bielfeldt, "Deification as a Motif in Luther's *Dictata super psalterium*," *Sixteenth Century Journal* 28 (Summer 1997): 416.

24. David C. Steinmetz, "Religious Ecstasy in Staupitz and the Young Luther," *Sixteenth Century Journal* 11 (Spring 1980): 23–24.

25. Martin Luther, *The Babylonian Captivity of the Church*, trans. A. T. W. Steinhaeuser, in *Selected Writings of Martin Luther, 1517–1520*, ed. Theodore G. Tappert (Philadelphia: Fortress Press, 1967), 461.

26. Steinmetz, "Religious Ecstasy," 36.

27. Milton, *De Doctrina Christiana*, in *The Works of John Milton*, 18 vols. in 21, ed. Frank Allen Patterson et al. (New York: Columbia University Press, 1931–38), 14:30; hereafter cited as CM followed by volume and page number.

28. "For God, as he is in himself, is far above human thinking, much more so of human senses." Milton's Latin can be read as suggesting that God is beyond both human understanding (abstract intellection) and human sense (felt perception or intuitive apprehension). In fact, *sensus* could be rendered in physical terms (feeling, perception, sensation), emotional terms (affection, emotion, feeling, sentiment), or in terms of human opinion or point of view (moral sense, opinion, thought). Thus, the difficulty of Milton's statement about just how far God exceeds human capacities is in knowing exactly which capacities are being referred to: in my view, Milton is taking full advantage of the multivalent quality of *sensus* in order to argue that *all* human capacities—intellectual, emotional, physical—are grossly insufficient for the most basic level of understanding, apprehending, perceiving, and relating to the divine.

29. Lewalski, *Life of John Milton*, 480. For an opposing perspective, see Clay Daniels, "Milton's Neo-Platonic Angel?" *SEL* 44 (Winter 2004): 173–88. Daniels argues that "whatever Neo-Platonism's influence on Milton, the ladder of love is not central to Milton's thinking and would not seem to merit divine endorsement, especially at this critical moment of the poem" (173).

30. Steinmetz, "Religious Ecstasy," 36.

31. Anna Baldwin, "Platonic Ascents and Descents in Milton," in *Platonism and the English Imagination*, ed. Anna Baldwin and Sarah Hutton (Cambridge: Cambridge University Press, 1994), 151.

32. Ibid., 154.

33. See Barbara Lewalski, John Shawcross, and William Hunter on this debate in "Forum: Milton's Christian Doctrine," *Studies in English Literature, 1500–1900* 32 (Winter 1992): 143–66.

34. Neil D. Graves. "Milton and the Theory of Accommodation," *Studies in Philology* 98 (2001): 251.

35. Quotations in this paragraph are from, respectively, ibid., 253, 252, 261, 262.

36. Plotinus, *Enneads*, 5.1.6, trans. Stephen MacKenna and B. S. Page, ed. Robert Maynard Hutchins, vol. 17, *Great Books of the Western World* (Chicago: Britannica, 1955), 211.

37. Lewalski, *Life of John Milton*, 420.

38. Ibid., 420.

39. Peter C. Herman, "*Paradise Lost*, the Miltonic 'Or,' and the Poetics

of Incertitude," *Studies in English Literature, 1500–1900* 43 (Winter 2003): 202–03.

40. Ibid., 203, 183; emphasis in the original.

41. Michael Bryson, *The Tyranny of Heaven: Milton's Rejection of God as King* (Newark, Del.: University of Delaware Press, 2004), 119–23.

42. John Meyendorff, *The Byzantine Legacy in the Orthodox Church* (Crestwood, N.Y.: St. Vladimir's Seminary Press, 1982), 174–75.

43. The dilemma was over how to speak of a God who cannot be known directly but can be known experientially, the latter a knowledge the Hesychast monks claimed to have achieved. Thus, the split between divine essence (*ousia*) and divine activities (*energeia*) was adopted: "If God was absolutely transcendent, but also could be 'experienced' and 'seen' as an uncreated and real Presence, one had to speak both of a totally transcendent divine 'essence' and of uncreated but revealed 'energies'" (ibid., 174).

44. "The novelty of Palamite theology consisted in the fundamental reinterpretation of emphases going back to Origen and Dionysius the Areopagite, despite a continuing reverence for Dionysius"; see Jaroslav Pelikan, *The Christian Tradition: A History of the Development of Doctine,* vol 2., *The Spirit of Eastern Christendom (600–1700)* (Chicago: University of Chicago Press, 1977), 262.

45. Christopher Hill, *Milton and the English Revolution* (London: Faber and Faber, 1977), 324. Hill goes on to put Milton in the context of the fifteenth century Neoplatonists and the Hermetic tradition, and also connects Milton, through the *ex Deo* theory of Creation, to such groups as the Familists—among whose members was John Everard, the seventeenth century translator of Pseudo-Dionysius—and such followers of Jacob Boehme as Charles Hotham, who "defended Boehme's doctrines at Cambridge, rejecting creation *ex nihilo* in favor of creation from the matter of the abyss" (329), and John Pordage, who "believed that he was summarizing Boehme when he argued, with Milton, that God created the universe out of himself" (330).

46. J. H. Adamson, "The Creation," in *Bright Essence: Studies in Milton's Theology,* ed. William B. Hunter, C. A. Patrides, and J. H. Adamson (Salt Lake City: University of Utah Press, 1983), 83.

47. For example, in *Paradise Lost* Raphael defines God as the one from whom "All things proceed, and up to him return, / If not deprav'd from good . . . / one first matter all" (5.469–72). Later, the Father himself claims to be the source of all matter: "I am who fill / Infinitude" (7.168–69). In *De Doctrina Christiana* (1.7), Milton argues that

> matter must either have always existed independently of God, or have originated from God at some particular point of time. That matter should have been always independent of God, . . . that matter, I say, should have existed of itself from all eternity, is inconceivable. There remains, therefore, but one solution of the difficulty, for which moreover we have the authority of Scripture, namely, that all things are of God. (CM 15:19, 21)

48. Proclus, *The Elements of Theology*, 29–43.

49. Analogous enough, in fact, that Regina Schwartz, *Remembering and Repeating: On Milton's Theology and Poetics* (Chicago: University of Chicago Press, 1993), 8–9, adopts Neoplatonist language when she describes "Milton's creation [as] an emanation of divine goodness." (Schwartz, however, argues cogently for a distinction between the way Milton treats the idea of Creation in the treatise and the way he treats the same idea in the poem: "When he objects to the doctrine of creation *ex nihilo* in *De Doctrina*, Milton tells us, with Lear, that nothing can come of nothing. Nonetheless, his chaos owes a far heavier debt to the Augustinian understanding of evil as privation than he would ever acknowledge in prose" (19). This privation can, as Schwartz suggests, be understood in Plotinian (or Neoplatonist) terms. Quoting from the first Ennead, eighth tractate, Schwartz argues for a strong resemblance between Plotinus's "expanded definition of evil" and Milton's poetic descriptions of chaos: "Evil is that kind whose place is below all the patterns, forms, shapes, measurements, and limits, that which has no trace of good by any title of its own but (at best) takes order and grace from some principle outside itself" (13).

50. See Merritt Hughes, "Milton and the Symbol of Light," *Studies in English Literature, 1500–1900* 4 (Winter 1964): 1–33; and Albert Cirillo, "'Hail Holy Light' and Divine Time in *Paradise Lost*," *Journal of English and Germanic Philology* 68 (1969): 45–56. The essential work along these lines, however, is in Michael Lieb's *Poetics of the Holy* (Chapel Hill: University of North Carolina Press, 1981). See especially 185–210.

51. Unless otherwise noted, all quotations of Milton's poetry are from the 1667 edition of *Paradise Lost* as presented in a facsimile edition by The Scolar Press, Menston, Yorkshire, England, 1968. I have modernized the typography, but have retained the spelling of the facsimile edition.

52. Lieb, *Poetics of the Holy*, 212, explains the tension between God *as* light and God *dwelling in* light in terms of the concepts that are used in the Greek and Hebrew scriptures, respectively.

53. For a thorough and provocative discussion of the role of "or" in *Paradise Lost*, see Herman, "*Paradise Lost*, the Miltonic 'Or.'" See, especially, his discussion of incertitude in the invocation to light of book 3 (186–87) and his argument that there are two raisings of the Son, whose priority cannot be decided, in books 3 and 5 (198–201). Herman's arguments are extended and expanded upon in his *Destabilizing Milton: "Paradise Lost" and the Poetics of Incertitude* (New York: Palgrave Macmillan, 2005).

54. For an overview of the debate over Milton's theology and whether it is most accurately described as "Arian," "Antitrinitarian," or "subordinationist," see (among many others) the following authors. For the Arian / Antitrinitarian Milton, see John Rumrich, "Milton's Arianism: Why It Matters," in *Milton and Heresy*, ed. Stephen B. Dobranski and John P. Rumrich (Cambridge: Cambridge University Press, 1998), 75–92. For longer and more in-depth arguments for Milton as Arian, see Michael Bauman, *Milton's Arianism* (Frankfurt: Peter Lang, 1987). On the "subordinationist" side of this controversy, the use of the term "Arianism," is disputed by John

Shawcross, "Forum: Milton's Christian Doctrine," *Studies in English Literature, 1500–1900* 32 (Winter 1992): 156. See also Shawcross, *With Mortal Voice: The Creation of "Paradise Lost"* (Lexington: University Press of Kentucky, 1982), 181 n. 2. For more in-depth treatments of the arguments for Milton as subordinationist (but not Arian or Antitrinitarian), see the individual chapters on Milton's relation to Arianism by Hunter, Adamson, and Patrides in *Bright Essence.*

55. Lieb, *Poetics of the Holy,* 186–87, describes "Milton's song to 'holy Light,'" as an "act of expressing the inexpressibility of the ineffable," and as "his way of declaring his devotion to the mysterium."

56. Henry Vaughan, "The Night," in *Major Poets of the Earlier Seventeenth Century,* ed. Barbara K. Lewalski and Andrew J. Sabol (New York: Odyssey Press, 1991), 579–81.

57. Stanley Fish, *Surprised by Sin: The Reader in "Paradise Lost,"* 2nd ed. (Basingstoke: Macmillan, 1997), 62.

58. In two articles, Michael Lieb has written persuasive arguments for Milton's God as a passible character: "Reading God: Milton and the Anthropopathetic Tradition," in *Milton Studies,* vol. 25, ed. Albert C. Labriola (Pittsburgh: University of Pittsburgh Press, 1989), and "Milton's 'Dramatick Constitution': The Celestial Dialogue in *Paradise Lost,* Book III," in *Milton Studies,* vol. 23, ed. James D. Simmonds (Pittsburgh: University of Pittsburgh Press, 1987).

59. It is, of course, true that all of the speeches of Satan, Raphael, Adam, Eve, and the others are delivered through the filter of the narrator. Thus it might be argued that the narrator's construction of God is also Satan's construction, and Adam's construction, and so on. Such an argument is entirely valid, but it does not address (much less obviate) the primary point: positive descriptions of deity abound in *Paradise Lost,* but not one of them penetrates "the truly mysterious darkness of unknowing" (*DN* 137). *Paradise Lost* offers numerous partial images, and partial descriptions of a God that, in the final analysis, it cannot express "unblamed."

60. In *Poetics of the Holy,* Lieb argues that Milton deliberately writes God as a deliverer of arbitrary—even irrational—commands: "Having categorically dismissed natural and moral laws as the underlying principle of the first prohibition, Milton postulates a situation in which a command is issued in order to impose upon man a deliberately arbitrary injunction that *by its very nature* runs counter to the dictates of human reason" (94; emphasis in the original). Take that description of the command not to partake of the fruit of the tree of the knowledge of good and evil, and transpose it to an angelic key, and you have a nice description of the command to Raphael.

61. *Meister Eckhart: A Modern Translation,* trans. Raymond B. Blakney (New York: Harper & Brothers, 1941), 204.

62. Herman, *Destabilizing Milton,* 203.

63. From a transcript by the Middle East Media Research Institute of a December 31, 2004, interview on Al-Majd television, clip no. 459; available at http://www.memritv.org/Transcript.asp?P1=459. The video is also available at http://memritv.org/Search.asp?ACT=S6&P3=3#.

64. From a transcript of the September 13, 2001, *700 Club* interview; available at http://www.commondreams.org/news2001/0917-03.htm. In the firestorm of controversy that immediately followed his remarks, Falwell seemed to backpedal, quoted in the *New York Times* the following day as saying that "he did not believe God 'had anything to do with the tragedy,' but that God had permitted it. 'He lifted the curtain of protection . . . and I believe that if America does not repent and return to a genuine faith and dependence on him, we may expect more tragedies, unfortunately." See Gustav Niebuhr, "Finding Fault: U.S. 'Secular' Groups Set Tone for Terror Attacks, Falwell Says," *New York Times*, September 14, 2001, A18. Falwell's position fell outside the mainstream of immediate post–9/11 thought, as is evidenced by the fact that so eminent a conservative commentator as William F. Buckley roundly condemned what he called the evangelist's "ignorant misapplication of Christian thought" in the *National Review* a mere five days after Falwell's televised remarks. See "Invoking God's Thunder: On the Reverend Jerry Falwell," *National Review Online*, September 18, 2001; available at http://www.nationalreview.com/buckley/buckley091801.shtml. Even the extraordinarily conservative *Washington Times* condemned the remarks: "Shortly after Sept. 11, the Revs. Falwell and Robertson distinguished themselves as the most noxious voices on the right of the American political spectrum"; see Tod Lindberg, "Osama bin Laden, meet Jerry Falwell; Extremism Must Be Defanged," *Washington Times*, October 23, 2001, A19. Falwell was hardly alone in the opinion that the attacks of 9/11 were a judgment from God, however. Outside the major media markets, letters to the editor appeared in smaller papers that supported Falwell. One example is by Amy Bradshaw, a letter writer from Blue Ridge, Virginia: "This was certainly a wake-up call from God. We take God out of our everyday lives. Then when tragedy strikes, we're down on our knees. Maybe if we spent a little more time in prayer before tragedy strikes, there would be a lot less hatred in this world"; see *Roanoke Times & World News*, September 18, 2001, A15.

65. Several years later Milton seems to remember, and make reference to, the hysteria of the mid-1660s in *Of True Religion*: "God, when men sin outragiously, and will not be admonisht, gives over chastising them, perhaps by Pestilence, Fire, Sword, or Famin, which may all turn to their good, and takes up his severest punishments, hardness, besottedness of heart, and Idolatry, to their final perdition" (YP 8:439). In other words, in Milton's view, God punishes sinners, not with natural disasters, but with the *spiritual* effects of their own sins, including—perhaps especially—idolatry, a sin in no short supply among those who create God in their own wrathful images.

66. See, for example, Stevie Davies, *Images of Kingship in "Paradise Lost"*: *Milton's Politics and Christian Liberty* (Columbia: University of Missouri Press, 1983).

67. See my *The Tyranny of Heaven: Milton's Rejection of God as King* (Newark: University of Delaware Press, 2004).

68. See, for example, William Empson, *Milton's God* (London: Chatto & Windus, 1961).

69. As in Dennis Danielson, *Milton's Good God: A Study in Literary Theodicy* (Cambridge: Cambridge University Press, 1982).

70. See Fish, *Surprised by Sin.*

Notes to Shawcross, *"That which by creation first brought forth Light out of darkness!"*

1. Stanley Stewart, "Milton Revises *The Readie and Easie Way,*" in *Milton Studies,* vol. 20, ed. James D. Simmonds (Pittsburgh: University of Pittsburgh Press, 1984), 221.

2. John T. Shawcross, *With Mortal Voice: The Creation of "Paradise Lost"* (Lexington: University Press of Kentucky, 1982), 1, 2.

3. See Elizabeth M. Pope, *Paradise Regained: The Tradition and the Poem* (Baltimore: Johns Hopkins University Press, 1944), and Barbara K. Lewalski, "Theme and Structure in *Paradise Regained,*" *Studies in Philology* 57 (1960): 186–220. The brief epic separates the motifs of the temptation of Jesus so that temptation 1 occurs in book 1, temptation 2 is spread over books 2–4, and temptation 3 takes place in book 4. The motif of *voluptaria* lies in book 2, as does the lure of wealth of the *activa* motif; the lures of glory and kingdom of the *activa* motif appear in book 3; and the lure of *contemplativa* in book 4. This treatment has led early commentators to assign the dream in book 2 to the first temptation and the storm of book 4 to the third temptation. The elements of temptation in the history set before Adam's eyes in original book 10 seem to have been little noticed by critics. Lewalski, "Structure and the Symbolism of Vision in Michael's Prophecy, *Paradise Lost,* Books XI–XII," *Philological Quarterly* 42 (1963): 25–35, importantly, discusses books 11 and 12 and the sins of "intemperance," "vainglory," and "ambition," which relate to the Matthew order of the temptations, in the parade of biblical events and personages.

4. Quotations (and linage) are from the first issue of the first edition of *Paradise Lost* (1667).

5. The strong contrast between the episodes of book 11 and those of book 12 is particularly noticeable in Paul M. Dowling, "Paradise Lost and Politics Gained: Milton Rewrites Scripture," *Cithara* 44 (2005): 16–31. The "six visions of Biblical events" in book 11 lead to a "political society" "suggesting human emancipation from the Creator" (16). The "six speeches of Biblical events" in book 12 lead to a "society governed by laws" (21); that is, "in the world outside Eden, dependence upon humans should replace dependence upon God." Thus seen, the epic, as it ends, can be seen to replace biblical paternalism with human interdependency. The separation of the books obscures the interrelated development of Milton's message that Dowling discerns that the original book 10 does not.

6. The biblical episode is fully discussed by Michael Lieb, *Milton and the Culture of Violence* (Ithaca, N.Y.: Cornell University Press, 1994), chapter 5, "The Court of Belial," 126–34. Noted by Lieb is "the disappearance of the old man and his daughter and the sudden and unexpected action of the

Levite" (128), who "simply loads her ['fallen down at the door of the house'] like merchandise onto his ass and transports her to his house" (129). See also Louise Simons, "'An Immortality Rather Than a Life': Milton and the Concubine of *Judges* 19–21," *Old Testament Women in Western Literature,* ed. Raymond-Jean Frontain and Jan Wojcik (Conroy: University of Central Arkansas Press, 1991), 145–73, and Lieb's following chapter 6, "The Exposure of the Matron," 135–55.

7. The 1667 text exhibits numerous textual errors, including verbal problems such as this. See also such examples as "Metal," 3.592 (1667) changed to "Medal" (1674); and "hear," 9.213 (1667) changed to "bear" (1674). Yet 1674 errs in omitting "fair" in 10.550, thus creating a defective line. Two needed verbal changes from 1667 were not caught in 1674: "fealty" for "realty" in 6.115–16, and "limn" for "limb" in 6.352–53. See my edition of *Paradise Lost* (San Francisco: The Arion Press, 2002), 392.

8. See sigs. C1–4, D2–4, G1–3, H1–4, L1–4, O1, 3, Q1, 3–4, R3, S2–4, Ee1, Kk1, Nn1–4, Oo1, 3–4, Vv1–2.

9. See *With Mortal Voice,* chapters 5 and 6, pp. 42–67. See also the essays by Michael Lieb and Joseph Wittreich in this collection for discussion of the expansion of books in the second edition. To be noted, first, is that the title pages *all* emphasize "TEN BOOKS" consistently in large capital letters and on a single line without other information, thus suggesting the importance of "TEN" rather than some other number (for example, the "standard" twelve books that will be created in 1674). Second, the title is consistently "Paradise lost."; that is, "lost" is lowercase, deemphasizing the losing and thereby emphasizing "Paradise." In 1674 not only is "TWELVE BOOKS" in smaller capitals but "Lost" is capitalized. In other words, in 1667 (and the manuscript records the same form) it is "Paradise" that is important, not the losing of it so much as the implied means of regaining it within the message associated with the Son / Jesus / the Christ in books 6 and 10 (12). And third, the question of where and what "Paradise" was was a major issue for the seventeenth century, the printing of the title of the poem in 1667 thus alluding to this religious concern. See specifically chapter 5 of Joseph E. Duncan, *Milton's Earthly Paradise: A Historical Study of Eden* (Minneapolis: University of Minnesota Press, 1972). Among many expositions of the question, see Alexander Ross, *Pansebeia; or, A View of All Religions of the World* (1653); Marmaduke Carver, *A Discourse of the Terrestrial Paradise* (1666); and Henry Hare, Baron Coleraine's *Situation of Paradise Found Out: Being an History of a Late Pilgrimage into the Holy Land* (1683), which alludes to and quotes from Milton's poem. See for the latter 8–9 (citations of *Paradise Lost* 4.214–23, 5.291–97, 4.236–41, and 4.543–45).

10. Michael Lieb, "Encoding the Occult: Milton and the Traditions of *Merkabah* Speculation in the Renaissance," in *Milton Studies,* vol. 37, ed. Albert C. Labriola (Pittsburgh: University of Pittsburgh Press, 1999), 68, 69.

11. See William B. Hunter, "The Center of *Paradise Lost,*" *English Literary Notes* 7 (1969): 32–34.

12. Louis L. Martz, *Poet of Exile: A Study of Milton's Poetry* (New Haven: Yale University Press, 1980), 158.

13. An English version of *Scriptum Dom. Protectoris Reipublicæ Angliæ, Scotiæ, Hiberniæ, &c. Ex consenu atque sententiä concilii Sui Editum; In quo hujus Republicæ Causa contra Hispanos justa esse demonstratur* was included in the edition of *Original Letters of His Excellency Sir Richard Fanshawe, During his Embassies in Spain and Portugal* in 1701, 1702, and 1724. Authorship of the Latin version of the Spanish Declaration, Columbia, State Paper No. 169, is ascribed to Milton. See also various articles by James Sims detailing Milton's influence from and possible echoes of Camões. Among these studies are "Camoëns, Milton, and Myth in the Christian Epic," *Renaissance Papers* (1971): 79–87; "Echoes of Camoëns' *Lusiads* in Milton's *Paradise Lost* (I–IV)," *Revista Camoniana* 3 (1971): 135–44; "*Os Lusiadas:* A Structural Prototype of *Paradise Lost?*" *Explorations in Renaissance Culture* 4 (1978): 70–75. There were also other works in ten books, for example, Lucan's *Pharsalia*, which appeared as *The Whole Ten Bookes Englished by Thomas May* (1627, 1630, 1635).

About the Contributors

Michael Bryson is assistant professor of English at California State University, Northridge. He is the author of *The Tyranny of Heaven: Milton's Rejection of God as King* (2004). He has also written on the dynamic relationship between sacrifice, death, and community formation in the Book of Judges (in *Religion and Literature*), and is currently at work on a new book on negative theology in Milton and Blake.

Stephen B. Dobranski is professor of Renaissance literature and textual studies at Georgia State University. He is the author of *Readers and Authorship in Early Modern England* (2005) and *Milton, Authorship, and the Book Trade* (1999). He also co-edited *Milton and Heresy* (1998) and most recently has completed *A Variorum Commentary on John Milton's "Samson Agonistes," 1671–1970*.

Phillip J. Donnelly is assistant professor of literature in the Honors College at Baylor University, where he teaches in the Great Texts program and the English department. He is author of *Rhetorical Faith: The Literary Hermeneutics of Stanley Fish*.

Richard J. DuRocher teaches English at St. Olaf College. He is the author of *Milton and Ovid* (1985) and *Milton Among the Romans* (2001). Currently he is working on a study of the emotions in Milton's poetry.

Achsah Guibbory is professor of English at Barnard College. Her most recent books are *Ceremony and Community from Herbert to Milton* (1998, 2006) and editor of *The Cambridge Companion to John Donne* (2006). She is completing "Imagined Identities: The Uses of Judaism in Seventeenth-Century England."

Bryan Adams Hampton is assistant professor of English at the University of Tennessee at Chattanooga, where he also serves as coordinator for the humanities program. He has previously published in *Milton Studies* and has also written on the Leveller John Lilburne in *The Age of Milton* (2004).

Laura Lunger Knoppers is professor of English at The Pennsylvania State University. She is author of *Historicizing Milton: Spectacle, Power, and Poetry in Restoration England* (1994) and *Constructing Cromwell: Ceremony, Portrait, and Print, 1645–1661* (2000). She has edited *Puritanism and Its Discontents* (2003) and co-edited, with Joan Landes, *Monstrous Bodies: Political Monstrosities in Early Modern Europe* (2004) and, with Gregory Semenza, *Milton in Popular Culture* (2006). She is currently completing a scholarly edition of Milton's 1671 poems.

Michael Lieb is professor of English and research professor of humanities at the University of Illinois at Chicago. He has recently published *Theological Milton: Deity, Discourse, and Heresy in the Miltonic Canon* (2006) as well as *Milton in the Age of Fish: Essays on Authorship, Text, and Terrorism*, which he has co-edited with Albert C. Labriola.

John T. Shawcross is professor emeritus at the University of Kentucky and the author of *Rethinking Milton Studies: Time Present and Time Past* (2005) and *Milton's Conceptual Development* (forthcoming). His compilation of the "Milton Bibliography, 1624–1799" is available on the Internet through *Iter* (2006).

Joseph Wittreich is Distinguished Professor of English at The Graduate Center of The City University of New York. His most recent books are *Shifting Contexts: Reinterpreting "Samson Agonistes"* and *Why Milton Matters*.

INDEX

Abdiel, 155–57, 180
Absalom and Achitophel (Dryden), 90
Accedence Commenc't Grammar (Milton), 37, 69, 73
Achinstein, Sharon, 55
Act of Uniformity (1662), 83, 149, 184–85
Adam: and clothing, 118–19, 174; and death, 21–23; education of, 172–74; and enlightenment, 49–50; fall of, 53, 136, 176–77; in the garden of Eden, 21, 129–37, 254n17; and God, 206; and labor, 124, 129–37, 253–54n7, 254n17; and Michael, 19–20, 88, 95, 119–20, 178–79; and Raphael, 17–18, 52, 85, 87, 137, 174; reader as, 13; and repentance, 138–39; separation of from Eve, 132–35; and virtue, 171
Adamson, J. H., 200
Addison, Joseph, 34
additions to text, 34–35, 75. *See also* front matter
Adeimantus, 167
advertisements, 35, 65–66
Aeneid (Virgil), 120, 159, 179
Aldrich, Henry, 120
Al-Fawzan, Fawzan, 210
Amory, Hugh, 71
Anabaptists, 144
Andrewes, Launcelot, 83
angels: and clothing, 117–18; dissenting, ix–x, 142; fallen, 113, 116, 145, 150–51, 169–70;

impossible tasks, 137; in *PL* first edition, 54, 239n52; and Sabbath observance, 152
Anglia Notitia (Chamberlayne), 108
Annus Mirabilis (Dryden), 73, 89–94
anonymous publications, 35–37, 40
anti-Sabbatarianism, 151–52
apocalypse, 51–52
Apology against a Pamphlet, An (Milton), 34, 163–64
apophatic theology, x, 186–87, 189, 199. *See also* negative theology
Areopagitica (Milton), 34, 36, 65, 68, 92, 158, 164
arguments: to further understanding of *PL*, 46–47, 52–54, 75; in *PL* first edition, 5, 223; in *PL* second edition, 6, 41, 78, 223
astronomy, 172
At a Solemn Music (Milton), 213–14
authorship, 35–37, 77
awakening, 49–51

Balaam, 102–03
Balak, 102–03
balance, sense of. *See* symmetry
Baldwin, Anna, 193
Baltimore, Lord, 104, *106*
Baptists, 142–43, 146, 155
Barrow, Samuel, 6, 41, 55, 68
Beale, John, 233n36
Beelzebub, 48, 205
beings, 117
Belial, 48, 205, 219

279

170; manifestations of, 48–49; and monarchy, 82; as Roman soldier, 120; as serpent, 136; tempting of Eve, 131, 135–36; and tyranny, 112–22
Savile, George, 144–45
S. B. *See* Barrow, Samuel
Schlichting, Jonas, 239n53
Schollers Purgatory, The (Wither), 66
science, experimental, 85–89
scientific progress, 85–89
Seaward, Paul, 145–46
Second Conventicle Act (1670), 149
Second Defense of the English People (Milton), 36, 97–98
sects. *See* Nonconformists
September 11 attacks, 210
serpent, 136
sexual profligacy, 128, 136
Shawcross, John, x, 9, 16, 213–23, 231n14, 278
Sheldon, Gilbert, 142, 145–48
Sidney, Phillip, 265n39
Simmons, Samuel, 4–6, 39–40, 42, 57, 67–78, 221, 230n9
sin, 169–70, 184, 220–21, 272n65
sleep, dissent from, 150–51, 153
social contract, 263n27
Socinians, 239n53
Socrates, 165–66, 168–70, 172–73, 175–78, 180, 260–61n14, 265nn37–39
Soest, Gerard, 104, *106*
Some Considerations touching the usefulnesse . . . (Boyle), 85
Somers, John, Lord, 8, 43
Somers edition. *See Paradise Lost,* fourth edition (1688) of
Son, the. *See* Jesus
Sophists, 260–61n14
speeches, table of, 34. *See also* front matter
Spencer, John, 29–30, 42
Spice Islands, 115
spirituality and corporeality of beings, 117

sponsorship, 43
Sprat, Thomas, 87–89
square, symbolism of, 234n47
Starkey, John, 40
State of Innocence (Dryden), 44–45, 79, 90, 231n12
stationers. *See* printers
Stationers' Register, 70–72
Steinmetz, David, 191–92
Stephens, Philemon, 84
Stewart, Stanley, 215
St. James's Park, 127–28
structural analysis, 16, 258n1. *See also Paradise Lost,* first edition (1667) of; symmetry
subscription list, 7, 34, 43
sultans. *See* tyranny, Oriental
sun, symbolism of, 175, 251n24
symmetry, 16, 30–32, 171–81, 222–23, 258n1
Symposium (Plato), 162
Synagogue, The (Harvey), 84

table, symbolism of, 234n47
Temple, The (Herbert), 84
temptation, 131, 135–36, 217–19, 273n3
Term Catalogues, The (Caryl), 75
Ternate, 115
theology, 52–54, 185–212, 239n53. *See also* Hesychast theology; negative theology
Thompson, Samuel, 74
Thrasymachus, 165–70, 262n20
Tidore, 115
Tillyard, E. M. W., 55
title pages: as advertisements, 65–66; of later *PL* editions, 7; Milton and, 34–36, 41–42; of *PL* first edition, 2, 4, 11, 27–28, 57–68, *58–63;* of *PL* second edition, 5–6
titles, 27–28, 34, 232–33nn29–30, 274n9
To the King . . . (Waller), 81
Tomkins, Thomas, 71
Tonson, Jacob, 9, 69, 95, 120